Understanding the
Development of
Inclusive Schools

Studies in Inclusive Education Series

Series Editor: Roger Slee, Dean of the Graduate School of Education, University of Western Australia

Understanding the Development of Inclusive Schools

Mel Ainscow

Falmer Press
Taylor & Francis Group

UK   Falmer Press, 1 Gunpowder Square, London, EC4A 3DF
USA   Falmer Press, Taylor & Francis Inc., 325 Chestnut Street, 8th Floor,
       Philadelphia, PA 19106

First published in 1999

A catalogue record for this book is available from the British Library

ISBN 0 7507 0735 6 cased
ISBN 0 7507 0734 8 paper

**Library of Congress Cataloging-in-Publication Data are available on
request**

Jacket design by Caroline Archer

Typeset in 10/12pt Times by
Graphicraft Limited, Hong Kong

*Printed in Great Britain by Biddles Ltd., Guildford and King's Lynn on
paper which has a specified pH value on final paper manufacture of not
less than 7.5 and is therefore 'acid free'.*

Contents

List of Figures

List of Acronyms

APEC	Anhui Provincial Education Commission
CASE	Cognitive Acceleration in Science Education
CFPS	Certificate in Further Professional Studies
CSIE	Centre for Studies on Inclusive Education
DHA	District Health Authority
GCSE	General Certificate of Secondary Education
ERA	1988 Education Reform Act
IQEA	Improving the Quality of Education for All
LEA	Local Education Authority
LMS	Local Management of Schools
OFSTED	Office for Standards in Education
PRA	Participatory Rural Appraisal
SFC	Save the Children
SLFA	Successful Learning For All
SNAP	Special Needs Action Programme
UNESCO	United Nations Educational, Scientific and Cultural Organization
UNICEF	United Nations Children's Fund
UPE	Universal Primary Education

Acknowledgment

I am grateful to the following for permission to reproduce figures:

Centre for Studies on Inclusive Education for figures 7.1, 7.2 and 7.3 from Index of Inclusive Schooling.

David Fulton for figures 6.2 and 6.4

Series Editor's Preface

In his concluding remarks Mel Ainscow refers to this text as an 'autobiographical' 'journey' in search of the 'illusive idea of inclusion'. Were I to borrow from the lexicon of the theatre critic, a phrase like 'tour de force' seems appropriate. This is indeed a vast journey that traverses considerable geographical and conceptual distance. Despite the fact that two of my favourite writers, John Lee Hooker and Van Morrison, suggest that we 'Don't Look Back', Ainscow surveys his professional work hitherto, and the theoretical struggles that underpin it, as an academic stock-taking to build successive theory and practice upon. Reflection has the capacity to be the most forward-looking activity we undertake. The result here is both impressive and instructive.

Paradoxically, while he describes the idea of inclusion as illusive, Ainscow establishes the idea and its forming principles early in this text. Inclusion is not assimilation, it is not an act of integrating or subsuming difference within the dominant culture of schooling. Inclusive schooling is a profoundly subversive and transformational undertaking. The aspiration is an overhaul of 'traditional forms of schooling no longer adequate for the task' of educating all children. It accepts as given Tom Skrtic's (1991) observation that 'special educational needs' as an 'artefact of the traditional curriculum'. To be sure, schooling never was, nor was it the intention, adequate for the task of educating the majority of students. While implausible statistical stabs suggest that 20 per cent of students in schools in England and Wales have Special Educational Needs, the inadequacy of schools for students from cultural/ethnic minorities, from non English speaking backgrounds and from disadvantaged working class communities (the list goes on) has been widely acknowledged.

Preferred is a 'language of practice' that personalizes schooling rather than individualizes differences as indices of defect. In his preface Mel Ainscow declares that the challenge of inclusive schooling strikes at the epistemological foundations of those schooled in special education. All educators need to become what bell hooks (1994) and Peter McLaren (1998) refer to as cultural workers transgressing the knowledge and consequent bureaucratic extrapolations that produce the 'twenty percenters'. It would seem that this text makes the demarcation of special and regular educator redundant. For Ainscow the challenge is to transform the structure and practices of schools so that the educational programme on offer speaks directly and personally to all children. In this way we may overcome the expensive deployment of considerable resources and energy to the measurement and classification of the multiple identities of children.

Understanding the Development of Inclusive Schools speaks to a very broad audience. The theoretical observations are carefully catalogued through reflection on the author's own teaching and school administrative practices, research projects and vignettes formed through observation of schools and classrooms from around the world. The writing is clear and engaging without reducing the theoretical complexity of the subject of inclusion and exclusion. Elsewhere I have been strident in my criticism of aspects of school effectiveness research and school improvement work that reduces the complexity of schools as 'messy organisations' (Ball, 1990), suggests the transferability of findings across cultural and national boundaries, and generates one dimensional lists as recipes for all (Slee, 1998). The methodology for research and practice developed in this book is deeply respectful of cultural and contextual specificity. Described are approaches to collaborative inquiry that seeks various representations of the school or the classroom from all constituencies to form a picture of inclusive practices, barriers to inclusion and the processes of exclusion. Critical reflecting upon his own work as teacher, headmaster, education adviser and academic researcher, Ainscow speaks directly to an expansive audience. This is essential reading for those engaged in the struggle for inclusive schooling. Indeed this text, though declaring its focus on disabled students, should not just be placed on 'special educational needs' reading lists. It is profoundly useful for all those engaged in the transformation required to make schools relevant to the requirements of all children.

References

BALL, S.J. (1990) *Politics and Policy Making in Education. Explorations in Policy Sociology*, London: Routledge.

HOOKS, BELL (1994) *Teaching to Transgress. Education and the Practice of Freedom*, New York: Routledge.

McLAREN, P. (1998) *Life in Schools. An Introduction to Critical Pedagogy in the Foundations of Education*, (3rd Ed.), New York: Addison Wesley Longman.

SKRTIC, T. (1991) 'Students with special educational needs: Artefacts of the traditional curriculum', in AINSCOW, M. (Ed.) *Effective Schools For All*, London: David Fulton.

SLEE, R. (1998) 'High reliability organisations and liability students — The politics of recognition', in SLEE, R., WEINER, G. & TOMLINSON, S. (Eds) *School Effectiveness For Whom? Challenges to the School Effectiveness and School Improvement Movements*, London: Falmer Press.

Preface

I have wanted to write this book for some years but, unfortunately, until recently other commitments have had to take priority. Specifically I have felt a need to bring together a whole range of ideas that emerged from my work over the last twenty years or so, in a way that would allow me to reflect upon and clarify my own thinking. This has meant that the book has involved a considerable amount of 'revisiting' of experiences and themes that I had written about previously, and, indeed, the re-working of many of these ideas.

The agenda of the book is very broad in that it is concerned with how schools and classrooms might be developed in order to make them more effective in fostering the participation and learning of all children and young people. The audience I wish to address is also broad, in two ways at least. First of all, in the sense that it includes all teachers in all kinds of schools, plus those like me whose work involves supporting teachers as they try to develop their practice. And, secondly, in that my concerns are with teachers and schools in all countries.

The ideas that are developed and the proposals that are made are, by their nature, intended to be challenging. In general they challenge the status quo of schools in relation to thinking and practice about organization and pedagogy. Then, in a more specific sense, they are a challenge to people like me and those of my colleagues who have made careers in the special education field. Indeed in some ways I believe it is our thinking which needs to be changed most fundamentally if we are to see significant movement towards the development of forms of schooling that are more inclusive. In this respect I hope that the accounts I provide into the development of my own thinking and practice will encourage colleagues to follow similar paths.

A central message of the book relates to the importance of human collaboration as a means of developing the conditions that are necessary for encouraging moves towards more inclusive arrangements. Perhaps more than anything else, therefore, my accounts are illustrations of the power of this way of working in that they all tell of experiences that have involved me in working closely with other people. However, this also presents some difficulties to the act of authorship, not least that of ensuring appropriate recognition of the many contributions of others to the ideas that are presented. So many colleagues are implicated that it is impossible to list them all. Nevertheless, there are certain of my collaborators who are so central to what I have written here that it would be deeply unfair if I did not acknowledge their contributions.

Two projects have provided the core experiences upon which the book is based and my partners in these initiatives have been particularly influential in the development of my thinking. First of all, my ideas about how teachers can be helped to reach out to all members of their classes have been much influenced by colleagues in many countries who have been involved in the UNESCO teacher education project 'Special Needs in the Classroom'. Here I owe particular thanks to Lena Saleh who was the instigator of the project and a continuing source of encouragement and inspiration. I am also conscious of the contributions of members of the international resource team associated with the project, especially my dear friends Anupam Ahuja in India, Cynthia Duk in Chile and Gerardo Echeita in Spain. We have learnt so much from each other, not least by exploring together the potential of cultural difference as a means of stimulating creativity.

Secondly, I must recognize the way in which my involvement in the 'Improving the Quality of Education for All' project has influenced my thinking about school development. Here the contributions of colleagues in the project schools were particularly important, as were, of course, those of the members of the outstanding team we were able to create at the University of Cambridge Institute of Education: Michael Fielding, David Hopkins, Judy Sebba, Geoff Southworth and Mel West. I must not forget, too, David Hargreaves who resisted our invitation to become a full member of that team but was frequently involved and became an enormous influence on our work.

A number of other close colleagues have made very significant contributions to my thinking. In particular, Dave Tweddle who has continued to be a powerful influence, not least in his insistence on the need for 'elegant explanations'; Susan Hart and Tony Booth, both of whom have questioned me in ways that have pushed me to engage with ideas in a more critical way; and Maggie Balshaw who has given support in so many different ways.

Colleagues in a number of other, more recent projects must also be mentioned, particularly Mark Vaughan and the other collaborators in the 'Index of Inclusive Schools' project; the members of the 'Understanding the Development of Inclusive Schools' network, not least since I adopted their name as a title for the book; Jill Martin and David Barrs who I have collaborated with in order to explore school-based staff development; Pam Holland, Dorothy Brown, John Harrington, and Ray Harris who I have worked closely with on two splendid school improvement projects in the Lewisham authority; Traian Vrasmas and my other friends involved in our UNICEF project in Romania; Alan Dyson (who has never forgiven me for that Cantona goal); and Climent Gine and our partners in the project 'Effective Schools for All' in Catalunya. Then, more generally, I must also not forget the influence of Keith Ballard, Peter Farrell (who will, I expect, find some of this book irritating), Anton Florek, the late Ron Gulliford, Janet Holdsworth, Alvaro Marchesi, Peter Mittler, Jim Muncey, Martyn Rouse, Tom Skrtic, Roger Slee, Sue Stubbs, Klaus Wedell and many others.

I must also thank colleagues and students in the Centre for Educational Needs at the University of Manchester for providing an intellectually stimulating environment that encourages me to continue pursuing the complex issues raised in this book, and Hilda Procter who tries so hard to protect my space. And, finally, my special thanks to lots of colleagues, too many to mention by name, in schools, colleges and education services in different parts of the world, for their friendship, inspiration and contributions. This book is dedicated to you all.

Mel Ainscow
September 1998

Chapter 1

Reaching Out to All Learners

The city where I work, Manchester, like many others around the world, is a city of diversity. For decades it has attracted people from all over the world. So much so that now it is possible to hear many different languages on our streets, eat wonderfully exotic dishes, listen to endless different kinds of music and buy fashions that reflect many cultures. In these and many other ways 'new' Mancunians have enriched the life of our community. Having said that, it would be foolish to ignore the tensions that all of this has created at certain times. Learning how to live with difference can be difficult. When we do so, however, it opens up rich possibilities that might otherwise be missed.

It was for reasons such as this that I have chosen to call this introductory chapter 'Reaching Out to All Learners'. In it I set out to stimulate and challenge those concerned with school effectiveness and improvement to consider how far their work really has taken account of the learning of *all* children. I also challenge those involved with what is currently referred to as special needs education to reconsider the roles they take. In this way I draw attention to the possibilities we can create for ourselves when we really do attempt to reach out to all learners.

The ideas that I explore and the suggestions I make in this book arise, in the main, as a result of reflections on the experience of working with teachers and schools over many years in this country and overseas. In particular, they have arisen from my involvement over the last ten years in two large-scale projects. The first of these was a school improvement project, 'Improving the Quality of Education for All' (IQEA), which involved a small team of university academics collaborating with English schools during what proved to be an unprecedented period of national educational reform. The experiences of this project led us to rethink many of our assumptions as to how school improvement can be achieved, noting in particular the way local histories and circumstances bear upon the improvement efforts of individual schools (Hopkins, Ainscow and West, 1994).

The second project was a UNESCO teacher education initiative to do with the development of more inclusive forms of schooling. This project, called 'Special Needs in the Classroom', originally involved research in eight countries (i.e. Canada, Chile, India, Jordan, Kenya, Malta, Spain and Zimbabwe), but subsequently led to dissemination activities of various kinds in over fifty countries (Ainscow, 1994). During the early phases it was assumed that materials and methods would be developed that could be distributed in a straightforward way for use in different parts of the world. Gradually, those of us leading the project came to realize, as others involved in international development activities in education have done (e.g. Fuller and Clark, 1994), that schooling is so closely tied into local conditions and cultures that the importation of practices from elsewhere is fraught with difficulties. In other words, learning from other people, particularly those who live their lives in far away places, is by no means straightforward!

The experiences of these two initiatives has had major implications for the development of my own thinking and practice. In particular, they have led me to reflect on how we can develop understandings that will be useful in encouraging the development of schools that will be successful in fostering the participation and learning of all pupils within a community. This raises questions such as, how do we make use of the diversity of experience and knowledge that exists within any given context to support the improvement of educational arrangements? Indeed, can we learn from the experience of others in ways that can support the development of practice? If so, what is the nature of the learning that might occur?

Keeping these questions in mind, in this book I use my own experiences to illustrate some ways in which an engagement with differences can stimulate our thinking about the issue of reaching out to all learners. In order to introduce the overall agenda for the book, in this first chapter I use vignettes based on observations made in schools and classrooms in various parts of the world in order to show how such experiences have stimulated a reconsideration of my thinking about practice in my own country. This leads me to argue that the power of comparison for the development of practice comes not from lifting approaches and moving them from place to place, but from using the stimulus of more exotic environments to reconsider thinking and practice in familiar settings (Delamont, 1992). It is about making what is strange familiar and what is familiar strange, as when seeing your own town in a new light when showing a visitor round. Features that are normally ignored become clearer, possibilities that have been overlooked are reconsidered, and things that have become taken for granted are subject to new scrutiny.

The shifts in my thinking that took place as a result of the two projects involved a reconceptualization of how some children come to be marginalized within, or even excluded from, schools. This, in turn, drew my attention to many possibilities for the development of schools that might easily have been overlooked. It also helped me to realize that a concern with local context had to be at the heart of any development activities, whether these are concerned with classrooms, schools or overall education systems. In this way I became aware of the importance of existing practice as the essential starting point for our efforts. Indeed, as my colleagues and I looked more closely at what was going on in the classrooms in which we worked we realized that very often much of the expertise that was needed in order to reach out to all learners was already there. Thus the strategy becomes less about importing ideas from elsewhere and more to do with finding ways of making better use of local knowledge. Put simply, our experience has been that teachers frequently know more than they use! The task of development, therefore, becomes essentially one of helping teachers, and those supporting them, to analyse their own practice as a basis for experimentation.

In what follows I illustrate what I have in mind by using stories from different parts of the world to show the potential of using local thinking and practice as a foundation for developing more inclusive schools. As I have already indicated, these accounts also demonstrate some ways in which we might learn from the experiences of others.

Vignette 1 — China

A primary school classroom in Inner Mongolia. There are approximately 75 children, sitting in rows of desks packed into a long, rather bleak looking room. The teacher stands at one end of the room on a narrow stage in front of a blackboard. In the back row of the classroom there are some pupils who look older than the rest. In fact, these are children who either started school later than the rest or, in some instances, are re-sitting the grade having failed in the previous year. Lessons are 40 minutes long and, although each is taught by a different teacher, mostly follow a common pattern. Typically this involves a process by which the teacher talks or reads and, frequently, uses questions to stimulate choral or individual responses from the class. Throughout the lesson the pace is fast and the engagement of pupils appears to be intense. Afterwards the teacher explains how she tries to help those who experience difficulties by directing many more questions to them and by encouraging their classmates to go over the lesson content with them during the breaktimes.

What, then, does an English observer make of such an experience? Does it suggest patterns of practice that might be relevant to teachers in my country where, despite much smaller classes, it is not uncommon to find groups of children whose participation in lessons is marginal to say the least? Why are these Chinese pupils so quiet and obedient throughout a day of lessons that appear so repetitive? It would be so easy to jump to simple conclusions that might appear to offer strategies that could be exported to other parts of the world. On the other hand there are so many other factors to consider. It is apparent, for example, that many other influences help to shape the events observed in this classroom. We are told that teachers are held in high esteem in Chinese society, although this is changing as a result of current economic reforms. It also seems that children are often under considerable pressure from their families to achieve success at school. Indeed in some parts of Asia there are signs in fast food restaurants which say 'No studying', presumably to discourage students from crowded home environments who are seeking space to pursue their schoolwork. Such community attitudes are but a part of a range of influences that help to shape the interactions that occur in local schools but which are difficult for the foreign visitor to determine.

Having said that, the Chinese story does point to the importance of teachers planning their lessons with all members of the class in mind. Here we bring into focus a central dilemma that confronts any teacher faced with their class. Put simply it is this: how do I work with the whole group and, at the same time, reach out to each member of the class as an individual? In the years since the right to educational opportunity was extended to all members of the community in many Western countries, it has become increasingly apparent that traditional forms of schooling are no longer adequate for the task. Faced with increased diversity, including the presence of pupils whose cultural experience or even language may be different from their own, and others who may find difficulties in learning within conventional arrangements, teachers have had to think about how they should respond.

Broadly speaking there seem to be three options:

- continue to maintain the status quo in the belief that those members of the class who do not respond have some problem that prevents their participation;
- make compromises by reducing expectations in the belief that some pupils will simply never be able to achieve traditional standards; and
- seek to develop new teaching responses that can stimulate and support the participation of all class members.

The problem with the first option, maintaining the status quo, is that it is likely to lead to conflict with some pupils and, possibly, their parents. It may also damage the working atmosphere for everybody, thus making life more stressful for the teacher. The second option, making compromises, involves a reduction in standards not least for some pupils who may already be vulnerable in our increasingly competitive society. The third option, demanding that it is, has the potential to bring about improvements that can enhance the learning of all pupils whilst at the same time reaching out to those who otherwise have been marginalized.

So, what kinds of practices might help teachers to 'reach out' to all members of the class? How might teachers develop their practice in order to make it more inclusive? These are major questions to be considered in subsequent chapters. At this stage a few introductory remarks will illustrate the directions I shall be taking. We have noticed that teachers who appear to be effective in providing experiences that facilitate the participation of all members of the class, whilst they each have their own style of working, do pay attention to certain key aspects of classroom life. First of all they seem to recognize that the initial stages of any lesson or activity are particularly important if pupils are to be helped to understand the purpose and meaning of what is to occur. Specifically, they aim to help their pupils to recall previous experiences and knowledge to which new learning can be connected. As one Italian teacher put it, 'I have to warm the class up — I want hot learners not cold learners'.

It is noticeable, too, the way that some teachers use available resources in order to stimulate and support participation. Most significantly they seem to be aware that the two most important resources for learning are themselves and their pupils. The idea of using the potential of pupils as a resource to one another seems to be a particularly powerful strategy but, regrettably, in some classrooms it is one that is largely overlooked. Certainly a striking feature of lessons that encourage participation is the way in which pupils are often asked to think aloud, sometimes with the class as a whole as a result of the teacher's sensitive questioning, or with their classmates in well managed small group situations. All of this provides opportunities for pupils to clarify their own ideas as they 'think aloud', whilst, at the same time, enabling members of the class to stimulate and support one another's learning.

It has taken me a long time to appreciate that existing practice represents the best starting point for development activities, not least because of my previous experience and training in the field of special education. It took me many years to recognize that the ways in which earlier attempts to develop integrated arrangements for pupils said to have special needs had often, unintentionally, undermined our efforts. As we tried to integrate such pupils into mainstream schools, we imported practices derived from earlier experience in special provision. What we learned was that many of these approaches were simply not feasible in primary and secondary schools. Here I am thinking, in particular, of the individualized responses, based on careful assessments and systematic programmes of interventions, that have been the predominant orientation within the special needs world. For many years this was very much the orientation that shaped my own work (e.g. Ainscow and Tweddle, 1979 and 1984). Gradually, however, experience has taught me that such approaches do not fit with the ways in which mainstream teachers plan and go about their work. For all sorts of sensible and understandable reasons the planning frame of such teachers has to be that of the whole class. Apart from any other considerations, the sheer numbers of children in the class and the intensity of the teacher's day makes this inevitable.

Consequently, when integration efforts are dependent upon the importation of practices from special education they seem almost certain to lead to difficulties. Indeed they are likely to lead to yet new forms of segregation, albeit within the mainstream settings (Fulcher, 1989), through the use of what Slee (1996) calls 'dividing practices'. For example, in England we have seen the proliferation of largely untrained classroom assistants who work with some of the most vulnerable children and their individual programmes in mainstream schools. When such support is withdrawn, teachers feel that they can no longer cope. Meanwhile, the legal requirement for individualized education plans has encouraged colleagues in some schools to feel that even more children will require such responses, thus creating massive budget problems in many parts of the country.

The gradual recognition that schools for all will not be achieved by transplanting special education thinking and practice into mainstream contexts has opened my mind to many new possibilities that I had previously failed to recognize. Many of these relate to the need to move from the individualized planning frame, referred to above, to a perspective that emphasizes a concern for and an engagement with the whole class. Thus as one teacher explained, what is needed are strategies that *personalize* learning rather than individualize the lesson. An understanding of what these might involve can be gained from the study of practice, particularly the practice of class teachers in primary schools and subject teachers in secondary schools. As my awareness of the value of such studies has developed, so my interest in observing and trying to understand practice has grown. Put simply, I am arguing that a scrutiny of the practice of what we sometimes call 'ordinary teachers' provides the best starting point for understanding how classrooms can be made more inclusive.

Vignette 2 — Ghana

A primary school in a rural district in West Africa. Here class sizes are much more manageable than those observed in the Chinese school. Typically there are 50 or so children in each class. On the other hand, the physical resources are noticeably poorer. Many of the children arrive in the morning carrying stools on their heads. It seems that for these children this is the equivalent of children in the West bringing a pen and a ruler from home. Apparently each evening the stools are taken home so that they can be used for domestic purposes. It may also be that some families are reluctant to leave them in school where they might be stolen, since the classrooms are open, having few walls. One of the teachers explains that his biggest problem is the lack of textbooks. In fact, for most lessons he only has one copy of the book and so frequently he has to write the text on the blackboard.

A surprising feature of the school from an English perspective is the presence of a number of pupils who are noticeably disabled. Further inquiries confirm that the headteacher assumes that it is his responsibility to admit all children in the district. 'Where else would they go?', he remarks. Apparently such examples of what Miles (1989) refers to as 'casual integration' can be found in a number of so-called developing countries, particularly in rural districts. Indeed they raise the question, is it significant, in some way, that it is a rural environment? A parent in Queensland, Australia, explained recently how she had found it necessary to move out of the city to find a school that would welcome her disabled daughter. Once again, however, there is the danger of jumping to simplistic conclusions and in so doing, perhaps, ignoring other factors that may well be influential in the context of Ghana? Can foreign visitors be sure of the conclusions they draw as they interpret their observations in the light of their previous experiences and existing frames of reference? Writing about the development of special education in Africa generally, Kisanji (1993) explains that there is evidence that the nature of provision is influenced by community perceptions of disabled children. He notes, for example, that in some countries disability is seen to arise as a result of the influence of factors such as witchcraft, curses or punishment from God, and anger of ancestral spirits. This being the case, it may be that some children will be hidden away from sight by the family in order to avoid feelings of shame.

It seems then that attempts to reach out to all learners will be influenced by the ways in which student differences are perceived. At the risk of oversimplifying what is undoubtedly a complicated issue, two possibilities come to mind. On the one hand differences may be seen in a normative way. This means that students are defined in terms of certain taken-for-granted criteria of normality, against which some come to be seen as being abnormal. Within such an orientation those who do not fit into existing arrangements are seen as needing attention elsewhere or, at least, assimilation into the status quo. Alternatively, perceptions may be guided by a view that all students are unique, with their own experiences, interests and aptitudes. Associated with this second, transformative orientation is a belief that schools have to be developed in ways that can take advantage of this diversity which is, therefore, seen as a stimulus for learning.

Here some of the traditional practices of many Western countries, including my own, may have discouraged movement towards a transformative approach. The tradition has been to perceive some pupil's differences as requiring a technical response of some kind (Ainscow, 1998; Heshusius, 1989; Iano, 1986). This leads to a concern with finding the 'right' response, i.e. different teaching methods or materials for pupils who do not respond to existing arrangements. Implicit in this formulation is a view that schools are rational organizations offering an appropriate range of opportunities; that those pupils who experience difficulties do so because of their limitations or disadvantages; and that *they,* therefore, are in need of some form of special intervention (Skrtic, 1991). It is my argument that through such assumptions, leading to a search for effective responses to those children perceived as being 'different', vast opportunities for developments in practice are overlooked.

I accept, of course, that it is important to identify useful and promising strategies. However, I believe that it is erroneous to assume that systematic replication of particular methods in themselves, will generate successful learning, especially when we are considering populations that historically have been marginalized or even excluded from schools. This over-emphasis on a search for 'quick-fix' methods often serves to obscure attention from more significant questions such as, why do we fail to teach some pupils successfully?

Consequently, it is necessary to shift from a narrow and mechanistic view of teaching to one that is broader in scope and takes into account wider contextual factors (Skrtic, 1991). In particular, it is important to resist the temptation of what Bartolome (1994) refers to as the 'methods fetish' in order to create learning environments that are informed by both action and reflection. In this way, by freeing themselves from the uncritical adoption of so-called effective strategies, teachers can begin the reflective process which will allow them to recreate and reinvent teaching methods and materials, taking into account contextual realities that can either limit or expand possibilities for improvements in learning.

It is important to remember that schools, like other social institutions, are influenced by perceptions of socioeconomic status, race, language and gender. This being the case, it is essential to question how such perceptions influence classroom interactions. In this way the current emphasis on methods must be broadened to reveal deeply entrenched deficit views of 'difference', which define certain types of pupils as 'lacking something' (Trent, Artiles and Englert, 1998). We have to be particularly vigilant in scrutinizing how deficit assumptions may be influencing perceptions of certain pupils.

Teaching methods are neither devised nor implemented in a vacuum. Design, selection and use of particular teaching approaches and strategies arise from perceptions about learning and learners. In this respect, even the most pedagogically advanced methods are likely to be ineffective in the hands of those who implicitly or explicitly subscribe to a belief system that regards some pupils, at best, as disadvantaged and in need of fixing, or, worse, as deficient and, therefore, beyond fixing.

In recent years, of course, the so-called deficit model has been subject to massive criticism in a number of countries (e.g. Ainscow, 1991; Ballard, 1995; Dyson, 1990; Fulcher, 1989; Oliver, 1988; Trent et al., 1998). This has helped to encourage a shift of thinking that moves explanations of educational failure away from a concentration on the characteristics of individual children and their families, towards a consideration of the process of schooling. Despite good intentions, deficit thinking is still deeply ingrained and too often leads many to believe that some pupils have to be dealt with in a separate way. In a sense it confirms the view that some pupils are 'them' rather than part of 'us' (Booth and Ainscow, 1998). This further encourages the marginalization of these pupils, whilst at the same time distracting attention away from the possibility that they can help to stimulate the development of practices that might well benefit all pupils. In other words, I am arguing that those who do not respond to existing arrangements should be regarded as 'hidden voices' who, under certain conditions, can encourage the improvement of schools. Thus differences can be seen as opportunities for learning rather than as problems to be fixed.

Vignette 3 — Austria

This example is set in a very different context, that of a primary school in Austria where class sizes are small and resources luxurious by any standards. Like a number of other European countries Austria has been moving towards a greater emphasis on the integration of children described as having special needs. As a result of recent legislation, the number of pupils in an 'integration class' is limited to 20: a maximum of four with disabilities and 16 others. A wide range of support personnel is also available to such classes. The school is in a small town in the eastern part of the country. There are 17 children sitting mainly in pairs at tables that are arranged informally, some pointing to the front of the room, others directed towards the centre of the room. One boy sits alone at a desk towards the rear of the room. There is thick snow outside and all the children wear slippers. The lesson is about Christmas and all the children have on their desks in front of them is a worksheet that has been prepared on a computer by the class teacher. After a short introductory presentation by the teacher the children carry out the tasks on the worksheet, chatting to one another as they work. Meanwhile, the boy sitting at the back of the room is being addressed by another teacher in a way that suggests that she perceives him as experiencing significant difficulties in understanding the spoken word. It seems that she is there to provide support to two pupils, who are seen as having special needs, one of whom is absent. This support teacher has her own desk, also located at the rear of the room. On this occasion she has designed a separate worksheet for the children she supports, one that deals with similar content but in a less demanding way.

This experience, like the earlier two, raises many questions. Certainly the boy in question is present in a regular classroom and, given his apparent learning difficulties, this would possibly not be the case in a number of other European countries. He also has the advantage of a large amount of individual attention of the sort for which parents in other countries have to fight. On the other hand, his physical location at the back of the room suggests that he remains somewhat marginalized, not least because the support teacher tends to stand between him and the rest of the class as she addresses him. So is he integrated or not? Can we take lessons from this encounter that might inform the development of more inclusive practices in other parts of the world?

The approach to inclusion that I am suggesting involves 'a process of increasing the participation of pupils in, and reducing their exclusion from, school curricula, cultures and communities' (Booth and Ainscow, 1998). In this way the notions of inclusion and exclusion are linked together because the process of increasing participation of pupils entails the reduction of pressures to exclude. This link also encourages us to look at the various constellations of pressures acting on different groups of pupils and acting on the same pupils from different sources.

For these reasons I am suggesting that yet another starting point for the development of practice within a school has to be the close scrutiny of how existing practices may be acting as barriers to learning. This means that attention has to be given to helping practitioners to develop a reflective attitude to their work such that they are continually encouraged to explore ways of overcoming such barriers. With this in mind, the approaches discussed in this book place considerable emphasis on the need to observe the process of schooling and to listen carefully to those involved. Many illustrations of what form this can take are provided, as well as examples of techniques that have been found to be helpful.

Vignette 4 — Laos

Laos is said to be one of the economically poorest countries in the world. Certainly this classroom has few material resources. The teacher spends the first ten minutes of the lesson talking to the children about a topic to do with nature. His presentation is illustrated by a lovely drawing he has done which is pinned to the blackboard. Suddenly the children move into groups of three to five and begin discussions. My interpreter explains that the teacher has set a question for them to address arising from his initial presentation. It is apparent from the speed with which all of this happens that the class are used to working in this way. What is also rather noticeable is the change in the atmosphere. The body language and facial expressions suggest that these children who had previously seemed rather passive were now much more engaged in the agenda that the teacher had set.

A feature of lessons like this that seem to be effective in encouraging pupil participation is the way available resources, particularly human resources, are used to support learning. In particular I am referring to a range of resources that is available in all classrooms and yet is often poorly used, that of the pupils themselves. Within any classroom the pupils represent a rich source of experiences, inspiration, challenge and support which, if utilized, can inject an enormous supply of additional energy into the tasks and activities that are set. However, all of this is dependent upon the skills of the teacher in harnessing this energy. This is, in part, a matter of attitude, depending upon a recognition that pupils have the capacity to contribute to one another's learning; recognizing also that, in fact, learning is to a large degree a social process. It can be facilitated by helping teachers to develop the skills necessary to organize classrooms that encourage this social process of learning. Here we can learn much from some of the economically poorer countries of the South, where limitations of resources have led to a recognition of the potential of 'peer power', through the development of 'child-to-child' programmes (Hawes, 1988). The recent interest in cooperative group work in a number of Western countries has also led to the development of teaching specifications that have enormous potential to create richer learning environments (e.g. Johnson and Johnson, 1994).

Vignette 5 — Nicaragua

A class of 45 twelve and thirteen year olds. Standing at the front of the classroom, five students are holding large posters that summarize conclusions about the local history projects they have been doing in groups. They take it in turn to summarize their ideas for the rest of the class. The teacher, a young male, comments on their presentations. Sitting at the back of the room is an older woman who, from her dress, is a nun; later I am told she is the deputy headteacher. After a time she interrupts the discussion to suggest to the teacher that he was perhaps placing too much emphasis on the ways in which the groups had been working. More attention needed to be given, she argued, to the actual content of the group discussions. They discussed this point across the room and, eventually, the teacher drew some of the students into a consideration of the deputy head's point. There was no impression given that the teacher or the students found these discussions in any way disturbing. Indeed, they seemed to be rather taken for granted as being part of normal activities.

Later I was told that this type of interaction is part of the school's overall strategy for encouraging improvements in teaching. Apparently each week the deputy headteacher holds meetings with staff to discuss aspects of classroom practice. Recently, for example, they had discussed the findings of a survey of student views about the teaching they receive. In these ways the school breaks down the traditional pattern of working within which teachers rarely have opportunities to discuss detailed aspects of their practice with their colleagues. In so doing, they are also helped to develop a language of pedagogy that enables them to reflect upon their own repertoires and to help one another to consider possibilities for further development.

   This experience reminded me of some of the ideas my colleagues and I have been exploring within our IQEA project, here in England. Much of our early work in schools involved attempts to introduce particular policies and, in so doing, to strengthen the schools' capacity to handle change (Ainscow, Echeita and Duk, 1994; Hopkins, et al., 1994; Hopkins, West and Ainscow, 1996). This has led us to look closely at schools where improvement efforts have led to changes in practice to see what lessons might be learned from their experiences. In stating that, however, I stress that I am not suggesting that our engagement with such a school will help to devise blueprints that can point the way forward for all schools. What I have learnt as a result of many years of working in schools, trying to support a variety of innovations, is that they are complex and idiosyncratic places. What seems to help development in one school may have no impact or even a negative effect in another. So, whilst we can, I believe, learn through vicarious experience, this learning has to be respected for its own qualities. Essentially it is a form of learning that provides a stimulus to reflect on existing experience and current understandings, rather than a means of providing prescriptions that can be transposed to other environments. Consistent with this view, throughout the chapters that follow I provide detailed accounts of classroom encounters and school processes that have provided me with such a stimulus.

Vignette 6 — India

The school serves a poor community in New Delhi. Having watched a wonderful lesson in which the children engaged in a role play activity about families I ask a couple of the teachers how this had been planned. They explain how for the previous year or so the headteacher had instigated occasional Saturday morning meetings to discuss their work. Around the walls of the school are beautiful posters developed during these gatherings. It was these discussions, the teachers explained, that had stimulated them to try out different approaches to teaching. However, they explained that it was not just the meetings. They had also developed the idea of what they called 'partnership teaching', whereby they occasionally have opportunities to work together in one another's classrooms. It was this, more than anything, they argued, that had stimulated their experimentation. I asked about how they found time given the numbers of children in each class. They explained that sometimes the headteacher would take a class to release a teacher to work with a colleague. Other times they might put two classes together but this usually meant that they would have to work outside since the classrooms were too crowded.

As can be seen, my interest in studying practice takes me beyond just a consideration of the work of individual teachers. Much of my research over the last few years convinces me of the importance of the school context in creating a climate within which more effective practices can be developed. The nature of such positive contexts can take many forms and, therefore, attempts at generalizations are very difficult. Nevertheless, the monitoring of developments in particular schools over time suggests certain patterns that are at least worthy of consideration. These suggest a series of organizational conditions that seem to facilitate the risk-taking that seems to be associated with movements towards more inclusive practices. More specifically they indicate that such movement is not about making marginal adjustments to existing arrangements, but rather about asking fundamental questions about the way the organization is currently structured, focusing on aspects such as patterns of leadership, processes of planning and policies for staff development. In this way the development of inclusive schooling comes to be seen as a process of school improvement (Ainscow, 1995b).

There is now considerable evidence that norms of teaching are socially negotiated within the everyday context of schooling (e.g. Keddie, 1971; Rosenholtz, 1989; Talbert and McLaughlin, 1994). It seems that the culture of the workplace impacts upon how teachers see their work and, indeed, their pupils. However, the concept of culture is rather difficult to define. Schein (1985) suggests that it is about the deeper levels of basic assumptions and beliefs that are shared by members of an organization, operating unconsciously to define an organization's view of itself and its environment. It manifests itself in norms that suggest to people what they should do and how. In a similar way, Hargreaves (1995) argues that school cultures can be seen as having a reality-defining function, enabling those within an institution to make sense of themselves, their actions and their environment. A current reality-defining function of culture, he suggests, is often a problem solving function inherited from the past. In this way today's cultural form created to solve an emergent problem often becomes tomorrow's taken-for-granted recipe for dealing with matters shorn of their novelty. Hargreaves concludes that by examining the reality-defining aspects of a culture it should be possible to gain an understanding of the routines the organization has developed in response to the tasks it faces.

Certainly my impression is that when schools are successful in moving their practice forward this tends to have a more general impact upon how teachers perceive themselves and their work. In this way the school begins to take on some of the features of what Senge (1989) calls a learning organization, i.e. 'an organization that is continually expanding its capacity to create its future' (p. 14). Or, to borrow a useful phrase from Rosenholtz (1989), it becomes 'a moving school', one that is continually seeking to develop and refine its responses to the challenges it meets.

It seems possible that as schools move in such directions the cultural changes that occur can also impact upon the ways in which teachers perceive pupils in their classes whose progress is a matter of concern (e.g. those nowadays usually referred to as 'having special educational needs'). What may happen is that as the overall climate in a school improves, such children are gradually seen in a more positive light. Rather than simply presenting problems that have to be overcome or, possibly, referred elsewhere for separate attention, such pupils may be perceived as providing feedback on existing classroom arrangements. Indeed they may be seen as sources of understanding as to how these arrangements might be improved in ways that would be of benefit to all pupils. If this is the case, as I have already suggested, the children sometimes referred to as having special needs represent hidden voices that could inform and guide improvement activities in the future. In this sense, as my colleague Susan Hart has suggested, special needs are special in that they provide insights into possibilities for development that might otherwise pass unnoticed (Hart, 1992).

It is important to recognize that the cultural changes necessary to achieve schools that are able to hear and respond to the 'hidden voices' is in many cases a profound one. Traditional school cultures, supported by rigid organizational arrangements, teacher isolation and high levels of specialisms amongst staff who are geared to predetermined tasks, are often in trouble when faced with unexpected circumstances. On the other hand, the presence of children who are not suited to the existing 'menu' of the school provides some encouragement to explore a more collegiate culture within which teachers are supported in experimenting with new teaching responses. In this way problem-solving activities may gradually become the reality-defining, taken-for-granted functions that are the culture of the inclusive school, i.e. a school that is attempting to reach out to all pupils in the community.

Learning from Experience

Even if we did not step foot outside our own countries, each of us already possesses extensive knowledge of the existence of differences in perspective on issues about processes of schooling, between pupils, parents and professionals, within and between a variety of cultural groups, and amongst academics and researchers. This knowledge should ensure that we avoid two common pitfalls of comparative discourse: the idea that there is a single national perspective on matters to do with education, and the notion that practice can be generalized across countries without attention to local contexts and meanings. In these senses this book builds on ideas developed recently as a result of a study I carried out with Tony Booth of processes of inclusion and exclusion in eight countries. In particular, it is intended to illustrate and further enhance an interest in the shaping effect on practice, of national and local policies, and cultural and linguistic histories (Booth and Ainscow, 1998).

The tendency to present single national perspectives is matched by a common failure to describe the way practice is to be understood within its local and national context. This is all part of a positivist view of social science in which research in one country can be amalgamated with that of another. The problem is compounded by differences of meaning of terms. Often this leads to the presentation of deceptively misleading international statistics, particularly in the case of special education, where data are frequently used to imply that the actual numbers of disabled children are the problem, leading to an assumption that solutions must focus on prevention, cure, and taking steps to make these children as normal as possible. In this way the statistics distract our attention from the ways in which attitudes, policies and institutions exclude or, at least, marginalize certain groups of children and young people (Stubbs, 1995).

All of this is in marked contrast to studies where there is a deliberate attempt to draw out nuances of meaning. An important contribution here is provided by the work of Susan Peters (1993 and 1995). Speaking as both a disabled person and a professional, she argues that educational concepts are by no means self evident in that they are culturally and context bound. Similarly, Miles and Miles (1993) use their experiences in Pakistan to outline how concepts such as childhood differ substantially between cultures; and Stubbs (1995) reports accounts that indicate that the concept of childhood does not even exist under Lesotho law. Rather, the population is divided into 'majors and minors', the latter being unmarried males and females who are not heads of families. As a result Lesothan primary school pupils may be in their late teens or even early twenties, having spent their younger years herding animals.

Such careful analyses of differences in perspective, context and meaning enhances rather than reduces the contribution that an examination of unfamiliar contexts can make to local practice, though they invalidate any attempt at simple imitation (Fuller and Clarke, 1994). As I have suggested, the power of comparison involves using the stimulus of more exotic environments to reconsider thinking and practice in familiar settings. In this way accounts of practice in other countries can present some of the opportunities afforded to travellers, particularly if they provide sufficient information to make practice transparent. But 'being there' is no guarantee of learning. One of my colleagues talked recently to a group of teachers from England who had visited Spain to see a school ostensibly similar to their own. When asked what they had seen on the trip, they said that they did not know. They had not armed themselves with the questions that they needed to ask about the Spanish system in order to make sense of the practice they saw. It seems, then, that visiting classrooms can be a disappointing experience, even in the most favourable circumstances, since most of what is interesting about what is going on is locked away in the heads of teachers and pupils (Booth and Ainscow, 1998).

Bearing these concerns very much in mind, this introductory chapter has attempted to illustrate how an engagement with less familiar contexts can stimulate a process of critical reflection, thus enabling previous experiences to be reconsidered and new possibilities for school improvement to be recognized. It also suggests and introduces a series of ideas that form the foundation of the proposals developed in subsequent chapters. These point to certain ingredients that can help in the development of more inclusive practices. Specifically, they suggest that movement in that direction is more likely in contexts within which improvement is seen as a process of **growth** that involves:

- using existing practices and knowledge as starting points for development;

- seeing difference as opportunities for learning rather than problems to be fixed;

- scrutinizing barriers to pupil participation;

- making effective use of available resources to support learning;

- developing a language of practice; and

- creating conditions that encourage a degree of risk-taking.

As I explain in subsequent chapters, these ingredients are overlapping and interconnected in a number of ways. Perhaps more than anything they are connected by the idea that attempts to reach out to all learners within a school have to include the adults as well as the pupils. It seems that schools that do make progress in reaching all pupils do so by developing conditions within which every member of the school community is encouraged to be a learner.

I do not pretend that any of this is easy. Profound changes will be needed if we are to transform schools, that were designed to serve a minority of the population, in such a way that they can achieve excellence with all children and young people. Some may argue that before investing in such an enormous project we need more evidence that it is possible. For myself, having seen what has happened in the schools referred to throughout this book, I see no need for further evidence. I have no doubt that amongst us we already have enough knowledge to develop schools that can be successful in educating all children. The big question is, do we have the will to make it happen?

Chapter Outlines

The chapters that follow further illustrate and develop the ideas that have been introduced. Their overall themes are as follows.

Chapter 2, 'Learning from Experience', is an account of the development of my thinking and practice in the years prior to the two projects that provided many of the examples and ideas presented in the subsequent chapters.

Chapter 3, 'Collaborative Inquiry', explores issues of methodology, looking, in particular, at what approaches to research can provide understandings that are directly relevant to the development of more inclusive practices.

Chapter 4, 'Moving Classrooms', considers what forms of practice can help teachers to reach out to all members of their class and how these might be conceptualized in a way that can help the process of development.

Chapter 5, 'Developing Practice', draws on the experience of the UNESCO Teacher Education project, 'Special Needs in the Classroom', in order to find ways of supporting teachers in extending their repertoires.

Chapter 6, 'Moving Schools', is mainly based upon the experience of the 'Improving the Quality of Education for All' project and is concerned with an understanding of the organizational conditions necessary in order to encourage the development of more inclusive practices.

Chapter 7, 'Developing Schools for All', uses the experience of a current project to develop an Index of Inclusive Schooling in order to explore what is involved in schools reviewing their existing arrangements in order to bring about improvements in practice.

Chapter 8, 'Supporting School and Teacher Development', provides an analysis of the skills needed by those inside schools whose task it is to lead development activities and those outside schools who are involved in supporting such initiatives.

Chapter 9, 'The Development of Inclusive Education Systems', moves the focus of attention to the overall national or district context in order to examine how more inclusive policies can be fostered.

Chapter 10, 'Some Final Reflections', provides concluding comments on the ideas that have been developed throughout the book.

Occasionally in the text I provide illustrative examples of activities that I have used as part of action projects in schools. These are mainly based on materials taken from the UNESCO Teacher Education Resource Pack, 'Special Needs in the Classroom' (available from UNESCO, 7 Place de Fontenoy, Paris), or the two manuals developed to support schools in the 'Improving the Quality of Education for All' project (i.e. Ainscow et al., 1994; Hopkins et al., 1997).

Chapter 2

Learning from Experience

The development of my own thinking and practice is at the heart of the ideas presented in this book. Indeed, a central argument is about the importance of reflecting on and learning from experience. With this in mind, therefore, this chapter provides an outline of some of the changes in my thinking that had occurred in the years *prior* to the two projects that are the main focus of attention. These provide a theoretical context for the experiences that are described and the proposals that are made in subsequent chapters.

The retrospective account presented in this chapter helped me to define certain ideas and assumptions that seemed to be significant starting points for the two projects. In preparing the account extensive use was made of various of my previous articles and books. Where it seems helpful I quote verbatim from these publications. Having said that, I am also conscious of Weick's warning about the limitations of retrospective explanations. Specifically he warns that they:

> . . . are poor guides to prospective action. We know relatively little about how we actually get things done. We don't know what works, because we misremember the process of accomplishment. We will always underestimate the number of false starts that went into the outcome. Furthermore, even though there were dead ends, we probably did learn from them — we learned more about the environment and about our capabilities. (Weick, 1985, p. 132)

He goes on to suggest that keeping records during times of change may help to avoid glossing over difficult experiences whilst striving for a particular outcome. In some senses the publications that I have drawn on in preparing this chapter provide such a record. Certainly revisiting them helped me to identify alternative explanations over and beyond those that were articulated when the writing was originally carried out.

Looking Back

Somebody said to me not so long ago, 'There are three kinds of people — people who make things happen; people who watch things happen; and people who wonder what the hell did happen!' If I look over my career in education I sense that I have at various stages been each of these.

My main professional interests have been and are with the difficulties that some children experience in school — and with attempts to find ways in which teachers can help all children to experience success in learning. Having worked as a teacher in secondary and special schools, I became a headteacher where my main role was to make things happen; I then worked as a local education authority adviser/inspector where I was able to spend more time observing practice in schools; and then, more recently, working in higher education, I have found myself looking back, reflecting on what I have learned from these experiences.

As I began work on the IQEA and UNESCO projects in the late 1980s, it was inevitable that these previous experiences would influence my decisions and actions. Whilst common sense suggests that everything that had occurred previously was likely to be an influence, two earlier experiences, in particular, seemed to be directly relevant to the task I faced. In this chapter, therefore, I provide reflective accounts of these experiences based upon my re-reading of my own writings during this time. The first of these experiences took the form of a curriculum development project in a special school; the other was an authority-wide staff development project related to the idea of special needs in ordinary schools. My accounts of these previous experiences provide the basis for an explanation of my thinking at the outset of the IQEA and UNESCO projects. They also indicate how this thinking had changed during the period of these earlier developments.

Curriculum Development in a Special School

During the 1970s I spent six years as headteacher of a special school in the Midlands for what were then referred to as ESN(M) (educationally subnormal, moderate) pupils (now designated as pupils with moderate learning difficulties). The population of the school consisted of pupils aged 5 to 16, most of whom were from economically poor families.

In collaboration with my colleagues in the school I attempted to develop an approach that would provide an educational experience suited to the needs of the pupils as we perceived them. We assumed that the children were in the school as a result of experiencing difficulties in ordinary schools and that in many instances these educational difficulties had come about, at least in part, as a result of social deprivation. Consequently, a strong influence on our thinking was a desire to compensate for the inadequacy of the children's experience. We were also keen to provide forms of intensive help that would accelerate their progress. Indeed, wherever possible, our aim was to bring the pupils to a level of achievement that would enable them to return successfully to ordinary schools.

Informed by these assumptions and beliefs, I saw it as my task to coordinate a team of people in developing and providing a curriculum that emphasized consistency and continuity. My view was that the best way to help our pupils to learn successfully was to provide teaching that was carefully planned and which co-ordinated the efforts of each member of staff. This work was going on during a period when the world of special education was subject to some criticism, particularly with respect to curriculum thinking and practices. This was part of a wider concern about the purposes and quality of schooling, leading to demands for greater accountability. There were, in addition, other more specific pressures that seemed to draw attention to the need for an examination of what happened in special schools. The Warnock Report had suggested that the quality of education offered to pupils in special provision was unsatisfactory, particularly with respect to the curriculum opportunities provided, and that many special schools underestimated their pupils' capabilities (DES, 1978). A number of other publications were also critical of existing practice (e.g. Brennan, 1979; Tomlinson, 1982).

Teachers in many special schools reacted to this new focus of attention on their work by taking a greater interest in the theoretical basis of their practice. Many became interested in curriculum theory, and in their search for guidance the staff in some special schools were influenced by the literature on planning with behavioural objectives, sometimes referred to as rational curriculum planning. This approach to planning, which was by no means new in the field of curriculum studies, had become popular in special education in North America, probably because of the strong influence of behavioural psychologists. Many of us working in special schools in the UK found the approach helpful as we sought ways of planning our teaching in a more systematic manner.

Initially, this interest grew as a result of our own discussions within the school, building upon the previous experience of the staff and was gradually affected by ideas from elsewhere. Dave Tweddle, who at that time was the educational psychologist attached to the school, was one such influence.

Over a period of years the staff established a pattern of meeting together on a regular basis to plan the curriculum for the whole school. Recently this sort of approach has become quite familiar in many schools, particularly with the introduction of staff development days, but at that time it was not that common. To provide a framework within which these discussions could take place we devised a simple curriculum model which consisted of the following two aspects:

1   The Closed Curriculum: this was an attempt to define those areas of skill and knowledge that were regarded as essential learning for all pupils in the school.

2   The Open Curriculum: this was viewed as being more open-ended, allowing content to be modified to take account of the needs of individual pupils.

It is important to note that within the school there was considerable commitment to the idea of providing a broad and enriching programme for all pupils. Indeed, there was very good work in areas such as creativity, personal and social development, environmental studies and outdoor pursuits — an orientation rooted in our desire to provide compensatory education. It is also important to recognize that whilst the Open/Closed framework was seen as a useful basis for planning, it was not the intention to use this distinction in planning actual classroom activities. In other words, it was acknowledged that pupils might well be engaged in tasks and activities related to Closed and Open Curriculum intentions at the same time.

Our detailed planning was based on agreed objectives. This involved taking broad goals and expressing them in terms of intended learning outcomes as a basis for planning and evaluating the teaching that was provided. It was also seen as a means of establishing the consistency and continuity to which we aspired. So, for example, a goal to do with teaching pupils to tell the time might lead to objectives such as:

1 reads aloud hours from the clock;
2 reads aloud minutes from the clock;
3 states that 60 minutes equals one hour; and
4 reads aloud time by half and quarter hours.

Within the Closed Curriculum, objectives were stated as relatively precise statements of observable behaviour that could then be used as a means of observing and recording pupil progress. Furthermore, these objectives were arranged in hierarchies of learning steps in the belief that progress would be accelerated by teaching the pupils in a step-by-step manner. Figure 2.1 is an example of how this approach was used as a basis for planning and recording progress. Further examples of this format, based on the work carried out in the school, can be found in two books that were written as a result of our work (i.e. Ainscow and Tweddle, 1979 and 1984).

In the Open Curriculum, planning was carried out in a less precise way, thus allowing individual teachers to provide opportunities that took account of the interests and experiences of their pupils. Consequently, a more flexible use of the objectives approach was encouraged, including the use of objectives that stated more general intentions and others which described experiences without predicting intended outcomes.

An Area Support Centre

A further development of the work of the school grew out of the then novel idea of the special school establishing a role as area support centre. This involved the creation of links with local primary and secondary schools in order to provide advice and support on dealing with learning difficulties. One element of this initiative was a series of inservice workshops, held in the special school for teachers from primary schools, with a main focus on developing individual learning programmes based on objectives and task analysis.

Further publicity for the work at the school was provided by a range of publications written by members of staff, including the book *Preventing Classroom Failure* (Ainscow and Tweddle, 1979), and the participation of colleagues in various conferences and courses. This publicity had an impact on teachers in special and ordinary schools around the country (Wolfendale, 1987). It also influenced the work of many educational psychologists and support services. I believe this influence was a positive one in a number of ways. It gave many teachers a means of talking about their work in ways that seemed practical and purposeful. It also had the effect of raising expectations about what certain pupils might achieve by

Name: *David*   **Date commenced:** *25th September*

Teaching goal: To develop the use of some basic sentence structures

Objective	Working on	Mastered	Checked	Comments
1 Uses an identity statement of the form 'This is a tree' in response to the question 'What is this?'		25th Sept. (assessed)	10th Oct.	
2 Uses the negation of objective (1), i.e. 'This is <u>not</u> a tree'.	25th Sept.	10th Oct.		Lang. Mast. cards introduced 2nd Oct. David is responding v. well.
3 Uses the identity statement 'The dog is black' in response to the question 'What colour is the dog?'		25th Sept. (assessed)	10th Oct.	
4 Uses the negation of objective (3), i.e. 'This is <u>not</u> black'.	12th Oct.	18th Oct.		Lang. Mast. cards used — prefers this to group puppet sessions.
5 Uses an action statement of the form 'The boy is running' in response to the question 'What is the boy doing?'		25th Sept. (assessed)	19th Oct.	
6 Uses the negation of objective (5), i.e. 'The boy is <u>not</u> running'.	19th Oct.			Expect rapid progress (i.e. 26th Oct.).

Figure 2.1 Format for recording progress using an objectives approach (Source: Ainscow and Tweddle, 1979)

focusing attention on those factors that teachers could influence. The emphasis placed on observing pupil progress within the classroom as opposed to the previous over-use of norm-referenced tests was also a significant step forward in many schools.

On the other hand, I came to recognize that the approach had a number of limitations and, indeed, potential dangers, particularly if used inflexibly (Ainscow and Tweddle, 1988). These concerns can be summarized as follows:

1   Planning educational experiences based on sequences of predetermined objectives tends to encourage a narrowing of the curriculum, thus reducing opportunities for learning.

2   Whilst the idea of individual programmes of objectives may be seen as a strategy for encouraging integration of pupils, it tends, in practice, to encourage segregation.

3   Where the approach is presented as a 'science of instruction' it tends to make teachers feel inadequate since it appears to give no value to their previous professional experience and expertise.

4   The idea of preplanning leaves little or no room for pupils to participate in decisions about their own learning. Consequently they are encouraged to adopt a passive role.

5   Programmes of objectives can become static, leading to them being used even when they are found to be inadequate or even redundant as a result of unexpected circumstances occurring.

In reflecting upon the work that was carried out by my colleagues in this particular special school, I came to the view that the successes that undoubtedly occurred were less to do with the idea of planning with objectives and more to do with group processes. In particular, I believe that the emphasis on staff discussion, leading to the creation of a common language that could be used to discuss matters of classroom practice, and the development of a more collaborative way of working in order to overcome difficulties, influenced the outlooks of individuals by raising their expectations and by providing a supportive social and professional environment. It also led to a strong sense of common purpose throughout the school, a factor which may be a common feature of all effective schools (see for example, Stoll, 1991). I should add that I have subsequently witnessed similar positive effects in other schools that have adopted this way of working (e.g. Ainscow and Hopkins, 1994; Hopkins et al., 1994).

A Local Authority Staff Development Programme (SNAP)

In 1979 I became adviser for special educational needs in Coventry. As part of my duties there I instigated and helped coordinate the development of a staff development initiative, 'The Special Needs Action Programme' (SNAP). This project had arisen as a result of a review of the authority's special education provision which led to a recognition of the need for significant change. (A detailed account of the development of SNAP is provided in Ainscow and Muncey, 1989.) In general terms the aim was to redirect special education provision and services away from ways of working that encouraged segregation of pupils towards a much more integrated range of responses. It was not seen as a revolutionary strategy but as an attempt to bring about gradual change in ways that would limit the risk of damaging existing good practice.

The development of the project was influenced by a number of significant factors. As part of a wider movement aimed at protecting the rights of minority groups in the community, there had been an increased recognition that the rights of children are significantly reduced if they are excluded from all or part of the programme of experiences generally offered in schools. There was also the impact of government legislation, particularly the 1981 Education Act. Whilst this had not come into effect at the outset of SNAP, the various consultative processes associated with its formulation helped to encourage the debate about special educational needs that had been fostered by the Warnock Report. In addition the influence of parental opinion was having an increasing impact upon the education service. In the special needs field in particular, the idea of 'parents as partners', as promoted in the Warnock Report, had become widely accepted if not implemented. Finally, developments in educational thinking generally were also influential. New ideas about curriculum, teaching and learning styles, forms of assessment and recording, and staff development had all enriched the discussion about how schools might respond to pupils experiencing difficulty.

The aims of SNAP were to encourage headteachers of ordinary schools to develop procedures for the identification of pupils with special needs; to assist teachers in ordinary schools to provide an appropriate curriculum for such pupils; and to coordinate the work of the various special education support services and facilities in ordinary schools. We did not see SNAP as an attempt to impose one model of achieving these aims. We felt that each school should develop policies and practices compatible with its situation and usual ways of working. With this in mind, each school in the authority was asked to designate one member of staff as coordinator for special needs, a strategy that was later adopted as part of national policy. Emphasis was placed on this person's task in the coordination of all staff in sharing responsibility for the progress of all pupils. Meanwhile, we attempted to disseminate examples of good practice that schools could use as vehicles for reviewing and, where necessary, extending existing procedures. This last point is important since some of the publicity given to SNAP nationally was based upon a misunderstanding of the ways in which the project operated in Coventry. For example, groups in some local authorities took some of the SNAP materials and used them as a means of imposing on teachers a particular way of working. Our emphasis was placed on helping schools to develop approaches that were consistent with their own traditions and philosophies.

The project focused initially solely on primary schools, but subsequently it had an impact in the secondary phase. The central strategy in both sectors was a series of inservice courses related to special needs in ordinary schools which were developed by teams within the authority. These were first presented to representatives from each school in the authority at the teachers' centre and then as part of school-based staff development programmes.

The early courses tended to be concerned with helping teachers to devise individualized teaching programmes, based very much on the ideas recommended in Ainscow and Tweddle (1979 and 1984). So, for example, the course for primary schools Teaching Children with Learning Difficulties involved a workshop guide, 'Small Steps'. This introduced procedures for developing individual programmes based upon planning with behavioural objectives in the form described earlier in this chapter. However, as SNAP developed, the courses gradually took on a much broader perspective. The course Problem Behaviour in Primary Schools, for example, examined issues related to school management and organization as well as examining principles of classroom organization. Similarly, the course Special Needs in the Secondary School attempted to get schools to review all aspects of policy and practice as a means of finding ways of meeting the individual needs of all pupils.

From starting in a small way, as just another inservice initiative, SNAP gradually grew until it became effectively the coordinating mechanism for the whole of the authority's policy on special needs. This was, in my view, an interesting example of how change can be facilitated provided the efforts of those involved are coordinated and supported over a period of years. Unfortunately, too often sound initiatives aimed at bringing improvements in educational contexts are less successful because this long-term commitment is not sustained.

Evaluating SNAP

Since the main purpose of SNAP was to help schools to review and develop their policies and practice this had to be the main focus of its evaluation. Extensive evidence from a number of sources, including detailed case studies of the work in schools and follow up evaluations of particular courses (e.g. Ainscow and Muncey, 1989; Arthur, 1989; Gipps, Gross and Goldstein, 1987; Moses, 1988), indicated that a series of features incorporated in the various courses developed as part of SNAP were particularly effective in encouraging staff development and change.

We found, for example, that the self-contained format of the course materials appeared to provide a relatively neutral stimulus that staff could use for reviewing existing practice. They did not imply that a school's existing approaches were redundant; but rather sought to build upon good practice. In addition, the emphasis on active learning approaches and group problem solving, as opposed to the traditional didactic teaching style of so much inservice education, encouraged participation and seemed to help overcome fear of change. Furthermore, involving all staff within a school in a process of review and development of policy helped facilitate a commitment to implement any changes that were agreed.

The courses attempted to present practical ideas and, in some cases, materials that could be used in the classroom. They also aimed to provide teachers with early success by getting them to try out strategies in their own classrooms. This was much appreciated by participants who suggested that too many inservice experiences provide theory without any attention to practical implications. The credibility of courses seemed to be enhanced by the fact that they were tutored by practising teachers and considerable efforts were made to support teachers as they tried out new approaches in their classrooms. This was provided by members of the various advisory and support services. A further source of help was created by emphasizing the importance of within-school support between teachers.

In reflecting upon the experience of SNAP in Coventry it seems to me that once again the major lesson to be learned relates to the importance of group processes. Whilst the inservice materials that developed were often quite impressive, the greatest impact may well have resulted from the collaborative problem solving that they encouraged and the way in which this helped to foster creativity and experimentation. This collaboration seemed to occur at different levels within the service. First of all the teams of people who came together to develop materials gained much from the professional dialogues that this process demanded. Then, those who acted as tutors gained in terms of their own confidence and expertise as a result of working together with representatives from the schools. Finally, where schools were able to use the project materials to facilitate review and development of policy and practice, this seemed to be an effective strategy for encouraging more coordinated whole-school approaches.

An Interactive Perspective

The period I spent in Coventry led me to change my views in a number of ways, particularly as a result of the many opportunities I had to observe teachers at work in primary and secondary schools. This gave me a much better understanding of the issues involved in attempting to respond to the needs of individual pupils in classes larger than those in the special schools in which I had previously taught.

My perspective was further influenced by my involvement in the planning of various other authority staff development initiatives (e.g. management; personal and social education). Consequently, I was able to review my ideas about the nature of educational difficulties. I began to recognize that much of my earlier work had been based on the assumption that these difficulties were to a large extent a result of within-child factors. I had tended to exclude from consideration causal explanations that might lie in contextual processes that are external to the individual child. Furthermore, I began to realize that this perspective leaves the organization and practice of ordinary schools untouched since they are assumed to be appropriate for the great majority of children. In other words, the provision of special education tends to confirm the assumption that difficulties occur in schools because certain children are special and this becomes a justification for the maintenance of the status quo of schooling.

In the light of these arguments I found myself increasingly joining others at the time (e.g. Wedell, 1981; Dessent, 1987) in adopting an interactive perspective to the special needs tasks. This position was summarized in the first chapter of a book I completed in 1988 with my colleague from Coventry, Jim Muncey (i.e. Ainscow and Muncey, 1989). In that book we contrasted what we called pre- and post-Warnock thinking with regards to special needs, using the publication of the Warnock Report into the future of special education as our reference point (DES, 1978). This led us to suggest what we referred to as a 'new approach based upon an acceptance of the Warnock argument that great numbers of children experience difficulties in the school system' (p. 10). We went on to state that most of these children are already present in ordinary schools and that we could anticipate a continuing trend towards youngsters with more severe difficulties being educated in mainstream provision.

The thinking associated with this interactive perspective to special needs is well summarized by the 'new assumptions' that Muncey and I put forward. I quote from these in some detail since they give a clear statement of our agreed position at that time.

New Assumption 1

Any child may experience difficulties in school at some stage

> It has to be recognized that experiencing difficulty in learning is a normal part of schooling rather than an indication that there is something wrong with a child. It is only when difficulties in learning cause anxiety to the child, the child's parents or teachers that particular attention needs to be paid. Furthermore, this can apply to any youngster whatever his or her overall attainments in comparison with others in the same class. So, for example, a child who is generally successful in learning may go through a period of boredom with the work presented by the class teacher. If this means that he or she is not applying effort to the task then it becomes a cause for concern. On the other hand, a child whose progress is generally slower than that of classmates may be getting on well and feeling generally positive about his or her work. The point is clear, therefore: our concern is with all children.
>
> This notion that any child can experience difficulties with learning is not of course confined to children. This was brought home to one of us recently when we were talking to a group of advisers, who, to their credit, pointed out that just as any child can experience a difficulty in learning so can any adviser, or indeed any adult.

New Assumption 2

Help and support must be available to all pupils as necessary

> Given that any child may experience some difficulty that causes concern at some stage of their school life, it makes sense that forms of support should be available as and when necessary.

With a traditional approach this would be difficult to achieve since the focus was on providing help for designated groups of children . . . this often necessitated complex and time-consuming processes of identification, which made it very difficult to make rapid and appropriate responses to pupils who might have a particular short-term difficulty in learning. In order to have a more responsive and flexible system we are now developing ways of providing support and extra attention through the normal and everyday processes of the life of the school — through the curriculum, through social encounters and relationships, and within the constraints and resources that are normally available. The aim is to make all the arrangements for teaching and learning as effective as possible. Indeed, since the principles of good practice for youngsters with special needs tend to be principles of good practice for all, a focus on special needs is a way of improving the delivery of education to all children.

New Assumption 3

Educational difficulties result from an interaction between what the child brings to the situation and the programme provided by the school

In moving towards a new way of working it is important to recognize its theoretical basis . . . In the traditional, pre-Warnock approach, the concern was with finding out what was wrong with the child. This approach, often characterized as a medical model, assumed that pinpointing the cause of the child's problems (i.e. diagnosis) would help us to determine an appropriate response (i.e. treatment or prescription). The new thinking, on the other hand, recognizes that, whilst the individual differences of children must influence their progress, what we as teachers do is also very important. Difficulties in learning occur as a result of the decisions teachers make, the tasks teachers present, the resources teachers provide and the ways in which teachers choose to organize the classroom.

Consequently, difficulties in learning can be created by teachers but, by the same token, can be avoided. This viewpoint is essentially an optimistic one since it points to areas of decision making, over which we as teachers have reasonable control, that can help children to experience success in the classroom and overcome whatever disadvantages or impairments they bring with them into school.

New Assumption 4

Teachers should take responsibility for the progress of all the children in their classes

. . . the message of the past was that special education was for experts. When children were seen as being in some way exceptional or special, teachers were encouraged to look for outside experts who could solve the problem, consequently, they tended to assume that there were certain members of the class that they could not be expected to teach. The work of some of the special education experts often encouraged this viewpoint by giving the impression that they had methods of working that were exclusive to them. This had the effect of further undermining the confidence of primary school teachers and implying that they need not take responsibility for certain pupils. The new thinking requires each of us to retain responsibility for all members of the class.

New Assumption 5

Support must be available to staff as they attempt to meet their responsibilities

Taking responsibility for all pupils does not mean that teachers should feel that they cannot look for help and advice. All of us are limited by our own previous experience and existing skills; all of us must expect to meet situations and challenges that we find difficult; and, indeed, all of us must be prepared to recognize our professional limitations. There is nothing to be gained by pretending to cope with something that is beyond our competence. So, in wishing to discourage the idea of special education experts who appear to take away certain of our responsibilities, we wish to argue that what is needed instead are approaches to teaching and learning that emphasize the sharing of expertise, energy and resources. Furthermore, as we argue in subsequent chapters, an emphasis on sharing and collaboration is a noticeable feature of successful schools.

Ainscow and Muncey (1989, pp. 10–12)

In the light of these 'new assumptions', Muncey and I characterized the way in which we believed schools should respond to the post-Warnock approach. We argued that the pre-Warnock emphasis on 'categories, care and segregation' should be replaced by ways of working that paid attention to 'needs, curriculum and collaboration'. We then want to note that the abolition of the formal categories of handicap had left something of a gap in the language of the education service. If we were not to describe a child as being maladjusted or educationally subnormal, how might we describe his or her difficulties and ensure the provision of appropriate help and support?

The 1981 Education Act had incorporated the concept 'special educational need', as proposed in the Warnock Report. On first sight it was an attractive idea in that it seemed to mean that we should think positively about the sorts of arrangements that need to be made in order to help individual children to gain access to the curriculum. Unfortunately, in the period following the implementation of the legislation, it was possible to detect a serious distortion of the original concept. From being an approach that attempted to pay particular attention to individuality, the term 'special educational need' increasingly became a super-label used to designate a specific group of pupils thought to have problems. In fact, what we had seen was a tendency to return to the old perspective of interpreting educational difficulties purely in terms of within-child deficits. Even worse, the category 'special educational need' was now being used in a fairly indiscriminate way to refer to a large minority of the school population. Thus, from a policy that was intended to facilitate the integration of pupils experiencing difficulties in learning, we had effectively seen an increase in the proportion of pupils labelled and segregated, at least in the sense that they were perceived by their teachers as being different.

An influence on this development was the wide acceptance of the idea that up to 20 per cent of pupils have special educational needs. This estimate was used widely in the early 1980s as a means of arguing for greater resources and the sharing of responsibility across the service. Unfortunately, from being an estimate of the number of youngsters who may experience difficulties of some kind at some stage in their school career, it became a target. Even worse, in some schools it became linked to crude notions of low general ability, so that teachers perceived the 'bottom 20 per cent' as having special needs. Hence the increase in labelling and segregation. Given these difficulties, Muncey and I concluded that it probably made sense to part company with the term 'special educational need'. Instead we felt that the aim should be to find ways of making schools responsive to pupils' individual needs in the belief that **all** children are special.

In the light of this analysis we decided that the central question to be addressed in the book was, 'How do we take account of the needs of individual pupils?' This being the case we went on to consider strategies and approaches for managing schools and classrooms that would enable all children to participate successfully in broadly the same range of experiences alongside others from their community. In this respect, we argued, our emphasis was on integration.

Encouraging Classroom Success

Meanwhile, almost ten years after completing the book *Preventing Classroom Failure*, Dave Tweddle and I met up again with a view to writing a revised second edition. After a series of meetings, over a period of months, we came to the view that this was now impossible. Our thinking had moved on so far as a result of our experiences and our assumptions had changed so fundamentally that we decided that it would be wiser to write a new book, *Encouraging Classroom Success* (Ainscow and Tweddle, 1988).

In this book we reflected on different approaches to the assessment of difficulties in learning. This led us to define two overall orientations that seemed to dominate practice. These were concerned with:

- analysing the learner; and

- analysing learning tasks.

Having considered the limitations and, indeed, potential dangers of each of these, we proposed a third possibility, that of:

- analysing the learning context.

In this way our attention was refocused away from a narrow perspective on individual learners towards the contexts in which learning takes place. This pointed us in the general direction of many of the approaches that are discussed in the later chapters of this book. It also led us to suggest a framework for reviewing practice as a means of finding ways of helping all pupils to experience success. It was an approach that replaced the rather closed prescriptions of our earlier work with a more open agenda that is intended to encourage teachers to take responsibility for their own learning. Our aim became one of helping all teachers to be 'reflective practitioners' (Schon, 1987). Classroom evaluation was central to this orientation. This is a process of gathering information about how pupils respond to the curriculum as it is enacted. The focus, therefore, is on areas of decision making over which teachers have a significant influence. Broadly speaking these areas are:

- objectives, i.e. Are objectives being achieved?

- tasks and activities, i.e. Are tasks and activities being completed?

- classroom arrangements, i.e. Do classroom arrangements make effective use of available resources?

Because of the complexity of classroom life and the importance of unintended outcomes, there is also a need to keep a further question in mind. This is:

- what else is happening? i.e. Are there other significant factors that need to be considered?

We recommended that the framework provided by these four broad questions be used by teachers and pupils to reflect upon the encounters in which they are engaged. In other words, the framework becomes an agenda for reflection. This approach was based upon our belief that success in the classroom is more likely to occur if objectives, tasks and activities, and classroom activities take account of individual pupils and are understood by all those involved. Thus classroom evaluation is seen as a continuous process, built into the normal life of the classroom and, furthermore, it requires collaboration and negotiation if it is to be effective.

Proposing this wider perspective, we argued, has major implications for the ways in which the education service provides support to youngsters experiencing difficulties in learning. It requires that the focus of assessment and recording should be children in their normal classroom environment; that information should be collected on a continuous basis; that pupils should have a key role in reflecting upon their own learning; and that the overall aim should be to improve the quality of teaching and learning provided for all pupils. It is perhaps worth adding that it is a perspective that does not lend itself to the provision of 'quick-fix' solutions to educational difficulties.

Implications

The account presented in this chapter provides an outline of the changes in my thinking that had occurred in the years prior to the IQEA and UNESCO projects that are at the centre of discussions in this book. My commitment to an interactive perspective on educational difficulties, in particular, represented a significant change from the predominant view in the special needs field. It means that educational difficulties have to be seen as being context bound, arising out of the interaction of individual children with a particular educational programme at a certain moment in time. Whilst being somewhat complex this definition has the advantage that it tends to encourage a sense of optimism. Unlike the traditional approach where the focus on child-centred causes of educational difficulty tended to create an air of despondency, the interactive perspective focuses attention on a range of factors that teachers can influence to encourage children's learning. It emphasizes the fact that what teachers do, the decisions they make, their attitudes, the relationships they develop and their forms of classroom organization, are all factors that can help children to experience success in school. By the same argument, of course, these factors can also help to **create** educational difficulties for some children.

This interactive approach to special education has major implications for the organization of schools and the work of teachers. In particular it has implications for provision made in ordinary schools. It argues for the development of primary and secondary schools that are responsive to children with a wide range of needs (e.g. Thousand and Villa, 1991; Wang, 1991). Indeed special education, instead of being seen as a search by specialists for technical solutions to the problems of particular children becomes a curriculum challenge shared by all teachers within every school (Ainscow and Tweddle, 1988).

Partly as a result of the influence of this type of argument, schools and school systems in many countries began to review their policies and practices (Hegarty, 1990). In many cases the aim was to move towards what had come to be called 'a whole school approach' to special educational needs (Ainscow and Florek, 1989). The idea was that all teachers within a school should accept responsibility for the development and progress of all its pupils, including those with difficulties and disabilities.

Across the whole range of provision the changes that were taking place had specific implications for the work of individual teachers, particularly those perceived as being specialists. Many teachers who had traditionally spent much of their time working with small groups of children withdrawn from regular lessons for intensive instruction in basic skills, now found themselves having to work collaboratively with colleagues in mainstream education, either providing support or working on joint curriculum initiatives (Ainscow, 1989).

As I look back, this account of developments during the 1980s sounds positive, rational and encouraging. It gives the impression that education services were marching in unison towards new ways of working, with agreement and understanding. Alas, this was far from being the case. As is usual with significant change, the service in many countries found it very difficult to come to terms with the new version of special education. In England, for example, government documents continued to encourage confusion between traditional and newer perspectives, whilst at local authority level the implementation of policies based on interactive perspectives remained in some confusion (Goacher, Evans, Welton and Wedell, 1988).

Inevitably, this general confusion was reflected in the practice of schools. Despite the rhetoric of whole school approaches for responding to individual needs, traditional views of special education persisted and the policies of many schools remained an uneasy amalgam of old and new (Clark, Dyson, Millward and Skidmore, 1997). This created contradictions and tensions that could be a major source of stress for individual teachers. Indeed, using the terms of Schwab (1969), it can be argued that there was evidence of a crisis of thinking in the field.

If education systems were to find a way successfully through this difficult phase there was a need for those involved, at all levels, to become clearer about the rationale upon which the new ways of working are based. As we know, change, particularly when it involves new ways of thinking and behaving, is a difficult and time-consuming process. Michael Fullan (1991) argues that for it to be achieved successfully, a change has to be understood and accepted by those involved. Understanding and acceptance take time and need encouragement.

How then could this be achieved? How could teachers and others involved in schools be helped to come to terms with a version of special education that was, in essence, about the development of the mainstream? The message that emerged from the analysis in this chapter, which was to become central to my own thinking, was that one way forward was to encourage teachers to take a more positive approach by learning how to investigate and develop their own classroom practice. The aim should be to facilitate understanding and to encourage professional development through processes of classroom evaluation and reflection, as Tweddle and I had recommended in 1988. In this respect the emphasis on collaboration that had emerged also represented an important message.

Chapter 3

Collaborative Inquiry

There is a story of a famous professor who, though he had written a number of significant papers about quality in education, had not visited a school for over 20 years. A new young colleague persuaded him to visit a local school that had acquired a reputation for the excellence of its work. On the journey back from the visit the young lecturer asked the professor to comment on what he had seen. After a moment's silence the professor replied, 'I'm just thinking, would it work in theory?'

In many ways my own work addresses the same question. Perhaps the major difference between me and the famous professor, however, is that I continue to spend significant periods of my working hours in schools. Over the last few years in particular, my work in this country and abroad has provided me with endless opportunities to reflect upon and engage with questions about how schools and classrooms can be developed in response to student diversity. How far these experiences represent what others regard as research in a formal sense is a matter of debate. What they have stimulated is a process of learning as I have sought to find meaning in and understand what I have experienced. In this respect, I echo Robinson (1998), in describing myself as a researcher who wishes to make a relatively direct contribution to the understanding and improvement of educational practice. Consequently, I have found it necessary to search for methodologies that can support this practical desire.

This chapter provides an account of my search for such a methodology. It leads me to argue that there is a need for much greater recognition of the power of practitioner research as a means of developing schools for all. I will argue, however, that such a move requires significant changes in thinking in the field about the nature of educational difficulties and how they should be investigated. It also has major implications for the ways in which educational researchers go about their business.

Rethinking Educational Difficulties

Over recent years my involvement in the school improvement project, 'Improving the Quality of Education for All' and the UNESCO teacher education project 'Special Needs in the Classroom', has heightened my awareness of the ways in which different perceptions of educational difficulties can influence and shape the responses of practitioners. This awareness leads me to assume that concepts of educational difficulty are socially constructed and must, therefore, be regarded as being highly problematic. As I engaged with these complexities I found my own position shifting, yet again, in ways that were, to say the least, both disruptive and disturbing. Inevitably, these changes in thinking are apparent in what I have written, thus, perhaps, leading those who read what I write to experience their own feelings of disturbance.

Some time ago Susan Hart and I attempted to map out some possible perspectives on educational difficulties in order to assist ourselves (and possibly others) in gaining a better understanding of our own current positions (Ainscow and Hart, 1992). In this context I take perspectives to mean those basic assumptions that determine our attitudes, values and beliefs, and lead us to predict the nature and meaning of incoming information (Nias, 1987). So the perspectives we defined are attempts to characterize alternative ways of looking at the phenomenon of educational difficulty, based on different sets of assumptions that lead to different explanations, different frames of reference and different kinds of questions to be addressed. In this sense they lead to assumptions that provide the basis of different theoretical positions.

We defined three overall perspectives. The first of these, we suggested, seeks to explain educational difficulties in terms of the characteristics of individual pupils. This remains the dominant perspective in the special needs field, where the nature of educational difficulties is explained in terms of particular disabilities, social background and/or psychological attributes. The frame of reference created by this perspective is the individual child, and responses are chosen that seek to change or support the child in order to facilitate participation in the process of schooling. Traditionally, responses informed by this perspective have taken the form of removal of the child from the mainstream curriculum for specialist help. However, more recently, responses have begun to develop which allow help to be provided in the context of the regular classroom.

The second perspective explains educational difficulties in terms of a mismatch between the characteristics of particular children and the organization and/or curriculum arrangements made for them (e.g. Wedell, 1981; Dessent, 1987). Here support may be directed towards helping the child to meet the demands and expectations of the system, if this is assumed to be fixed or — for the time being at least — unchangeable. Or it may be directed towards making modifications to the system in order to extend the range of pupils that can be accommodated. In many respects current 'state of the art' responses (e.g. whole-school approaches, differentiation) are informed by this perspective. Further, it is a perspective that is seen as arising as a result of dissatisfaction with the first perspective, which is seen as being a 'deficit model' (Dyson, 1990). The frame of reference in this interactive perspective once again focuses attention on individual pupils but this time is concerned with the ways they interact with particular contexts and experiences, so much so, that those adopting this perspective have, in recent years, tended to argue for the use of the term 'individual needs' rather than 'special needs', as I suggested in the previous chapter. Responses chosen in the light of this perspective include curriculum adaptations, alternative materials for pupils, or extra support in the classroom.

Sometimes, these responses are also seen as being of benefit to pupils other than those designated as having special needs.

The third perspective explains educational difficulties in terms of curriculum limitations, using the term curriculum in a broad sense to include all the planned and, indeed, unplanned experiences offered to pupils. Thus in this perspective there is a concern with what can be learnt from the difficulties experienced by some children about the limitations of provision currently made for all pupils. The assumption is that changes introduced for the benefit of those experiencing difficulties can improve learning for all children (Hart, 1992). Those adopting this perspective are critical of the limitations of an individual frame of reference, even where this is used to raise questions about the adequacy of curriculum organization and practice as currently provided for individual pupils. They argue that a wider frame is needed, focusing on curriculum organization and practice as currently provided for all pupils. The task involves continually seeking ways of improving overall conditions for learning, with difficulties acting as indicators of how improvements might be achieved (Ainscow, 1994; Cohen, 1997; Hart, 1996). Those who adopt this perspective are likely to favour approaches that encourage enquiry as a means of achieving improvement, e.g. various forms of partnership teaching, action research.

It is important to recognize at this stage in the argument that, whilst the adoption of a particular perspective tends to encourage the choice of certain types of organizational and curriculum responses, the responses are in themselves often neutral as to their orientation. So, for example, support teaching (i.e. the provision of additional staff who work alongside regular teachers within the mainstream classroom in order to support the participation of pupils seen as having special educational needs), which has become a very fashionable response in recent years, might be used by teachers favouring any of these three perspectives. In this case, those adopting a characteristics perspective would see support teaching as a means of providing an individual pupil with extra teaching, albeit in the context or framework of regular classroom activities; those who take an interactive view, on the other hand, would see support teaching as a way of making modifications to existing arrangements in order to accommodate certain pupils experiencing learning difficulties; whereas the curriculum limitations perspective would encourage the idea that additional adults could facilitate the review and development of existing arrangements in the light of a scrutiny of the difficulties experienced by certain pupils.

I can now relate this general map of perspectives to my own work, including my continuing involvement with teachers and schools in the various projects with which I am involved, particularly the UNESCO project. In those contexts I am continually provoked into reconsidering my own thinking and practice as a result of being confronted by what seem strange situations. In particular I find that the unusual situations that I meet as I work in different countries have the effect of making the familiar seem strange. As I have suggested, this seems to be consistent with the view of Delamont (1992) who argues that familiarity can act as a barrier when carrying out research, suggesting that it is possible to make use of national differences in educational experience and organization to illuminate features that might otherwise be taken for granted.

As the UNESCO project developed, I gradually became aware that my position had changed from one that I characterized in the previous chapter as being based upon an interactive perspective, to one that that can be seen as being informed predominantly by a curriculum limitations view (Ainscow, 1995b). At the heart of this shift was a growing concern about the limitations and, indeed, potential dangers of an individual frame of reference when addressing educational difficulties. In particular, I saw this as leading to a narrowing of opportunity and lowering of expectations for children, not least in that it masked possibilities for developing practice.

Much of current thinking regarding the improvement of work in the special needs field, set within the context of what I am describing here as an individual frame of reference, treats educational difficulty as primarily a technical issue (Iano, 1986). Consequently, solutions to problems of academic underachievement and exclusion tend to be formulated in methodological and mechanistic terms, dislodged from the wider contextual realities that shape them. As a result, the special needs task is often reduced to a search for the 'right' teaching methods, strategies or packaged materials that will work with those pupils who do not respond to the teaching arrangements generally made.

As I suggested in Chapter 1, the systematic replication of particular methods, in and of themselves, are unlikely to generate successful learning, especially when we are considering pupils that historically have been alienated in or excluded from schools. An overemphasis on searching for effective methods often seems to distract attention from more significant questions such as, why in a particular society or, indeed, school, do some pupils fail to learn successfully? Consequently, it is, I believe, necessary to shift away from this narrow and mechanistic view of educational difficulties to one that is broader in scope and takes into account wider contextual factors, including both cultural and structural dimensions (Ainscow, 1995a).

As I have argued, teaching strategies are neither devised nor implemented in a vacuum. Design, selection and use of particular teaching approaches and strategies arise from perceptions about learning and learners. I contend that even the most pedagogically advanced methods are likely to be ineffective in the hands of teachers who implicitly, or explicitly, subscribe to a belief system that regards certain pupils, at best, as disadvantaged and in need of fixing, or, at worst, as deficient and beyond fixing.

In recent years this deficit model has been subject to massive criticism in the special needs field and, in consequence, we have seen some changes in thinking that seek to move explanations of educational failure away from the characteristics of individual children and their families towards the process of schooling. As I have explained, this has led to the introduction of approaches based upon an interactive view of educational difficulties. However, my involvement in schools during this period leads me now to argue that despite good intentions, approaches informed by this perspective and the frame of reference it encourages, often give rise to a kinder, more liberal, and yet more concealed version of the deficit model that views 'special children' as being in need of special teaching, i.e. approaches that other children do not require in order to achieve in school. Thus, despite moves towards the integration of children seen as having special needs, with an emphasis on approaches such as curriculum differentiation and additional adult support in the classroom, the deficit orientation towards differences continues to be deeply ingrained in many schools and classrooms.

For these reasons I have come to the view that progress towards the creation of schools that can foster the learning of all children will only occur where teachers become more reflective and critical practitioners, capable of and empowered to work together in order to investigate aspects of their practice with a view to making improvements. Only in this way can they overcome the limitations and dangers of deficit thinking; only in this way can we be sure that pupils who experience difficulties in learning can be treated with respect and viewed as potentially active and capable learners. This analysis indicates, therefore, a need to consider what forms of inquiry are relevant to this task.

Investigating Practice

The reconceptualization of the special needs task that is implicit in my argument so far, then, necessitates the use of forms of inquiry that will enable those involved to investigate aspects of their existing practices as a basis for further development. Unfortunately, the dominant tradition of research in the field is, I will argue, unsuitable for this task. Once again, therefore, what is needed is a radical change, following the advice of others who have argued for the introduction of new approaches to research in the special needs field (e.g. Barton, 1988; Clough and Barton, 1995; Iano, 1986; Schindele, 1985; Skrtic, 1986).

Traditionally, research in special education has been influenced by theories derived from psychology and biology. This was largely consistent with the idea of special education being seen as a search for effective methods to solve a technical problem (Iano, 1986). As a result, the aim was to establish, through carefully controlled experiments, the existence of generalized laws that teachers could use as a basis for their interventions. Indeed much of teacher education, particularly in the special needs field, is still based upon this orientation. Teachers attend courses to learn about theories derived from such research in order that they can then use these to inform the development of their practice.

The emphasis within this dominant research tradition is on the use of experimental or, more likely, quasi-experimental designs of a quantitative type. Typically, these involve the study of the relationship between sets of variables with a view to making generalizations that apply across settings (Harre, 1981; House et al., 1989). So, for example, research might be carried out in order to consider the impact of teachers' use of praise upon the social conduct of pupils. The aim would be to demonstrate relationships between the two variables, praise and behaviour, in order to establish the existence of laws that would apply in the classsrooms of other teachers.

Such investigations are based upon a number of assumptions that remain matters of dispute (e.g. Heshusius, 1989; Iano, 1986). In particular they assume that variables such as praise and social conduct can be defined in ways that could be said to apply across different contexts, times and people. The problem with this is that classrooms are complex places, involving numerous social encounters, the significance of which comes to be understood separately by each participant. So much so that the idea of generalizable interpretations is always subject to doubt, at least (Bassey, 1990).

While special education was framed as a series of technical tasks concerned with finding solutions to the problems of particular children or groups of children seen as sharing similar characteristics and, by implication, experiencing similar difficulties, this dominant research tradition seemed to provide a good fit. Although issues of methodology, not least to do with rigour, continued to encourage argument, the idea of seeking to establish laws of cause and effect that could be used to make generalizations about classroom life seemed appropriate. The arguments I have outlined above, however, argue that progress in the field will be more likely if the task is reformulated in order to pay attention to the uniqueness of contexts and encounters. Thus the focus is on children's interactions with particular people, at a particular time and in a particular situation, looking, specifically, at barriers to their participation and how these can be overcome. The idea of establishing predictions across people, time and contexts is, therefore, to say the least, inappropriate. Rather what is needed is a deeper understanding of the nature and outcomes of individual educational events and situations. In this sense reality is assumed to be something that is created in the minds of those involved in the event or situation, rather than something that can be defined objectively, observed systematically and measured accurately. This change in orientation is, of course, indicative of a shift from the positivist to the interpretative paradigm, and assumes very different ideas about the nature of reality and the relationship of knower to the known (Lincoln and Guba, 1985).

In the light of these arguments my own research has involved an exploration of forms of inquiry that have the flexibility to deal with the uniqueness of particular educational occurrences and contexts; that allow social organizations, such as schools and classrooms, to be understood from the perspectives of different participants, not least the pupils themselves; and that encourage teachers to investigate their own situations and practices with a view to bringing about improvements (e.g. Ainscow, Hargreaves and Hopkins, 1995). Similarly, within my work in higher education I have encouraged course participants to carry out school-based assignments based on these ideas whilst, at the same time, addressing issues of direct relevance to the development of their classroom practice (Ainscow, 1989). Indeed the overall aim of this work has been to encourage teachers to see themselves as 'reflective practitioners', skilled in learning from experience and, as a result, more responsive to the feedback offered by members of their classes.

Action Research and Reflection

As I have continued to work in these ways, encouraging teachers to study aspects of their own practice, I have gradually come to recognize the significance of this experience for my own learning. In this respect, my experience seems to mirror that of Lanzara (1991) who, as a result of a similar process, notes: 'To my surprise, I discovered that as I was helping my partners to reflect on their own practice, I was also reflecting on my own' (p. 287). In my own case the recognition of this process was stimulated as a result of keeping a research diary as a means of recording procedures adopted and decisions made as part of the on-going evaluation of the UNESCO project (Ainscow, 1995a and b). Within the project the idea of the research diary was combined with the notion of a learning journal (Holly, 1989), used by all participants as part of continuous evaluation of their professional development. As a consequence, this placed considerable emphasis on the value of writing as a means of making sense of experience.

Initially, despite my good intentions, I found it difficult to establish the discipline of writing in the journal on a regular basis. I found that there were phases during which I was regularly making entries but then long periods would occur when the journal was ignored. Over time I also became aware that the nature of my engagement with the journal changed. Whilst I was continuing to record events and decisions I also found that I was using the journal to hold conversations with myself. Comments about personal feelings started to appear, as did expressions of confusion or uncertainty. I also began re-reading earlier entries and annotating them with afterthoughts. In this way I gradually became involved in what Lanzara (1991) refers to as a process of 'self-study', using what he calls 'backtalk' in order to reconsider events and situations that had previously occurred in order to explore the kinds of knowledge that might emerge.

Lanzara notes that in more conventional forms of research backtalk might be seen as feedback to be used as a corrective device or control mechanism in order to achieve a more rigorous account. However, in what he characterizes as 'second order inquiry', it performs a more radical function as a reflective mechanism to interrogate the categories and procedures used in generating earlier accounts. In his work he extends the idea of backtalk to involve other participants and, indeed, my continued interaction with colleagues and participants in the UNESCO project can be seen as providing a similar function.

What then is the nature of second order inquiry? How does it fit into overall thinking about educational research? Indeed, how far does it qualify as a legitimate form of research at all? All of these questions are complex and I am aware that my engagement with them remains uncertain and somewhat tentative. Nevertheless, my experience of this way of working so far has convinced me of its potential for informing the development of thinking and practice, whether or not we choose to regard it as research in a formal sense.

The approach I am describing bears much resemblance, of course, to action research, a form of inquiry that in its original form sought to use the experimental approach of social science with programmes of social action in response to social problems (e.g. Lewin, 1946). More recently action research has come to refer to a process of inquiry undertaken by practitioners in their own workplaces. Here the aim is to improve practice and understanding through a combination of systematic reflection and strategic innovation (Kemmis and McTaggart, 1998). Action research is sometimes dismissed as not being 'proper' research by researchers working within more traditional research paradigms. Others, whilst acknowledging it as a worthwhile activity for practitioners, are anxious that claims for the validity of findings should not be made beyond the particular contexts in which the investigation is carried out (e.g. Hammersley, 1992).

Proponents of action research, on the other hand, have responded to these criticisms by rejecting the conceptions of rigour imposed by traditional social science, and by mounting their own counter-criticism of the methodology and assumptions about knowledge upon which these conceptions of rigour are dependent (e.g. Winter, 1989). They claim, for example, that the notions of rigour to which both positivist and interpretative researchers aspire are oppressive, restrictive and prescriptive, designed to perpetuate the hierarchical divisions between the producers and users of research (Iano, 1986). Many of those who argue for action research see it as an alternative to traditional forms of research which, they suggest, have been notoriously unsuccessful in terms of bringing about improvements in schooling (e.g. Kemmis and McTaggart, 1998; Elliott, 1981; Ebbutt, 1983). Action research, it is claimed, leads to improvements in the quality of education because teachers themselves take responsibility for deciding what changes are needed, and teachers' own interpretations and judgments are used as a basis for monitoring, evaluating and deciding what the next stage of the investigation will be. Thus action research addresses the crucial issue of 'ownership' over the process of change in schools.

Drawing attention to the limitations of research carried out within positivist and interpretative paradigms, some writers have argued that action research could become a new paradigm in itself (Carr and Kemmis, 1986; Winter, 1989). This new paradigm assumes a different view of professional knowledge and of the relationship between theory and practice. As I argued earlier in this chapter, traditional social science research seems to assume a relationship between theory and practice within which practice involves the application of theory in specific applied contexts. The overall effectiveness of practice is thus limited by the adequacy of the available theory, plus, of course, the practitioners' understanding and skill in applying it. By implication, improvements in practice will follow from the development of more adequate theory and enabling practitioners to apply it effectively. Those who see action research as an alternative paradigm argue that this is a model based on knowledge in the natural sciences and that teachers' professional knowledge cannot be applied with the same degree of certainty — not because the body of knowledge is less adequate but because the process of application of knowledge is of a different order (Winter, 1989).

Action research tends to assume that all knowledge produced through a reflective process of inquiry is necessarily provisional, and that the relationship between theory and practice is dialectical rather than prescriptive. This means that practice is not treated as dependent upon theory to tell it what to do, but that both theory and practice confront and question one another in an on-going dialogue, consequently, all judgments and interpretations are regarded as open to question and the practitioner-researcher's accounts are accorded no privileged status over those of other participants in the situation under investigation. All are regarded as 'data', i.e. as resources for reflection and critique. Inevitably, within the field there are different viewpoints, even amongst those who are generally sympathetic to the idea of action research. For example, Adelman (1989) argues against 'overblown claims' for action research as a new paradigm. He also argues that it lacks an adequate theory of learning that is capable of explaining how new insights come to be generated through the research process. Furthermore, he suggests that the method-ology of action research has become a substitute for an adequate account of how learning occurs through the action research cycle. Action research that aims for improvements in practice but does not confront the values implicit in these goals 'may have no more intrinsic educational significance than much of the psycho-statistical research to which (it) is seen as a radical popular alternative' (Silver, quoted by Adelman 1989). What counts as an 'improvement' in understanding? How do we know that we have really learnt something through the action research process and not simply confirmed our existing prejudices or interpretations?

Writers such as Carr and Kemmis (1986), Lather (1986) and Winter (1989) have begun to address these questions, suggesting that central to an understanding of the process of reflection must be the notion of 'critique'. Carr and Kemmis proffer the concept of critical self-reflection, suggesting that the process requires collaboration as a basis for exploring and questioning interpretations within a 'critical community of enquirers into teaching'. Winter also invokes collaboration as an essential element, but goes further in terms of elucidating the process itself as, 'questioning what is taken for granted by reconsidering neglected possibilities' (p. 44) and developing in some detail a set of principles derived from a non-positivist theory of knowledge for understanding and carrying the process through.

My own experience leads me to endorse the shift in emphasis which can be detected in recent thinking on teacher development generally towards reflection on experience as the basis for development, rather than reliance on procedures of 'research' (of whatever complexion). Action research offers one means of enabling this to happen, but once the emphasis shifts from research to reflection it becomes clear that teachers' working contexts offer many more. Incidental observations, examples of children's work, instances of misunderstanding or miscommunication, can all provide a stimulus for reflection, without the constrictions associated with traditional research procedures or the predetermined stages of a cycle of the sort recommended in the action research literature. Most significant of all in terms of the agenda of this chapter, barriers to participation experienced by pupils can create an ever-present opportunity to 'reconsider neglected possibilities', provided the difficulty is treated as an occasion for professional development and learning.

It is important to add that the outcomes of traditional social science can also provide important resources for reflection on practice and, therefore, for profes-sional development. The significant difference is that the research is treated by a 'reflective practitioner' (Schon, 1987) not as a prescription for practice but as a contribution to the resources upon which teachers can draw in order to generate knowledge and understanding through processes of reflection.

Understanding Schools from the Inside

In the light of the analysis described in this chapter I have found it essential in my own work to engage in forms of inquiry that are to a large degree located within schools and classrooms, and that require me to work in partnership with teachers. The overall aim is to understand difficulties experienced in schools from the points of view of insiders and to explore together how these can be addressed in ways that attempt to support the growth of those involved. In this section I provide accounts of two, very different experiences, that illustrate what this may involve and, at the same time, give a flavour of the potential advantages and difficulties of such ways of working.

The overall aim of the IQEA project has been to explore how schools can develop in ways that support the learning of all students (Hopkins et al., 1994). I see this as contributing to understandings that are central to the development of thinking in the fields of school improvement and special needs education, in that the concern is with how schools can become more inclusive. As part of this research programme we recently looked in detail at developments that had occurred in a small group of secondary schools over a period of five or six years, focusing in particular on the perceptions and interpretations of insiders. Our detailed knowledge of these developments represented a starting point for the study but we were keen to enrich our understandings and, indeed, have our outsiders' accounts challenged by accounts constructed from the inside. What we were confident about was that all these schools had gone through a period of at least five years of sustained attempts to bring about organizational restructuring and developments in classroom practice, and that there was evidence that actual changes had resulted.

The aim of the study was, therefore, to find ways of 'digging deeper' into the experiences of the five schools. However, we also wanted to make use of methods of inquiry that would enable us to follow their developing stories over those years from the perspectives of different participants. We were conscious that our own impressions and interpretations had probably been influenced, if not shaped, by the relatively small group of people we normally met during our school visits. This study would, we hoped, sensitize us much more to different interpretations of the same range of events, as well as giving richer accounts of the social and cultural complexities that influence change efforts. Finally, we were very committed to the use of methodologies that would be helpful to our colleagues within the schools as they continue their improvement efforts. To quote our own rhetoric, we wanted to 'work with the schools, not on them' (Ainscow and Southworth, 1996).

In devising a suitable methodology we were aware of others who have attempted to follow a similar path. For example, Poplin and Weeres (1992) report a study called 'Voices fom the Inside', carried out by students, teachers, administrators and parents in four schools. Here the aim was 'to create strategies that allowed everyone at the school site to speak and insured that everyone be heard'. Thus the research allowed all participants to be both the researchers and, at the same time, the subjects of the research. Since the study began with the assumption that academics had already 'misnamed the problems of schooling', the roles of outsiders had to be rethought so that those on the inside could come to know and articulate the problems they experience. The use of this process was reported to have led to many changes in the schools, although it was also found to be extremely time-consuming.

Two other studies also seemed to be near to what we had in mind. First of all, in their 'School Change Study', Wasley and her colleagues (1996) used what they call 'collaborative inquiry' to study the work of five schools that had taken part in the 'Coalition of Essential Schools' project for at least four years. Their interest was in how the schools had used the project ideas and values to drive change; how they had sustained and developed the process; and whether the changes made were having an impact on the educational experiences of students. In addition to a large external research team, a teacher in each school was paid to act as a coordinator for the study and two students at each school were paid to write weekly journals. The stated aim was 'to bridge the worlds of practitioners and scholars'. However, whilst there was clearly insider involvement in the research process, the locus of control remained with the outsiders. Finally, Levin's (1993) account of his use of what he calls 'empowerment evaluation' as part of the 'Accelerated Schools Project' seems to have many similarities with our approach, particularly his emphasis on the idea of widespread involvement as a school is 'taking stock'.

In designing our own study we too were keen to develop a way of working that might be characterized as 'collaborative inquiry' (Reason and Rowan, 1981; Reason, 1988). At a meeting of representatives of the five schools a set of groundrules was worked out. In our summary of these groundrules we stated that 'the intention is to produce rich, authentic descriptions of individual "cases" as a basis for subsequent analysis and comparison'. It was agreed that each school would form a team of three to five members of staff to carry out the inquiry. The team was to be reasonably representative of 'different levels and viewpoints in the school'. It was also agreed that each account would attempt to include the full range of views available within and around the school, including, if possible, those of students, parents, LEA officers and governors. In the final accounts it was not necessary to reconcile or judge the value of the various perspectives.

All matters of policy within the study were openly debated with the school teams and on a number of key issues our original plans were subject to substantial modifications. As Wasley, Hampel and Clark (1996) found, 'even when a collaboration works, it is full of surprises'. So, for example, we were keen to use a series of research techniques, known as 'Mapping Change in School', developed by members of our group (Ainscow et al., 1995). During discussions, however, the teams, which included the headteachers of four of the schools, resisted our proposals, agreeing only to consider the possible use of some of these approaches if they proved to be relevant at a later stage.

The initial phase of the study, involving the collection of data and the production of the initial accounts, took about a year to complete. During this period the approaches used gradually took on very different forms in each of the schools. Such diversity is, of course, somewhat disturbing to a research team attempting to carry out some form of cross-site comparison. It does, however, seem inevitable in a study that is seeking to allow insiders to conceptualize their own versions of what has occurred. In a more positive sense, of course, these diverse formulations are in themselves interesting in that they provide an illustration of how a school goes about getting things done. Furthermore, they illustrate the dangers of researchers attempting to reduce these differences between schools into some form of cross-site, generalized explanation.

All the draft accounts were read by the inquiry teams in the five schools and debated during a whole day meeting in which they all took part. This, in itself, led to some very interesting discussions, with individuals using the experiences of other schools to reflect on their current understandings of their own situations. It also confirmed our view that, despite the vast differences in the ways in which data were collected, analysed and reported, the case studies provide rich, complex and, at times, challenging accounts, based on an impressive range of perspectives in the schools. In addition, as a result of these experiences we are now considerably clearer about both the advantages and, of course, the difficulties involved in carrying out such a study.

In terms of advantages, from the point of view of the schools there was strong evidence that those involved found the process to be both informative and stimulating. They found that a specific need to engage with multiple interpretations of events in their schools had forced them to think much more deeply about their own perceptions. Furthermore, exploring ways of valuing points of view that they might more usually ignore, or even oppose, also seemed to stimulate them to consider previously ignored possibilities. At the same time they found the process to be affirming, giving them an opportunity to celebrate many achievements in their schools.

Turning to difficulties, the experience of this study highlighted some of the problems that can occur when practitioners take on the task of carrying out what might be referred to as insider research. We found, for example, that despite the commitment to reporting a wide range of opinions, some of the accounts revealed little evidence of alternative voices, thus giving the impression of what seemed to us a most unlikely level of consensus. There was also very little evidence presented from students and parents, gaps that seem particularly regrettable when we read the findings of the Poplin and Weeres' study, reported earlier. All of this may explain, in part at least, the comment of one headteacher who, after reading the account of his own school, felt that it failed to reveal the 'soul of the place'.

Finally, there remained some concerns about confidentiality. As the accounts are read by more people in the schools, can we be sure that the views of certain individuals will remain anonymous? And, in one case, in particular, we remained anxious that some of the views expressed could have led to considerable distress to at least one colleague in one of the schools.

From our own point of view, as we have explained elsewhere (West, Ainscow and Hopkins, 1997), the account led us to question some of the assumptions we had been making about these particular schools. They also threw up more general questions about processes of school and teacher development that we wanted to pursue. In particular, they suggested a series of contradictions which needed to be addressed in our subsequent work.

Evaluation through Collaborative Inquiry

An experience in a very different context provides further illustration of what is involved in using what I am calling collaborative inquiry to develop understandings that can help to facilitate movement towards more inclusive practices. It involved the evaluation of a project in Anhui, a province in China, to integrate children seen as having special needs into local kindergartens. The evaluation was carried out by a team that included a project officer from the Anhui Provincial Education Commission (APEC), a Chinese special education specialist and an integrated education adviser from Save The Children (SCF), the organization that has supported the project since 1988. Present also were two interpreters, both with backgrounds in educational development activities, and the chief of the APEC Elementary Education Division.

Prior to the evaluation, terms of reference had been agreed. These specified the objectives, information to be collected and a list of indicators that were intended to guide the teams' investigations. However, it was made clear that these indicators might need to be adapted during the process. Arrangements had been made for the team to gather information in six kindergartens and one primary school over a two-week period.

On the way to Anhui the SCF adviser and I discussed issues related to the style of the evaluation. We were in broad agreement that a participatory approach would have a number of advantages, although somewhat anxious that our fellow team members might not necessarily agree. I had recently read a report given to me by Cheng Kai-Ming of Hong Kong University in which he described his difficulties in attempting to utilize ethnographic research approaches within a team carrying out a similar evaluation task in Chinese schools during the 1980s. In the paper he referred in particular to problems of status that occurred within the evaluation. For example, it had been suggested that he should not have meals with his fellow evaluators because he was the 'foreign expert'. He also described the difficulties of getting teachers to speak openly to him after he had been given a formal reception as part of what was clearly seen as a visit by government officials.

All of this heightened my sense of anticipation as we prepared for this work, not least as a result of a previous visit I had made to the Anhui project in 1994. On that occasion I had attended a conference in connection with the same project and visited a small number of the kindergartens involved. These experiences had drawn attention to how the local ways of orchestrating such events seemed to create expectations of what is to occur and, indeed, constraints as to what is possible. In saying this it is important to note that these arrangements seem to be driven by a strong desire to make respected visitors welcome and to make efficient use of time.

The nature of this orchestration and its likely impact can be best illustrated by providing a description of what, in my experience, is the usual format for visits to Chinese schools by teams of visiting 'dignitaries'. The team arrives shortly after school commences and is met at the front gate by a group of local leaders. Introductions are usually made in the street. Meanwhile parents and others passing by stare curiously, particularly where the visitors include foreigners. This scene is filmed by one or two video crews and, in addition, there is at least one photographer. Following the introductions the whole party march into the grounds of the school, passing a freshly painted sign in Chinese and English welcoming the 'visiting experts'. The visitors are then escorted into an office where they sit at a large meeting table. Around the walls are examples of children's and, sometimes, teachers' paintings. Tea is served in mugs with lids, on the table are plates of nuts, fresh fruit and sweets and, in addition, there are new packets of cigarettes.

The meeting begins with a brief welcome from the most senior leader who then invites the headteacher to provide a 'briefing on the situation in the school'. Written copies of this report that have been prepared for the visitors are distributed but, nevertheless, the headteacher reads it aloud without interruptions. After the meeting the visitors go outside to watch the children do their morning exercises. They are then escorted to a classroom where rows of chairs have already been laid out at the back of the room where they are to sit as they observe the lesson. The impression is that considerable attention has been given to lesson preparation, with attractive teaching aids used and the teacher providing what seems to a Western eye to be a rather dramatic performance. Children regarded as having special needs may be pointed out by one of the leaders, all of whom sit and observe the lesson with the visitors. Later the group are shown to another classroom for a second observation. This may be followed by an escorted tour of the rest of the school, including exhibitions of toys and aids made by staff. Throughout, the video crews and photographers continue to make a record of the proceedings. The visit concludes with a final meeting at which one of the visitors offers the leaders and the headteacher some brief comments. The visitors are then thanked for their advice, which, it is noted, will be followed.

How, then, to conduct the evaluation in such a way as to penetrate the inevitable barriers created by such arrangements seemed to be a major challenge facing the team as we set about planning our methodology? Implicit in the terms of reference was an expectation that the team would try to gather authentic views from teachers, parents and administrators. How could such views be collected if our style of working gave strong messages that we were an élite group whose interpretations might lead to unknown yet significant outcomes for those involved?

Against this background the team held a whole day planning meeting. During the first part of this meeting those who had been closely involved in the project explained its history. The newcomers occasionally prompted this process by asking questions to elicit clarification. Particular attention was given to the content and format of the inservice training given to project teachers and to issues regarding the choice of pupils suitable for integration. The SCF adviser explained the guidelines that had been developed in order to brief schools joining the project. After I had commented about how directive these instructions sounded from a Western perspective, the team had the first of many discussions about cultural factors and how they influence processes that occur in educational contexts. In this instance Chinese colleagues argued that in their context people were willing to accept directions when they were faced with new circumstances. This was, they suggested, in the nature of 'Chinese pragmatism'.

Having dealt with the history of the project the meeting moved on to consider themes and issues that needed to be addressed during the evaluation. A starting point for this discussion was, of course, the terms of reference referred to earlier. However, I was keen at this early stage to emphasize the general idea of participation, first of all in respect to decisions faced by the team. With this in mind, I argued that it was important that each team member should contribute to the evaluation agenda, using their experiences and perspectives as a resource that could enrich our overall understanding of the contexts we were to examine. I noted, for example, that within the team we had the possibility of drawing upon both insider and outsider perspectives, male and female, Chinese and English, and so on. In order to demonstrate the potential of these possibilities I suggested that each of us spend ten minutes or so making notes of our own ideas about what the evaluation should address. Then each person was asked to number their proposals in order of importance, using an abridged 'nominal group technique' (Ainscow, 1994). A list of each person's first priority was then written on a flip chart in both Chinese and English. After a long debate about the content of this list, including further consideration of its relationship to the terms of reference, the team agreed an overall typology that could guide the enquiry. This consisted of three major categories: experiences, outcomes and lessons.

These three headings were written on a sheet in order to frame discussions of possible methods of enquiry. At this stage I outlined experiences of evaluations carried out elsewhere; in particular, a previous evaluation study of a similar integration project in schools in Lesotho, carried out by Stubbs (1995). I went on to suggest four principles that might be helpful in guiding the enquiry. These were that the evaluation should:

- be of direct help to people in the schools visited;

- inform the development of policy elsewhere;

- demonstrate rigour such that the findings would be worthy of wider attention; and

- inform the thinking of the team members.

These ideas were received with smiles and nods by my colleagues, but no comments were made. However, what occurred subsequently suggested that in the main they were seen as being useful. For example, on many occasions during the following two weeks members of the team made reference to how far our actions were in line with 'our' agreed principles.

The planning proceeded with more detailed discussions of what methods of enquiry would be relevant to our three major categories. Against the category 'outcomes' what was described as 'traditional practice' was noted. Specifically this involved 'interviews with headteacher and staff; classroom observations; checking records and files; and discussions with parents'.

This done I outlined some examples of so-called participatory methods, emphasizing, in particular, the value of group processes and visual methods of recording. My proposals here were influenced to a large degree by experiences of using collaborative inquiry methods in English schools, including some of the techniques we had developed as part of IQEA (e.g. Ainscow et al., 1994; Ainscow et al., 1995). A further source was the notion of 'participatory rural appraisal' (PRA), as developed by Chambers (1992) and refined by Stubbs (1995) for use in school contexts. Gosling and Edwards (1995) argue that PRA is a particular form of qualitative research that can be used to gain an in-depth understanding of a community or situation.

These proposals led to considerable discussion and, indeed, a degree of uncertainty about the willingness of Chinese teachers to contribute to participatory methods. Eventually it was agreed that use could be made of the idea of school 'timelines'(Ainscow et al., 1995), as the basis for focused interviews with staff. However, various other group data collection suggestions were rejected since these were felt to be too time consuming, but a full programme for the first school visit was agreed, to include classroom observations, interviews with staff, parents and administrators (discussions with children were to be added a few days later, following the visit to the first kindergarten), and scrutiny of various documents. Finally, there was discussion of roles and responsibilities, including a consideration of issues of confidentiality and how the final report would be prepared.

This whole process had taken almost eight hours. Towards the end of the meeting some participants looked very tired. Afterwards one of the interpreters commented that meetings of such intensity rarely occur in China, apart from in situations of 'crisis'. Nevertheless, everybody seemed relaxed and comfortable with the decisions that had been made.

For my own part, I was aware that during these early discussions competing positions had been in evidence and that compromises had probably been made. In my notes I commented that there remained the question of meaning, i.e. did we all mean the same things when we agreed the approaches to be used, particularly those that assumed a significant level of teacher participation? I noted, for example, my 'slight suspicion' that certain team members still regarded evaluation as a form of school inspection.

Undertaking the Evaluation

Over the next few days a pattern of activity gradually emerged as the team travelled from kindergarten to kindergarten. This meant that typically a full day was spent collecting data in each kindergarten and then team members spent the early part of the evening writing up their field notes. Later in the evening the team would have a meeting to review the visit and plan for the next day. Where process changes were agreed these were recorded on a computer so that each person could have their own copy of the new plan. In addition, of course, the notes had to be prepared in two languages. All these activities had to be arranged around travel between districts, including settling into new hotels and taking part in frequent banquets hosted by local leaders.

As this pattern developed so, gradually, did the shape of the enquiry in each kindergarten. By the later visits use was made of all of the following techniques.

Classroom observations

Each team member spent most of the morning observing alone (or where necessary with an interpreter) in one of the classrooms. Care was taken to cover different age groups and classes were observed that did and did not include children categorized as having special needs. The focus was on the whole process of these lessons but with particular attention given to noting evidence of implementation of ideas and strategies introduced as part of the integration project. Of specific interest here were the teachers' strategies for encouraging pupil participation in lesson activities, including those children seen as having special needs. Field notes tended to take the form of general accounts of the lesson with more detailed descriptions of what were perceived as being significant events and interactions. In addition, video recordings and photographs were made of some sessions. These were processed immediately in order that they could be discussed by team members as soon as possible after the events recorded. Whenever possible periods of classroom observation were followed almost immediately by informal discussions with the teachers involved. Here the team member would feedback aspects of their observations and invite the teachers to comment. The intention was to gain greater insight into the teachers' thinking, particularly with respect to processes of planning and lesson modification in respect to pupil differences. In carrying out these discussions team members had agreed to avoid making remarks that might be perceived as being critical of what had been observed.

Timeline interviews

In each kindergarten two members of the team carried out an interview with the headteacher and the project coordinator in order to design a visual timeline illustrating the most significant events that had occurred as the project developed. Typically timelines included items such as meetings, courses, visits and pupil admissions. A sample of staff, including the headteacher, was then interviewed individually. After an initial demonstration of what was required each teacher was asked to draw a line on a copy of the timeline indicating their perceptions of the 'ups and downs' of the project. Once they had had time to think, the teacher was asked to tell the story of the project from their own point of view, using the completed timeline as an *aide-mémoire*. During this process the roles of the team members were to make notes and to provide an occasional prompt. At the end of the discussion, which usually took about 15 minutes, the key points noted were read back to the teacher who was asked to make any necessary corrections or modifications. It was the view of all members of the evaluation team that this format was enormously successful in encouraging teachers to talk frankly and was highly efficient in terms of use of time.

Group discussions

Each site visit included a programme of discussions with members of key stake-holder groups. These discussions were loosely structured around the themes and issues emerging from the enquiry within a particular kindergarten and, at the same time, taking account of the wider evaluation agenda. Frequently, such discussions were used to check interpretations and gain deeper insights into findings. Groups taking part in these discussions usually involved local leaders and educational administrators, pupils and parents, including those of children perceived as having special needs.

Factor posters

As the study developed it became increasingly apparent that there was considerable variation in progress between kindergartens. Consequently, the team became interested in trying to define factors that seemed to be influencing these differences in implementation. With this in mind the evaluation team developed a group discussion technique aimed at collecting teachers' views on this matter. This was focused around a poster format. A large piece of paper was placed on the wall in front of the group of teachers. The paper was divided into two by a vertical line, one side of which was headed 'factors that support', whilst the other was headed 'factors that hinder'. After a brief explanation the teachers were each given two sets of small paper slips, each set of a different colour. They were then asked to write one idea on each paper, using one colour for supporting factors and the other for factors that seem to have hindered the progress of the project. The team member leading the activity collected all the slips and these were grouped around themes and stuck on the poster. Whilst all these individual written responses remained confidential, the group was then invited to discuss the themes suggested by the completed poster. A note was kept of the content of these discussions which, with the poster, provided a record of what occurred.

Documentation

The final main source of evidence was various documents kept in each school, a sample of which was analysed by one member of the team. The documents examined usually included policy documents, research reports written by members of staff, lesson plans and records kept about individual pupils.

A deliberate strategy within the evaluation design was that of using 'triangulation' as a means of checking and exploring the significance of data. Three forms of triangulation were used. These involved comparing and contrasting evidence from:

1   different people within a particular kindergarden;

2   different methods of data collection; and

3   different team members.

Indeed, much of the discussion within the team was stimulated by attempts to find common meaning within the mass of data that was accumulated in each kindergarten.

At the evening meeting following the first site visit the team discussed how the process of data analysis might be handled. Three possibilities were considered: (i) try to agree an immediate common framework for analysis; (ii) stay completely independent until much later; (iii) keep one another informed about emerging ideas with a view to moving gradually towards a common framework. The second option was quickly rejected and after further discussion it was agreed that the third approach was an appropriate way of using our individual differences in a way that was consistent with our principles and yet sensible in moving towards some agreed conclusions. Certainly it proved to be an excellent approach in terms of our own learning as a team.

After one of the team meetings to share our findings I made the following notes in my learning journal:

> . . . we had a meeting to review our findings about yesterday's school. It was wonderful. Each person took it in turns to talk about the things that had struck them most. In this way we gradually built up a rich account of the school, putting together complementary and, at times, contradictory material that enabled us to engage one another in a debate about the significance of our experiences. It was a pity the discussion could not have been taped. In future evaluations of this type I would recommend at least a day's writing up time between schools in order to draw together and make a record of these perspectives. This is the potential power of this methodology, I feel.

Overall, then, the methodology described here can be characterized as essentially a social process. It required a newly formed group to engage in a search for a common agenda to guide their enquiries and, at much the same time, a series of struggles to establish ways of working that enable them to collect and find meaning in relevant data. All of this was carried out in a way that was intended to be of direct benefit to those in the contexts under consideration. In so doing the members of the group were exposed to manifestations of one another's perspectives and assumptions. At its best all of this provides wonderful opportunities for developing new understandings. However, such possibilities can only be utilized if potential social, cultural, linguistic and micro-political barriers are overcome.

In my notes after the final meeting of the team I commented on what I described as an 'amazing learning experience for me'. In particular, I noted that I felt I had been learning about 'ways of working within Chinese traditions'. This points to an important point to bear in mind when electing to adopt participatory approaches to inquiry. It seems likely that such ways of working will take on very different forms as a result of the influence of particular cultures. In this respect the actual methods adopted may not be the most significant factor. Rather, as Chambers (1992) notes, 'the behaviour and attitudes of outside facilitators are crucial, including relaxing not rushing, showing respect, "handing over the stick", and being self-critically aware'.

Implications

The experience of these two studies and, indeed, others that have involved the use of a similar orientation, has confirmed my commitment to the argument I have developed in this chapter for the use of collaborative forms of inquiry that emphasize practitioner research as a means of encouraging the development of more inclusive practices. It leads me to believe that greater understanding of how educational contexts can be developed in order to foster the learning of all children is most likely to emerge from studies in which outsiders, such as myself, work alongside teachers as they attempt to work out 'what works in theory'.

Such an orientation helps to overcome the traditional gap between research and practice. As Robinson (1998) argues, it has generally been assumed that this gap has resulted from inadequate dissemination strategies. The implication being that educational research *does* speak to issues of practice, if only the right people would listen. She suggests an alternative explanation, pointing out that research findings may well continue to be ignored, regardless of how well they are communicated, because they bypass the ways in which practitioners formulate the problems they face and the constraints within which they have to work.

As we have seen, practitioner research is fraught with difficulties. On the other hand, the potential benefits are enormous, not least in that the understandings gained may have an immediate impact on the development of thinking and practice. In the chapters that follow I explore what is involved in moving towards forms of classroom practices and school organization that can effectively reach out to all pupils, using evidence from a range of activities that have made use of collaborative inquiry methods of the type discussed in this chapter. In essence this requires teachers and those who work with them to work together in order to examine existing practices within their own school and classroom contexts, including the thinking *behind* the thinking that informs these arrangements.

This orientation may be disappointing for some readers in that it does not result in generalizations and lists of strategies that can be lifted and transported across educational contexts in order to inform improvement efforts. Rather it leads to fine grained accounts that illustrate practices within the particular contexts in which they occurred. Their greatest value is in their potential to stimulate us to scrutinize and reflect on our own ways of working, and to challenge the assumptions that inform and shape those practices. Consistent with this position, my discussions and arguments make extensive use of examples from my observations in schools and classrooms, plus interpretations of these descriptions from those taking part. In this way I attempt to avoid the traditional academic pitfall, that of 'misnaming the problems of schooling'.

Chapter 4

Moving Classrooms

Recent years have seen extensive efforts in many countries to ensure that the right to educational opportunity is extended to all members of the community. As this has happened it has become increasingly apparent that traditional forms of schooling are no longer adequate for the task. Today's pupils live in a world of remarkable interest and excitement. Many have opportunities to travel, whilst even those who do not are accustomed to a rich diet of stimulation through television, films and computers. In this sense they present challenges not faced by earlier generations of teachers. The pupils of today are, therefore, demanding and discriminating; they also, of course, bring to the classroom experiences and ideas that can provide important foundations upon which lessons can be planned.

Faced with this increased diversity, including the presence of pupils whose cultural experience or even language may be different from their own, and many others who may experience barriers to their learning within conventional arrangements, teachers have had to think about how they should respond. So, what kinds of practices might help teachers to 'reach out' to all members of the class? What does research suggest about how teachers and schools might develop practices that will make them more inclusive? In addressing these issues I draw extensively on my own experience of working with schools and teachers using notions of collaborative inquiry to make sense of how movement can be achieved.

Starting with Existing Practice and Knowledge

Recently I watched a reading lesson taught by Janice, the deputy headteacher of an inner city primary school in the south of England. Also present was one of her colleagues, a recently qualified teacher named Felicia. After the lesson the three of us spent time together discussing our impressions.

The lesson involved 27 year 4 pupils. During the initial phase the children were sitting on a carpet in a circle, each holding their reading book. In her lesson introduction Janice discussed the idea of the 'main characters' in a story. She used questions to draw out the children's existing knowledge, e.g. 'What do we call the person who writes a book?' Then they were asked to work in pairs, talking about the main characters in their own books. Janice moved round the circle of children indicating who each child should partner. She then explained that eventually each person would be required to talk about what their partner had said. One boy, Gary, was to work with her.

After a few moments of this activity it became evident that quite a few members of the class remained uncertain as to what was required. Consequently, Janice stopped the class and gave further clarification of the task. The children then talked in their pairs for about five minutes.

Eventually the class members were asked to finish talking to their partner and then each person took it in turn to report to the class. After listening to each child's summary Janice wrote certain words on a flip chart. Occasionally she questioned them to elicit suitable vocabulary, e.g. 'Would you like him? . . . Why not?' Many of the questions seemed to be aimed at making connections with children's day-to-day experiences, deepening their thinking and, at the same time, extending their vocabulary, e.g. 'Getting expelled — what does that mean?' Despite the fact that this phase of the lesson took some time and involved a lot of listening, the children remained engaged. Indeed, towards the end of the process Janice congratulated all the children on their concentration. She then got them to read the words she had listed choral fashion.

The class were told that they now had to return to their tables and carry out a writing task about what would happen if their character visited the school. As they moved to their places one child, clearly feeling very involved in what had been discussed, asked if this was really going to happen!

The children were seated at five tables, apparently grouped on the basis of their reading attainment. As they began work Janice distributed various worksheets. Then she moved to certain tables helping individuals to get started. After a while she stopped the class and asked them to listen to one boy reading his text aloud so that they could all help him to determine where the full stops should be located.

After the lesson the three of us reflected on various things that had happened. We talked, for example, about the care Janice seemed to take with language and her use of questioning to probe the children's own understandings. We also discussed her use of paired discussion. Apparently the children are familiar with this approach since it had been used in previous lessons. Certainly we were all impressed by their concentration and their ability to express themselves. I mentioned about the way she had chosen to work with Gary. This had happened by chance, although she had steered him to the front of the class so as to 'keep a close eye on him'. It seems that Gary can be disruptive sometimes. We talked about different tactics for keeping an eye on potentially difficult pupils.

Perhaps the most interesting aspect of our discussion, however, concerned ways of catering for differences within the class. I expressed my worry that sometimes so-called 'differentiation' strategies of the type that are currently fashionable can set limits on our expectation of certain children in such a way as to lower their performance. Janice explained how an experience early on in her career had made her aware of this danger. She noted, 'All children have things in them to surprise us . . . all can surprise us'. Felicia and I recalled different ways in which this lesson had allowed opportunities for 'surprises' whilst, at the same time, offering individuals varied degrees of support in order that they could participate. We recalled, for example, the way in which some children were encouraged to respond by the use of carefully judged questions. We also noted how Janice had quietly offered different levels of support once the children began the writing task. So, for example, she immediately moved to give further oral instructions to those she assumed would need them. She also gave additional written prompt sheets to some children but in a way that did not draw attention to their need for further support (in fact, I had not noticed her doing this). In these ways all the children took part in a common lesson, within which they shared a similar agenda, but in a way that attempted to respond to their particular needs.

I think we all three felt that our discussions had helped us to reflect in detail on aspects of our own thinking and practice. In this sense the experience demonstrated the value of having an opportunity to observe practice, and quality time to participate in detailed discussion of the shared experience, a theme to which I return later. For me, too, it was yet another example among many of how much expertise is available within schools that can form the basis for improvement efforts. Indeed, my experience over the years leads me to believe that in most schools the expertise needed in order to teach all the pupils effectively is usually available amongst the teaching staff. The problem is that the people in most schools know more than they use. Thus the task of moving things forward becomes one of finding ways of making better use of existing knowledge and skills, including the often dormant skill of working together in order to invent new possibilities for overcoming barriers to participation and learning. Another example, this time from a secondary school classroom, further illustrates what I am suggesting.

As part of a study I am carrying out with my colleagues Tony Booth and Alan Dyson, I watched a Year 7 geography class in an urban comprehensive school in the north of England (Booth and Ainscow, 1998). The students were seated in rows, two at a table, each with a text book in front of them. The teacher began the lesson by explaining, 'This is the first of a series of lessons about the USA'. He went on to say that before they opened their books he wanted to know what the class already knew about this subject. Immediately lots of hands went up and within minutes the blackboard was full of lots of information. Despite the fact that none of these young people from a poor city estate had ever been out of the country, their regular viewing of films and television programmes meant that their knowledge of the American way of life was extensive. Sitting on the front row was James, a student who has Down's Syndrome. Next to him was a classroom assistant who is there to support this student's participation. James raised his hand and, when called on by the teacher, said, 'They have yellow taxis'.

So, here the teacher was using a familiar tactic to 'warm up' his class; that of using questioning to draw on existing knowledge, prior to introducing new material. It is an approach that many teachers use. Certainly it is not 'special education' but, nevertheless, it proved to be a means of facilitating the participation of members of the class, including one who is seen as needing a permanent adult helper.

This story further illustrates what I see as the most important starting point for development and learning; that is the knowledge and understandings that already exist in any context. Interestingly, this seems to apply to the learning of both pupils and teachers. Current thinking in cognitive psychology emphasizes the idea that learning is a personal process of meaning-making, with each participant in an event 'constructing' their own version of that shared experience (Udvari-Solner, 1996). The implication is that even in what might be seen as a rather traditional lesson, with little apparent concession being made by the teacher to the individual differences of members of the class, each pupil experiences and defines the meaning of what occurs in their own way. Interpreting the experience in terms of their own mental frames, individuals construct forms of knowledge which may or may not relate to the purposes and understandings of the teacher. Recognizing this personal process of meaning-making leads the teacher to have to include in their lesson plans opportunities for self-reflection in order that pupils can be encouraged to engage with and make a personal record of their own developing understandings.

It has taken me a long time to appreciate that existing practice represents the best starting point for development activities, not least because of my previous experience and training in the field of special education. It took me many years to recognize that the ways in which earlier attempts to develop integrated arrangements for pupils said to have special needs had often, unintentionally, undermined our efforts. As we tried to integrate such pupils into mainstream schools, we adopted practices derived from earlier experience in special provision. What we learned was that many of these approaches were simply not feasible in primary and secondary schools. Here I am thinking, in particular, of the individualized responses, based on careful assessments and systematic programmes of interventions, that have been the dominant orientation within the special needs world. As I have explained, for many years this was very much the orientation that shaped my own work (e.g. Ainscow and Tweddle, 1979 and 1984).

Often when I visited schools to offer advice on how to respond to those pupils seen as having special needs, I would help teachers to develop individualized programmes of work. Then, some weeks later, when I carried out my follow-up visit, I would often be greeted in a somewhat uncomfortable manner. Reasons might be offered as to why the programmes had not been followed: 'we have been busy with the Christmas play'; 'a lot of staff have been absent with the flu'; 'it's been windy and the kids have been hell for the last week'. In essence, the teachers were explaining that there had simply not been time to implement the detailed, individualized plan that we had agreed. Gradually, however, I came to the view that there was another, much more fundamental problem associated with my approach. Experience taught me that it did not fit with the ways in which mainstream teachers plan and go about their work. For all sorts of sensible and understandable reasons the planning frame of such teachers has to be that of the whole class, rather than the individualized frame that I had learnt to use during my years working in special education contexts. Apart from any other considerations, the sheer numbers of children in the class and the intensity of the teacher's day makes this inevitable.

As a result, when integration efforts are dependent upon the importing of practices from special education they seem almost certain to lead to difficulties. They also tend to foster the development of yet new, often more subtle forms of segregation, albeit within the mainstream settings. So, for example, recent years have seen the introduction of support teachers who work alongside the class teacher in order to facilitate the presence in the room of those pupils categorized as having special needs, as they carry out their separate individualized tasks. When such support is withdrawn, teachers may feel that they can no longer cope. And, of course, the formal requirement for individualized education plans laid down by legislation in English schools has encouraged colleagues in some schools to feel that many more children will require such responses, thus creating the massive budget problems currently faced by some local education authorities.

The gradual recognition that schools for all will not be achieved by transplanting special education thinking and practice into mainstream contexts opened my mind to many new possibilities that I had previously failed to recognize. Many of these relate to the need to move from the individualized planning frame, referred to above, to a perspective that emphasizes a concern for and an engagement with the whole class. Thus as one teacher explained, what is needed are strategies that *personalize* learning rather than individualize the lesson. An understanding of what these might involve can be gained from the study of practice, particularly the practice of class teachers in primary schools and subject teachers in secondary schools. As my awareness of the value of such studies has developed, so my interest in observing and trying to understand practice has grown. Put simply, I am arguing that a scrutiny of the practice of what we sometimes call 'ordinary teachers' provides the best starting point for understanding how classrooms can be made more inclusive.

Our own observations of planning processes used by teachers who seem to be effective in responding to diversity suggests certain patterns that might be borne in mind (Ainscow, 1995a; Hopkins, West and Ainscow, 1997). Usually experienced teachers have developed a range of lesson formats that become their repertoire and from which they create arrangements that they judge to be appropriate to a particular purpose. Here they seem to take account of a range of interconnected factors, such as the subject to be taught, the age and experience of the class, the environmental conditions of the classroom, the available resources and their own mood, in order to adapt one of their usual lesson outlines. Such planning tends to be rather idiosyncratic and, indeed, often seems to be conducted at a largely intuitive level. In this sense it is unlike the rather rational procedure introduced to student teachers in that it consists, to a large degree, of an on-going process of designing and re-designing established patterns.

Much of this planning, therefore, goes on incidentally in the background as teachers go about their day-to-day business. Whilst some of it may occur over the weekend or in the evening, it also continues on the way to school in the morning and on into the building as the teacher gathers things together for the lesson. Indeed it sometimes strikes me that final adjustments are still being made as the teacher enters the classroom and judges the mood of the class.

All of this may sound rather informal, even hit and miss, but my observations indicate that for many experienced teachers it involves an intellectually demanding process of self-dialogue about how best to stimulate the learning of the class. Attempts to encourage and support further improvements in practice in this area must, therefore, take account of the nature of this complex approach to planning.

There is a rather obvious limitation to this approach to classroom planning that arises from the largely private way in which it is conducted. This is that the teacher is confined to the range of possibilities that is suggested from earlier experiences. This is why within our IQEA project schools were encouraged to develop organizational conditions that lead to discussions of teaching and sharing of experiences about how lessons might be planned (see Ainscow et al., 1994, in particular Chapter 7). It is also essential to recognize that planning does not conclude when the lesson commences. Indeed, often the most significant decisions are those that are made as the lesson proceeds, through what I have characterized as a process of improvisation that is somewhat analogous to the practice of jazz musicians (Ainscow, 1995a). Let me illustrate what I mean.

Recently I spent three days observing teachers in the modern languages department of an English secondary school. The teachers explained to me their total commitment to what they referred to as 'the target language approach'. Put simply, this involves immersing the pupils in the language being studied throughout the whole period of a lesson. In this way they are expected to find ways of establishing meaning in the language much as young children do as they develop their first language in their homes. The approach is very intensive, placing great demands on staff and pupils. My observations confirmed that the teachers in this particular school were tremendously skilful in this way of working with pupils at all levels of achievement. As I watched their lessons, however, I noted that despite their obvious belief in the target language approach they would occasionally 'break the rules' by speaking to the class in English. I sensed that this occurred when the teacher interpreted the situation as needing a brief change of medium. So, for example, a teacher might sense that some members of a class had been unable to comprehend a detailed instruction as to how a task should be carried out. A brief clarification, in English, quickly solved the problem. On other occasions the teacher might sense a need to lighten what had been an intensive period of engagement by an amusing aside in English. As far as I could see, none of this was planned, and, indeed, the teachers hardly recognized my descriptions of its use as a tactic. It was, I felt, a form of 'improvisation' made at a largely intuitive level as the teachers played their familiar tunes and, in so doing, responded to the reactions of their audience.

Another researcher uses a different set of images to explain the way teachers adjust their established ways of working in an attempt to reach out to members of a class. He compares the work of teachers to that of artisans (Huberman, 1993). An example will illustrate the point he makes. Faced with a leak in a sink an experienced plumber sets about the task in the certain knowledge that he (or she) has the wherewithal to solve the problem. Since he has fixed many similar leaks before he is confident that one of his usual responses will do the trick. Occasionally, however, he experiences a surprise — his usual repertoire proves to be inadequate. What does he do? Does he go on a course? Call for help? Read a manual? More likely he will 'tinker' with the problem pipes until he is able to invent a solution. In this way he adds a new way of working to his repertoire, which, of course, he can then take with him to the next leaking sink.

The suggestion is that this is something like the way in which teachers develop their practices. Arguably, the key difference is that teaching is far less predictable than plumbing; so much so that during each lesson there are many 'surprises' to be dealt with and, therefore, far more possibilities for 'tinkering'. For example, there is the pupil who suddenly wants to tell the teacher about something interesting that happened the previous night; another who asks a question about the subject of the lesson that the teacher has never thought of; and, inevitably, those who lose interest or misbehave in some way. All of these unexpected events require an instant decision. Just like the plumber, the teacher has no opportunity to take advice. In this way new responses are trialled and, where they are found to be of value, added to the teacher's range of usual approaches. Through this form of 'planning in action' teachers learn how to create classroom arrangements that can be more effective in responding to individuals within their classes (Ainscow, 1996).

My colleague Susan Hart has developed a helpful framework that can be used by teachers to probe more rigorously and systematically into classroom situations that have not previously responded to their intuitive responses (Hart, 1996). Her approach, which she calls 'Innovative Thinking', is a means of generating new ideas to support children learning. It is based on the following 'interpretive modes':

- Making connections, i.e. 'What contextual influences might have a bearing on the child's responses?'

- Contradictions, i.e. 'How else might this response be understood?'

- Taking a child's eye view, i.e. 'What meaning and purpose does this activity have for the child?'

- Noting the impact of feelings, i.e. 'How do I feel about this? What do these feelings tell me about what is going on here?'

- Suspending judgment, i.e. 'This move involves recognizing that we lack information on resources to have confidence in our judgments, and therefore making holding back from making judgments about the child's needs while we take steps to acquire further resources.' (Hart, 1996, pp. 8–9)

In her book Susan demonstrates how together these questions can be used to develop the 'thinking-on-the-feet' that teachers carry out within lessons in order to identify further possibilities for action.

Seeing Differences as Opportunities for Learning

Recently I watched a wonderfully gifted teacher conduct a French lesson with a year 7 class in the school I mentioned earlier, where the teachers use the target language approach. It struck me that her style took the form of a 'performance' in which she used a range of what I saw as dramatic techniques to create high levels of engagement amongst all the pupils. This started even as they arrived, in that as they walked into the classroom they immediately joined in choral chanting of days of the week, the alphabet, numbers and so on. This gradually became more directed once they were all seated, making the whole introduction to the lesson feel fluent and engaging. There were 23 pupils, eleven of whom were girls. They were scattered around the room, mostly sitting next to boys. Later the teacher explained that she had imposed the seating arrangements at the start of term, arguing that 'it's important to create patterns'.

Having completed the class register the teacher moved quickly into a session of questions and answers, practising vocabulary. Little use was made of English and the pace set by the teacher was very quick. Sometimes the impression was of a 'market salesman', with rapid fire patter; other times she was like a 'conjuror', taking objects from her rucksack and asking, 'what's this?'. Occasionally, she pointed to illustrations and captions on the wall display in order to prompt a pupil's response. At one stage she invited the pupils to sing jingles about the days of the week. Much to my amazement boys and girls readily volunteered to do this individually.

A wide range of vocabulary was used during what was almost 30 minutes of intensive teacher-led emersion in the target language. Variety of content seemed to be one way in which the pupils' engagement was maintained. However, variety of task was also evident. At one point, for example, a large soft plastic dice was thrown around the room from pupil to pupil. As it landed the number indicated which word the pupil was required to read aloud from the blackboard. Much use was made of first names to call on individuals and there were many expressions of celebration by the teacher. Given the pace and the slight sense of uncertainty that she created, such that at any moment a pupil might be called on to respond, there was little room for distraction and, in fact, little was evident. It seemed, however, that the pressure of all of this was compensated for by the atmosphere of support that she was able to create.

During the final moments of the lesson I became aware of Geoffrey, who was sitting just behind me. It was obvious that he was unclear about what he should be doing. Indeed, at one point he leaned forward and asked me for help. A girl sitting next to me whispered, 'he's a bit slow'. After the lesson the teacher explained that Geoffrey often has difficulty in following instructions. 'He's my failure', she explained. She then went on to describe her attempts to encourage him by inviting his responses. On reflection I recalled her doing this although it had not struck me as being particularly significant at the time.

It seemed to me that these comments summed up her approach to her work. Clearly she felt that it was her responsibility to help all members of the class to learn and that if individuals experienced difficulties it was her 'failure'. In this way she saw them as stimulating her to think about how her repertoire might be adjusted in order to overcome the barriers they faced. I contrast this with the apparent ready willingness of some teachers to presume that difficulties that occur in their classes are a direct result of the limitations or home circumstances of some of their pupils.

Once again, some of the traditions of the special needs field may have encouraged this type of response. As I explained in Chapter 2, the introduction of the concept 'special educational needs' during the 1980s was to a large extent an attempt to move away from an emphasis on the categorization of pupils by disability or inability, focusing on impairment or defect, to an examination of what each child might need to overcome his or her educational difficulties. This involved a broadening of concern from a small group of learners categorized as 'handicapped', and usually placed in special schools, to an engagement with all pupils who experience difficulties in education, inside or outside the mainstream. In practice, those of us involved in this reformulation found it very difficult to escape from the legacy of our past, where pupils were divided into the 'normal' and the 'less than normal' in order to provide the latter group with a different form of education often separate from, but always additional to that provided for the majority of pupils.

The approaches developed as part of what is now referred to as special needs education have, despite good intentions, continued to create barriers to progress as schools have been encouraged to adopt them. In particular, the preoccupation with individualized responses has deflected attention from the creation of teaching approaches that can reach out to all learners within a class and the establishment of forms of school organization that will encourage such developments. The grouping together of pupils on the basis of the special educational needs label has continued and, indeed, has expanded, thus exaggerating the differences between these and other learners. In some instances this can even create a sense of fear amongst teachers about their ability to deal with pupils who have certain characteristics. For example, I was recently told the story of how impressed teachers in one English primary school were when they observed a video recording of two of the school's unqualified classroom assistants 'teaching' three children who were described as having moderate learning difficulties in a corridor. It was reported that teachers were 'uncertain' about their own abilities to work with these pupils.

Sometimes the label 'special educational needs' also becomes a repository for various groups who suffer discrimination in society, such as those from minority backgrounds (e.g. Artiles and Trent, 1994). Some years ago I watched an impressive musical production performed by pupils from a residential special school in Hungary. My questioning confirmed my suspicion that all of these pupils were from a Romany background. Rather paradoxically given the characterization of so-called gypsies in many European countries, the performance was of the musical 'Oliver' and included an excellent rendition of the song, 'Gotta pick a pocket or two'. It seems, then, that special education can sometimes be a way of hiding discrimination against some groups of pupils behind an apparently benign label and, in so doing, justifying their low attainments and therefore, their need for separate educational arrangements.

Scrutinizing Barriers to Participation

The approach I am adopting to inclusion involves a process of increasing the participation of pupils in, and reducing their exclusion from school curricula, cultures and communities. In this way the notions of inclusion and exclusion are linked together since the process of increasing participation of pupils entails the reduction of pressures to exclude. This link also encourages us to look at the various constellations of pressures acting on different groups of pupils and acting on the same pupils from different sources. It draws our attention to the 'comedy' played out in some schools as pupils previously sent off to special schools are welcomed in through the front door whilst others are ushered out at the back. Meanwhile other schools seem to have revolving doors which allow pupils to enter with one label, such as 'learning difficulty', only to be relabelled and then excluded with another such as 'emotional and behavioural difficulty'.

Arrangements for sorting pupils into groups or classes based upon their assumed common abilities for learning remain common practice in many schools despite the massive warning evidence we have that suggests the negative influence they can have upon the motivation and achievement of large groups of pupils (e.g. Mehan, Villanueva, Habbard and Linz, 1996). Recently one of my students carried out a detailed study of practice in an inner city primary school that illustrated yet again the ways in which these negative influences occur (Vamvakdou, 1998). She explained how pupils in the reception class were arranged in groups according to their ability. The pink group included children seen as having higher ability and, on the whole, the older ones; the red group comprised the children of medium ability; and the blue group were those of lower ability and, mainly, the younger ones. The teacher, who was very experienced, explained that ability grouping 'makes organization and planning very much easier', adding that it 'allows time for both, depending on the aim of the lesson'. All the activities of the class were orchestrated on the basis of these groups, including all their lesson activities and social encounters. Indeed, the only time when pupils operated outside the groups was during circle time, which involved the whole class working together, and at playtimes.

The children were clearly aware of how they came to be in their groups. For example, one boy commented, 'We are the blue group, we don't know how to write'. Another boy from the red group, commenting upon the work of a girl in the pink group said, 'She is in the pink group. I bet she's done well'. In fact, the teacher noted that this boy really should have himself been in the pink group but because there was no room for him he remained with the reds where he could 'help the others'. It is worth remembering here that these children who have already developed such a firm view of their relative strengths as learners are still only aged four or five!

Often the processes that lead to some pupils feeling marginalized are subtle ones that occur as part of normal classroom interactions. So, as I watched lessons in one school recently I noted how 'throw away' remarks by teachers appeared to suggest that a low level of participation was anticipated. For example, a teacher appeared to have targeted one boy as somebody who was unlikely to make much of a contribution: 'Grant, homework, I assume you didn't do it — you never do, despite letters home to your mum.' Similarly, an English teacher on calling the class register remarked, 'Amazingly we have Shula here'. It can be argued that such interactions help to reduce expectations and shape the pupils' views of themselves as learners. In so doing, they also discourage participation and learning. For these reasons, therefore, I am suggesting that yet another starting point for the

In any classroom some students will experience barriers to participation that limit their learning. In order to improve practice it is necessary to examine what barriers exist. This information can then be used in order to create the conditions that will help to overcome such barriers.

Barriers can take many forms. Some arise because of circumstances that are outside the control of teachers. For example, poor material resources or very large classes can create barriers. Also, some children arrive at school feeling tired or upset because of experiences in their homes. However, many barriers result from the way schools and classrooms are organized. Examples of possible barriers to participation include:

- a curriculum that does not relate to children's experiences;
- lessons that are poorly prepared;
- use of an unfamiliar language; and
- teachers who reject some children because of certain of their characteristics.

Some barriers are major and may inhibit the participation of many students; others are minor and may only inhibit one or two students.

The aim of this activity is to help you and your colleagues to focus on classroom factors that may hinder children's participation in lessons.

Step 1
Work with a small group of colleagues (three or four) to generate a list of possible barriers to children's participation in learning. For each item on the list make some notes as to how teachers can take actions to overcome these barriers. Produce a poster that summarizes your ideas.

Step 2
Fasten the posters to the wall around the room. Form new groups, each of which has one member from the working groups in step 1. The new groups now move around the room from poster to poster discussing the ideas that are presented.

Step 3
Write a short memo to yourself that completes the following sentence:

'From these discussions I have learnt that . . .'.

Discuss your ideas with your colleagues.

Figure 4.1 Workshop activity — barriers to participation

development of more inclusive practices within a school has to be with a close scrutiny of how existing arrangements may be acting as barriers to learning.

As part of my work with schools I encourage teachers to examine their practices carefully and systematically in order to consider possible barriers to participation. Figure 4.1 is an example of a staff development activity used to encourage this approach. Ideally it should be carried out with all members of staff together.

A current area of practice in the English education system that seems to lead to feelings of exclusion concerns the role of classroom assistants (i.e. unqualified adults who work alongside teachers to support the learning of pupils categorized as having special educational needs). Here it is important to stress that the idea of having extra adults around who can help facilitate the participation of pupils is an excellent one. The problem is that many schools have yet to work out how to make such a strategy work effectively. Recently with colleagues I looked closely at the impact of the work of a team of assistants on pupil participation in one secondary school (Booth et al., 1998). In art, for example, two pupils with 'statements' completed the tasks of the lesson even though they were both absent! In fact, the classroom assistant did the work for them. Meanwhile there was another group of pupils in the same lesson who had no support and spent most of the lesson talking. Presumably the assistant had been told to concentrate her efforts solely on the targeted pupils.

In general our impression was that whilst those pupils seen as having special needs were following broadly the same activities as their classmates, the constant presence of a 'helper' meant that often the challenges posed by these activities were significantly reduced. For example, the assistant might hold the paper for a pupil with a physical disability, write the words for a pupil experiencing learning difficulties, and so on. In these ways it seemed likely that at some point the continual availability of adult support would cease to ensure participation in the lesson, whilst at the same time effectively trivializing the activity. To take a specific example, Carol, a student with Down's Syndrome, was observed in a series of lessons. Given the level of support she received 'she' always completed the set tasks, although it seemed apparent that some of these held little meaning for her. Having said that, in many other ways she presented as a full participant in the classroom.

The constant presence of an assistant may well, of course, be socially reassuring for a student and we saw examples of how this can facilitate interactions between students. On the other hand, however, we saw many instances where the assistants' actions acted as a barrier between particular students and their classmates. This was particularly the case where assistants elected to group students with special needs together. This tended to encourage these students to talk to and seek help from the assistant rather than their classmates or, indeed, the teacher. As a result it was evident in some classes that the teacher spent little time interacting with students seen as having special needs and would more often address their remarks to the assistant. Thus the presence of an assistant acting as an intermediary in communication and supporter in carrying out the required tasks means that the teacher may, in effect, carry less responsibility for some members of the class than might otherwise be the case. Furthermore, this means that the lesson can continue in the usual way knowing that the implications for these students will be dealt with by the assistant. This being the case it can be argued that the existence of support may eliminate the possibility that the demands of these individuals could stimulate a consideration of how practice might be changed in an attempt to facilitate their participation.

The way forward, therefore, has to be with the development within a school of a policy for working with assistants that does not fall into these traps. An analysis of existing practice can often provide examples that can be used to encourage further developments within a school. An example illustrates some possibilities. I watched a year 2 class lesson in an English inner city primary school where a teacher and an assistant worked well together. At the start of the lesson the children were all sitting together on a carpet at one side of the classroom. The teacher engaged with the whole class, asking them to come up with suggestions about what they would do when they were 99 years old. Lots of interesting ideas were generated, such as, 'I would eat gallons of ice cream and jelly'. During this time the assistant was sitting at the back of the group, occasionally joining in with discussions. Eventually the children moved to their tables where they were to sit in groups working on individual writing tasks. It was made clear that all sentences were to start with, 'I would . . .'. As they began work the teacher went over and began working intensively with one group, who, she felt, needed more detailed discussion about what they were going to write. Meanwhile the assistant moved around the other five groups, encouraging individuals, providing help where necessary and keeping an overall eye on the class. After about 10 minutes the two colleagues exchanged roles, with the teacher moving to work with the class as a whole and the assistant giving further attention to the group that was seen as needing more assistance. All of this was carried out in a relaxed and fluent way, suggesting that the two partners had established prior agreements as to how each of their contributions would be made in such a way as to offer maximum support to all members of the class.

Planning of how the benefits of two adults in one classroom can be achieved is, therefore, essential and schools need to develop a policy that encourages such planning processes. In a new edition of her influential book *Help in the Classroom*, Maggie Balshaw provides helpful principles that should guide the development of such a policy. She suggests that classroom assistants or, as she refers to them, learning support assistants should:

- be clear about their roles and responsibilities;
- be included in and understand the communication system of the school;
- be seen positively as part of the school's provision;
- be part of a working team;
- be encouraged to make use of their personal and professional skills; and
- be supported in the development of their professional skills. (Balshaw, in press)

Using Available Resources to Support Learning

A feature of lessons that seem to be effective in encouraging pupil participation is the way available resources, particularly human resources, are used to support learning. An example illustrates what I have in mind. A history teacher recently described to me how he had been using highly structured group learning methods in order to improve achievement in his lessons. He explained how he had planned one particular lesson around the idea of the 'jigsaw classroom' (Ainscow, 1994;

Johnson and Johnson, 1994). Briefly this involves the use of small 'expert groups', each of which study separate texts related to the overall themes of the lesson. Then new groups are formed consisting of at least one member of each of the expert groups and they pool their material.

When he arrived at the classroom the teacher was surprised to find that the classroom assistant who was usually there to help communication with a deaf boy in the class was absent. Despite this he pressed ahead with his carefully planned lesson. His evaluation was that not only had the lesson been successful in facilitating the learning of the class but that also it had been the first occasion on which the deaf pupil had really seemed to be fully involved. Apparently, the carefully planned social processes of the lesson plan had opened up opportunities for the other pupils to overcome communication barriers that had previously left this individual rather marginalized during lessons.

This example illustrates the potential of approaches that encourage cooperation between pupils for creating classroom conditions that can both maximize participation, whilst at the same time achieving high standards of learning for all pupils. Indeed, there is strong evidence to suggest that where teachers are skilful at planning and managing the use of cooperative group learning activities as part of their repertoire, this can have a positive impact upon achievement. Furthermore, there is evidence suggesting that the use of such practices can lead to improved outcomes in terms of academic, social and psychological development (Johnson and Johnson, 1994; Slavin, Madden and Leavey, 1984). They have also been found to be an effective means of supporting the participation of 'exceptional pupils', e.g. those who are new to a class; children from different cultural backgrounds; and those with disabilities. However, it is important to stress again the need for skill in orchestrating this type of classroom practice. Poorly managed group approaches usually involve considerable waste of time and, indeed, present many opportunities for increased disruption.

Given the strengths of the arguments for cooperative learning it would be reasonable to assume that the use of such approaches would be widespread. However, my own observation supports earlier evidence that this is not the case (e.g. Galton et al., 1980). In English primary schools, for example, there has been a long tradition of discovery learning and problem solving within the curriculum, so it might be expected that teachers would make considerable use of approaches that require pupils to work collaboratively on common tasks or activities. In fact, whilst it is common to see children in primary schools sitting around tables in groups, a closer look confirms that often they are working on individualized tasks. In this sense they may be getting the worst of both worlds. Individual work requires concentration that may well be disturbed as a result of incidental group discussion that is encouraged by such seating arrangements.

Effective group work can take a variety of forms, but the central feature is that the completion of the task necessitates the active participation of all individuals within a working group and that one member of the group cannot succeed without the success of the others. It is essential, therefore, that group members perceive the importance of working together and interacting in helpful ways. Johnson and Johnson

(1994) suggest that this can be accomplished by incorporating the following elements into small group experiences:

- Positive interdependence — where all members of a group feel connected to each other in the accomplishment of a common goal, such that all individuals have to succeed for the group to succeed.

- Individual accountability — which involves holding every member of a group responsible to demonstrate their contributions and learning.

- Face-to-face interaction — where members are close in proximity to each other and have dialogue that promotes continued progress.

- Social skills — involving the use of interaction skills that enable groups to function effectively (e.g. taking turns, encouraging, listening, giving help, clarifying, checking understanding, probing).

- Processing — where group members assess their collaborative efforts and target improvements.

It is important to recognize that asking pupils to work collaboratively involves presenting them with new challenges. As a result, this aspect of the curriculum has to be as carefully planned and monitored as any other. The most important aspect of cooperative working must be an acceptance amongst members of a group that they can achieve their objectives only if other members achieve theirs. We can refer to this as positive interdependence, the idea that 'one cannot learn without the others'.

Positive interdependence can be achieved in different ways depending upon the nature of the set tasks, the content of the lesson and the previous experience of the pupils. For example:

- pupils may be required to work in pairs preparing a joint statement about a topic which they will be responsible for giving to a larger group or, possibly, the whole class;

- a group may be involved in a task that can only be completed if separate materials that are held by individual members are pooled;

- individual members of a group may be assigned to particular roles, e.g. chairperson, recorder, summarizer, reporter;

- each member may be asked to complete the first draft of a task that has to be completed by the whole group; and

- a group may be told that they will be scored or graded as a result of the aggregate performance completed by individual members.

In asking pupils to work cooperatively we are, in effect, introducing an additional set of objectives to be achieved. As well as trying to achieve their academic objectives they are required to bear in mind objectives related to their skills in working with others. This means that the complexity and demands of working collaboratively must be introduced carefully and increased in a gradual fashion. Initial difficulties can be minimized, for example, by simply asking each pupil to work with one familiar classmate on a relatively straightforward task. The nature of the task demands, and group size and complexity, can then be increased gradually as the pupils grow in competence and confidence. Where written materials are to be used as part of group work these have to be carefully selected and presented. On the other hand, I have found that well thought out group processes, of the sort recommended by Lunzer and Gardner (1984), for example, can be a powerful way of helping pupils to use reading more effectively, whilst, at the same time, providing support to those within a class who may find difficulty in engaging with the texts that are being used. This approach is rooted in the view that reading should be seen as a strategy for learning. As such, it involves decoding of a text, making sense of what it is saying and relating this to the reader's existing understanding. By these processes judgments are made and knowledge is extended and modified. In other words, learning takes place.

Pupils will, of course, need to learn how to work cooperatively in order to gain meaning from written materials. This may involve teaching them particular strategies for analysing a piece of text. So, for example, as part of a science or humanities lesson they might be asked to work with other students to:

- Locate and identify particular information in the material. This may involve underlining parts of the text to indicate where particular information can be found.

- Mark the located information in some way as an aid to understanding. Here sections of the text may be grouped into categories of particular significance.

- Organize the information and present it in a different form, perhaps by making a list of items located in the text or by filling in information on some form of table or graph. Groups may also be asked to consider questions or issues that are not dealt with in the text or not dealt with adequately. This may well require them to think beyond the actual written material by considering questions such as, 'What might have happened if . . . ?', or 'What would be the result of . . . ?'

Other useful techniques involve some modifications of the texts to be used. For example:

- activities that involve the group in completing material that has words or sections deleted;

- the presentation of a text cut up into separate sentences or paragraphs that the group have to put into sequence; or

- prediction of likely outcomes before going on to read the next page or section.

It is important to note that all these approaches rely on the teacher providing effective explanations and, possibly, demonstrations of what the processes involve before groups are asked to start work.

It would be foolish to pretend that this type of approach to finding meaning in written material using group strategies solves all the problems faced by pupils who have limited reading skills. However, at the very least it can help them to participate in curriculum experiences from which they might otherwise be excluded. The experience of collaborating with more effective readers can be a means of helping them to recognize the potential usefulness and, indeed, enjoyment of reading, whilst at the same time supporting processes of personal and social development (Moss and Reason, 1998).

I am arguing that child-to-child support represents an under-used resource that can be mobilized to overcome barriers to participation in lessons and contribute to improved learning opportunities for all members of a class. Interestingly, it should be noted that the essential resources for this to take effect are already there in any classroom. In fact, the larger the class the more potential resources that are available. The key factor is the teacher's ability to mobilize this largely untapped energy. My argument is that teachers need help and encouragement in order to develop the necessary skills to make this happen. This takes us on neatly to my next theme.

Developing a Language of Practice

A couple of years ago I had a meeting with the deputy headteacher of one of the schools in the IQEA project. We were discussing the remarkable improvements that had occurred in the overall working atmosphere of the school following the appointment of a new head two years earlier. As we talked he explained how, despite these undoubted improvements, the style of teaching used around the school remained largely the same. He explained how over recent years the school had gone through a period of considerable difficulty, including a rather painful inspection, as a result of which a kind of house-style had developed. Basically this meant that some of the best teachers in the school had adopted a style of teaching that did not make too many demands on the pupils. In his words, 'they had stopped playing their best shots'. This ensured that the forms of teaching used now involved teachers in not taking any risks. Clearly such an emphasis is unlikely to foster the use of responses that reach out to all learners.

Much of our early work in schools like this within the IQEA project involved attempts to introduce particular policies and, in so doing, to strengthen the schools' capacity to handle change. Gradually we recognized, however, that even where such initiatives were successful they did not necessarily lead to changes in classroom practice. Other similar studies point to similar conclusions (e.g. Elmore, Peterson and McCarthy, 1996). The evidence suggests that developments of practice, particularly amongst more experienced teachers, are unlikely to occur without some exposure to what teaching actually looks like when it is being done differently along with exposure to someone who can help teachers understand the difference between what they are doing and what they aspire to do (Elmore et al., 1996; Joyce and Showers, 1988; Hopkins et al., 1994). It also seems that this sort of problem has to be solved at the individual level before it can be solved at the organizational level. Indeed, there is evidence that increasing collegiality without some more specific attention to change at the individual level can simply result in teachers coming together to reinforce existing practices rather than confronting the difficulties they face in different ways (Lipman, 1997).

At the heart of the processes in schools where changes in practice do occur is the development of a common language with which colleagues can talk to one another and indeed to themselves about detailed aspects of their practice. It seems that without such a language teachers find it very difficult to experiment with new possibilities. Frequently when I report to teachers what I have seen during their lessons they express surprise. It seems that much of what they do during the intensive encounters that occur is carried out at an automatic, intuitive level. Furthermore, there is little time to stop and think. This is why having the opportunity to see colleagues at work is so crucial to the success of attempts to develop practice. It is through shared experiences that colleagues can help one another to articulate what they currently do and define what they might like to do. It is also the means whereby taken-for-granted assumptions about particular groups of pupils can be subjected to mutual critique.

Figure 4.2 provides the guidelines for the types of activities I encourage in schools in order to encourage the idea that learning from one another is an essential element of school improvement, and that mutual observation is an important way in which this can be encouraged. This means that it is vital to create the climate within which colleagues will feel able to be in one another's classrooms. It is also necessary for those involved to develop the skills of observing and recording practice, and giving feedback in a constructive way.

In addition to direct observation I find the use of video recordings of lessons helpful in stimulating discussions of the all important details of classroom practice. Once again this has to be introduced sensitively since initially, at least, colleagues may be anxious about having their work recorded. A useful guideline here is that when a lesson is recorded it should be first seen by the teacher in private in order to decide whether it is suitable for their colleagues to view.

The deputy headteacher of one secondary school explained how he had viewed a recording of one of his maths lessons at home with his wife. He was very pleased with his performance, arguing that it was a really good lesson. Apparently his wife was rather less impressed. She drew his attention to the fact that sometimes he would ask a pupil a question and then, if it was not answered almost immediately, he would provide the answer himself. 'Why don't you give them more time to

This activity is aimed at identifying the features of lessons that will encourage the participation and learning of all students. In order to develop your ideas you will be asked to observe colleagues as they teach their lessons. Your observation will need to focus on the details of their practice. For example:

- the materials they use;
- the ways in which they introduce the lesson;
- their use of questioning;
- their encouragement of children's talk;
- use of small group activities;
- how children are praised for their efforts and achievements;
- the ways in which children are helped to record and review their learning;
- the social climate of the classroom; and
- the support given to students who experience some difficulty.

The activity will also help you to develop your skills in observing practice and talking to colleagues about your work.

Step 1
Working alone, make a list of features you would expect to see in an effective lesson. After a few minutes join a colleague and share your ideas. Each of you must listen carefully so that you can report on what your colleagues has said.

Step 2
With your partner, form a working group with two other pairs. Each person takes it in turn to provide a short summary of what their colleague has said. The group then work together to develop a small number of 'indicators'. These are descriptive statements of what we expect to see during an effective lesson. Examples of indicators might be:

Questions are used to help students connect the topic of the lesson to their experiences.
The teacher praises children's efforts and achievements.
Children are encouraged to talk to one another about their work.
A variety of teaching methods are used.

Notice that each indicator refers to one feature only and is written in the present tense. It is a clear statement of what we want to see happening.

Step 3
In your working group, plan how a lesson might be observed in order to collect information about each indicator. What kind of information is needed? How can it be recorded? (If possible, you might practise observation using a video recording of a lesson.)

Step 4
Working in pairs, each person has a chance to observe their partner, using the indicators as a guide. Remember, this observation is *not* a form of evaluation. It is a way of helping you both to think about your teaching and how it might be developed.

Step 5
After the observation you should meet together, in private, to talk about what happened in the lesson. The observer starts the conversation by giving feedback. The feedback should be positive and constructive.
Helpful phrases for giving positive feedback are:

- I liked the way you . . .

- I noticed that you . . .

- Why did you . . . ?

- Have you thought of . . . ?

- Some teachers find it helpful to . . . ?

- Thank you for letting me watch your lesson. I enjoyed it!

At the end of the discussion agree some targets — things that you each want to improve about your classroom practice.

Figure 4.2 Workshop activity — reviewing classroom practice

think?' she asked. Whilst accepting the point that his wife had made, the deputy head reiterated to me that it was still a good lesson!

Video recordings can help teachers to examine aspects of their practice that might otherwise be overlooked. The teachers in the history department of an English secondary school watched a recording of one of their colleagues, Russell, teaching a lesson about the conditions of women working in factories in nineteenth century England. After viewing the lesson the teachers discussed with Russell how he had used questions to get the class to recall themes they had discussed in a previous lesson. One teacher noted how Russell tended to call on those pupils who did not put their hands up. This was, apparently, a deliberate ploy to find out what these pupils could remember. As he explained all of this, Russell seemed rather pleased that his colleagues had noted and admired this technique he used. After a few minutes, however, he became rather agitated, saying, 'Do you think the students have worked it out? Perhaps they've realized that if you don't know the answers it's best to put your hand up.' It struck me as a splendid example of how a shared experience can stimulate everybody involved to think in detail about how apparently minor aspects of their practice can influence the learning of individuals within their classes.

In many fields and professions opportunities for such sharing of expertise through observation and discussion happen quite incidentally on a regular basis (Schon, 1987). So, for example, young doctors shadow experienced practitioners during their training; architects often work in open-plan studios where problems can be aired; and professional musicians and sports people have regular opportunities to observe one another in ways that encourage peer coaching and detailed discussion of technique. A significant aspect of the forms of school organization that we have inherited from our predecessors is that many teachers rarely, if ever, have the opportunity to consider in detail how their colleagues deal with the day-to-day challenges of classroom life. It is this tradition of professional isolation, perhaps more than anything else, that prevents the risk-taking that seems to be essential to the creation of more inclusive forms of pedagogy.

Chapter 5

Developing Practice

Jiauzhan Normal School in Shandong province, China, prepares teachers to work in primary schools. It caters for some 1 000 student teachers, all in the age range 15 to 20. The visitor to the school is struck first of all by the neat, orderly appearance of the campus, with its modern buildings and attractive grounds. Students, who all wear multicoloured track suits, live in hostels nearby. Relationships between them and the staff of the school seem relaxed and friendly.

Classes are usually conducted in a formal manner, with lecture presentations given by the teacher, sometimes followed by periods of student questioning, although these are usually short. By and large Chinese students seem reluctant to ask questions during the lesson. This reluctance was explained to me by one teacher when he commented, 'we are taught that the tallest tree in the forest is usually the first one to be cut down'. Certainly to the European eye the classrooms have a somewhat regimented appearance, seeming to provide little or no opportunity for students to make individual contributions.

In the midst of this predominant style of working, a small group of the teaching staff are experimenting with some alternative teaching approaches that are intended to focus much more attention on the individuality of the students. Mr Hu, an education teacher, is a member of this group. A brief account of one of his classes gives a flavour of the approaches being used.

The purpose of the class is to explore ways of responding to pupils who may be experiencing learning difficulties during a lesson. There are 59 third year student teachers, sitting in groups of about eight, around tables. In preparation for the class they have each studied a story which tells of an imaginary island where gracefulness is seen as the most important and necessary attribute for educational success. In this context it is children who are clumsy who are perceived as experiencing difficulties in school. Known as 'gawkies', these children present considerable problems to their teachers and there is much debate as to how they should be dealt with. Indeed some feel that they should either be given an adapted form of curriculum in the same school or be placed in separate types of school.

Mr Hu's class consists of a series of activities, stimulated by the story, during which the students are encouraged to reflect upon their own experiences and attitudes, and to discuss their ideas with their colleagues. Initial discussions are carried out in pairs and then this is followed by the sharing of ideas in larger working groups. Occasionally, Mr Hu interrupts the discussions to take feedback from members of the class and then to refocus the discussion. Otherwise he moves around the room listening to the student conversations, sometimes joining in to help clarify a point or to introduce further questions.

The class lasts one hour. Towards the end of this time the various groups are asked to summarize their conclusions, relating these to the situation in Chinese schools. Volunteers from each group take turns to go to the front of the class and present their findings. For this purpose each group has prepared a drawing that illustrates their main ideas. One of the drawings shows a teacher lecturing to the blackboard even though there are no students in the room. Another has the teacher talking to a class that consists solely of large ears. Yet another illustrates schooling as a long narrow bridge leading to the university, with lots of students falling off into a deep valley below. All of the pictures and presentations focus on the need to reform schools in ways that encourage forms of teaching that recognize student individuality.

A remarkable feature of the presentations is the confident way in which the students express themselves. They are obviously used to addressing their class-mates in this way, and they speak with expression, conviction and, occasionally, a sense of humour. During the presentations members of the class listen attentively, sometimes applauding what is said.

At one point a discussion occurs when one student expresses his disagreement with a point made by a presenter. An argument develops, during which a number of students contribute their points of view. The disagreement is about the role of assessment and whether all children should be judged against common criteria. During this debate Mr Hu stands back, allowing the argument to continue without his involvement. The smile on his face suggests that he approves of the inter-change. After a while, however, he intervenes to summarize the main points and then to move the discussion forward.

During the final moments of the session Mr Hu asks the class to reflect on the activity and to write a short memo summarizing what they feel they have learnt. In particular, he asks them to write about factors that inhibit children's learning and how such barriers can be overcome. Finally, at the end, he instructs the students to do further reading for the next session of the course. His approach is new to teacher education in China and, as we have seen, is in sharp contrast to the usual teaching experienced by these students. A researcher from Beijing describes it as the fresh air that is coming in because 'the window has been opened'. A local official com-ments: 'We have been asking for reform in teacher education for years — at last we see it in action'.

The UNESCO Teacher Education Project

The materials and approaches used by Mr Hu and his student teachers were developed as part of the UNESCO teacher education project, 'Special Needs in the Classroom'. This project began in 1988 with the aim of producing and disseminat-ing a resource pack of materials that could be used within pre-service and inservice contexts to help teachers to respond positively to children experiencing difficulties in learning, including those who may have disabilities. Pilot materials were field tested and evaluated by a resource team in eight countries (Ainscow, 1994). Subsequently, the project has expanded throughout the world, with initiatives in over 50 countries. Apart from the development of the project materials, all of this experience has thrown light on how the tasks of preparing and helping teachers to respond to pupil diversity might be best conceptualized. This conceptualization represents a major challenge to the status quo in many countries, not least my own.

Before explaining the nature of this reconceptualization, however, it will be helpful to consider the place of teacher education with respect to special needs within the context of the education system as a whole. In particular, it is important to consider the place of special needs work within the wider international discussions of 'Education for All', as stimulated by the 1990 World Conference held in Jomtien, Thailand. During the years since Jomtien, thinking in the field has moved on. The rather token mention of special needs within the early Education for All documentation is being gradually replaced by a recognition that the special needs agenda should be seen as an essential element of the whole movement. Thus, instead of an emphasis on the idea of *integration*, with its assumption that additional arrangements will be made to accommodate pupils seen as being special within a system of schooling that remains largely unchanged, we now see moves towards *inclusive education*, where the aim is to restructure schools in response to the needs of all pupils (Sebba and Ainscow, 1996).

This inclusive orientation is a strong feature of the Salamanca Statement on Principles, Policy and Practice in Special Needs Education, agreed by representatives of 92 governments and 25 international organizations in 1994 (UNESCO, 1994). Arguably the most significant international document that has ever appeared in the special needs field, the Statement argues that regular schools with an inclusive orientation are 'the most effective means of combating discriminatory attitudes, building an inclusive society and achieving education for all'. It goes on to suggest that such schools can 'provide an effective education for the majority of children and improve the efficiency and ultimately the cost-effectiveness of the entire education system'.

Implicit in this orientation is, therefore, a paradigm shift in respect to the way we look at educational difficulties. This shift in thinking is based on the belief that methodological and organizational changes made in response to pupils experiencing difficulties can, under certain conditions, benefit all children. Within such a formulation, those pupils who are currently categorized as having special needs come to be recognized as the stimulus that can encourage developments towards a richer overall learning environment.

The approaches to teacher education developed as a result of the research carried out within the UNESCO project are consistent with the Salamanca orientation. Specifically, they involve a move away from what I am describing as an integration perspective towards an inclusive approach. Within the project this shift came about as a result of a realization that the ways in which earlier attempts to develop integrated arrangements had, unintentionally, undermined our efforts. As I have explained, earlier attempts to integrate pupils seen as having special needs into mainstream schools were often based on practices derived from earlier experiences in special provision. Many of these approaches are simply not feasible in primary and secondary schools, certainly in poorer countries with their massive classes and scarce resources.

The UNESCO project, therefore, took as its starting point existing practice within mainstream classrooms. This also assumes a particular view of how teachers develop their practice. Specifically, it assumes that the development of practice occurs in the main through a largely 'trial and error' process within which teachers extend their repertoires as a result of finding out what works for them. Their previous experience as pupils themselves may be very influential in shaping this developmental process, in addition to their observations of other practitioners — including those who lecture to them in teacher education contexts. In this way, teachers create their own individual theories of teaching that guide their day-to-day practice. Such theories are largely unarticulated (Iano, 1986). They represent the 'tacit knowledge' that has been created through what seems to be a mainly intuitive process of learning from experience using the idea of improvisation or tinkering, as described earlier.

Within the UNESCO project we have attempted to work in ways that are consistent with this view of how teachers learn. We try specifically to encourage teachers to become more confident and skilful in learning from experience through processes of reflection, in ways that we hope will stimulate further tinkering. Rather than simply leaving this to chance, we believe it is possible to create workshop contexts that enable them to recognize the value of this form of learning and to gain greater control of the processes involved. For example, Figure 5.1 is an activity from the project that I have used in many countries as a basis for such a workshop session. It encourages participants to share their experiences and ideas, whilst, at the same time, exposing them to participatory learning approaches that can be adapted for use with classes in their schools later. Indeed, towards the end of such an activity I would help participants to debrief the experience by analysing the steps, showing how each had been planned to maximize participation, encourage collaboration and personalize the learning that had taken place for each group member. I would also encourage them to consider how the approaches used might be tried in their classrooms.

There is a rather obvious weakness in the emphasis I am placing on learning from experience. It may lead to situations where individuals are left alone to make sense of their experience and to draw whatever conclusions they can determine. It is, therefore, potentially a restricted and restricting source of learning. Consequently, within the UNESCO project we have placed considerable emphasis on the exploration of the power of collaboration in order to widen the resources available to teachers as they seek to develop aspects of their thinking and practice. Here the aim is to encourage them to experience the value of dialogue with others in order to gain better understanding and to see further possibilities for improvements in practice. In this respect 'others' may include colleagues, pupils, parents and, of course, teacher educators. All of these are seen as sources of inspiration and support that can be used to facilitate learning. In addition, they are all seen as offering alternative

Teachers in many countries have found it helpful to organize workshops in the school where all members of staff can help each other to develop practice. This activity is taken from the UNESCO Teacher Education Resource Pack 'Special Needs in the Classroom' which provides lots of other materials and ideas for organizing such workshops.

The aims of school-based workshops are as follows:

1   to help you to develop a detailed language of practice;
2   to encourage you to share ideas with your colleagues; and
3   to learn new teaching techniques that you can use in your classroom.

It is important that all participants in a workshop are prepared to listen to colleagues, even when they make suggestions that seem strange or unrealistic. Discussion of unusual ideas can help you to be much more creative in your work.

The example below is of a workshop session from the UNESCO Resource Pack. It looks at factors in classrooms that can help children to participate in the lesson activities.

Step 1
How do you teach the whole class and at the same time make each student feel welcomed and valued? This is a central question faced by any teacher. Look at the diagram. It includes some suggestions as to the ways teachers do this. Spend a few moments thinking about your own teaching style. Can you add any more suggestions to the diagram?

Step 2
Put stars against *three* ideas — ones that you think are most important. Make groups of four or five and take turns to explain your three choices. Listen carefully to your colleagues and, at the end, together choose one theme for detailed attention.

Step 3
Use 'brainstorming' to list ideas. The aim is to produce a long list of suggestions. One person acts as a scribe and writes down on a large sheet all the ideas that are suggested. Group members take turns to speak. The rules of brainstorming are:

• all ideas are valued;
• aim for a long list;
• no discussion until later.

Classroom strategies chart (from UNESCO Resource Pack, 'Special Needs in the Classroom')

Setting individual tasks		Talking to individuals
	Giving pupils choice	Praising children's effort
Getting to know parents	Varied materials	Small group work
	Listening to individuals	Recording progress

Step 4
After five minutes, normal discussion takes place. The group should use the ideas listed to develop a series of practical suggestions regarding the theme of the discussion. Each person makes their own copy of these suggestions in preparation for the next step.

Step 5
New groups are formed with one member of each of the old group. Each person has three minutes to explain the ideas they have worked on.

Step 6
Write a note to yourself about what aspects of your teaching you want to work on as a result of this activity. Bear in mind:

- topics that have been discussed;
- the group learning process used in the session.

Share your thoughts with colleagues and think about how you can support one another in experimenting in the classroom.

Figure 5.1   Workshop activity — discussing classroom practice

perspectives that can help individuals to interpret their experiences in new ways, not least by challenging taken-for-granted assumptions that may be influential in guiding their practices. Information from articles and books provide yet further resources that can be used to inform and extend this process of learning through experience.

These two ideas then, *reflection and collaboration*, are at the heart of the approaches that have been developed within the UNESCO project. Our experience of using them in many countries suggests that they can be influential in encouraging teacher and teacher educators to see improvement as a fundamental area of their work. We have also found that these ways of working can encourage teachers to adopt a more flexible view of the difficulties experienced by pupils in their classes — a view that sees such difficulties as sources of feedback on existing classroom arrangements. Indeed, as I have already argued, this feedback can be used as a stimulus for adjusting classroom arrangements in ways that may well be beneficial to the whole class. In this way, schools can be helped to provide teaching that is more effective in responding to the experience and existing knowledge of individual pupils.

The materials for the UNESCO project are provided in a Resource Pack that is presented in a loose-leaf form. This was a deliberate decision made in order to encourage flexibility in their use. Those using the materials are encouraged to modify them to suit the needs of particular contexts. In the same way they are informed that elements of the pack can be ignored, or additional materials added.

The pack is arranged in four modules as follows:

Module 1   — An introduction to 'Special Needs in the Classroom'
Module 2   — Special needs: definitions and responses
Module 3   — Meeting individual needs in the classroom
Module 4   — Help and support

Individual modules can be used independently of one another or, indeed in any order. Each module had a set of study materials that provided an overall introduction to the issues to be considered. To help readers to study this material a number of features are incorporated. These are:

Guides

Introductions that help focus the reader's attention on the topic to be presented.

Points to Consider

These questions encourage readers to question the material they have read and relate it to their own experience.

Brief Summaries

At the end of the Study Material a single page summary is provided. (Figure 5.2 is an example from Module 2). They can be made into transparencies for use on an overhead projector. In some contexts, however, course leaders might feel that these should be used instead of the full version.

The units attached to each module provide the basis for course activities. Their purpose is to focus attention on practical implications of the ideas raised in the Study Material. The format for the units is as follows:

Instruction Sheets

These include the unit aims, explanation of activities and evaluation issues. Usually course participants are given these sheets in order to encourage them to take an active role in the activities.

Discussion Materials

This material provides the basis for course activities (Figure 5.3 is an example). Often participants are asked to study these materials prior to the course session in which they are to be discussed. Not all units contain discussion materials.

It is stressed that individual units can be used independently of one another.

Using the UNESCO Resource Pack

Through the original research carried out to develop the Resource Pack we became aware that it had to be introduced with considerable care. The implementation of

Special Needs in the Classroom

Module 2 — Special Needs: definitions and responses
Brief summary of the study material

Two ways of looking at educational difficulties

1 The Individual Pupil View

(i.e. difficulties defined in terms of pupil characteristics)

Based upon the following ideas:

* A group of children can be identified who are special

* These children need special teaching in response to their problems

* It is best to teach children with similar problems together

2 The Curriculum View

(i.e. difficulties defined in terms of tasks, activities and classroom conditions)

Based upon the following ideas:

* Any child may experience difficulties in learning

* Such difficulties can point to ways in which teaching can be improved

* These improvements lead to better learning conditions for all pupils

* Support should be available as teachers attempt to develop their practice

This course aims to help you to become a better teacher.
It is about finding ways of helping *all* children to learn.

Figure 5.2   Example of a brief summary from the UNESCO Resource Pack

these approaches to teacher development is by no means straightforward, particularly in contexts where they are fundamentally different from existing ways of working. In addition, our experience has been that teacher educators in some countries are not used to the idea of strategic thinking, nor do they necessarily see the actual implementation of changes in classrooms as being part of their responsibility. Great care has to be taken, as a consequence, in establishing a project design that includes arrangements to provide optimal support for those involved over a period of years.

With this in mind, we have found it helpful during the initial stages of such an innovation to work in a small number of contexts in order to establish local models of practice. These can be used later to illustrate what is possible. This strategy

---

What do we know about learning?

1 *Learning is never complete*

Even as adults, our understanding continues to develop as we test our new ideas against previous knowledge. Old ideas can be changed in the light of new experiences.

2 *Learning is individual*

Even if a whole group of children — or adults — are exposed to the same experience, the learning that takes place will be different for each individual. This is because each individual, child or adult, brings to every situation a unique blend of previous experience.

3 *Learning is a social process*

Some learning takes place in a group. Sharing learning with others can be stimulating.

4 *Learning can be enjoyable*

This is something that many adults seriously doubt, when they think back to their own schooling. However, learning can be hard, and enjoyable at the same time. Even making mistakes can be part of the fun — how many times did you fall off when you learned to ride a bike?

5 *Learning is active*

Someone else can teach us, but no one else can do our learning for us. Learning requires our active engagement, in doing and talking.

Figure 5.3   Example of discussion material from UNESCO Resource Pack

is also a means of establishing teams of resource people that have competence and confidence in using the recommended approaches. They can be used later to lead wider dissemination activities.

The preparation of these teams is a vital factor in the development of an initiative. A model of preparation that we have used in a number of countries seems to be effective (Ainscow, 1994; Jangira and Ahuja, 1992). Usually this takes approximately a year to carry out. Initially participants take part in a two-week introductory workshop/seminar led by a small team of teachers who are experienced in the use of active methods. The first week consists of a workshop that is planned in order to demonstrate a range of approaches that are based upon the overall rationale. Sometimes local school teachers are included as additional participants during these sessions in order that the teacher educators are reminded to bear in mind the day-to-day problems of life in schools. Following this demonstration workshop, a short seminar is held to debrief the experience and to explain the rationale that has informed the activities. Video recordings of other similar workshops may also be viewed at this stage.

Participants then work in twos or threes to prepare workshop sessions that they will be asked to lead during the second week. These practice sessions are followed by feedback from other participants and the leaders of the workshop. Towards the end of the two weeks time is set aside to allow participants to plan strategies for their follow-up implementation activities.

Sometimes this period of initial preparation, involving as it does demonstration, analysis, practice, feedback and forward planning, is spread over a period of weeks, which allows participants to carry out interim practice activities in their own workplaces. This design has been found to be generally more powerful as an introductory strategy.

Follow-up activities are usually characterized as a process of action research. In this way participants are encouraged to work in small, local teams in trying out the approaches, collecting evaluation data and, in doing so, making modifications to fit in with their circumstances. Adaptations, improvisations and new ideas that arise can be used to refine overall thinking and practice within the project. A deadline is set for this follow-up work and the teams are expected to produce a detailed evaluation report within a predetermined protocol (Ainscow, 1994). During this period occasional meetings of the various teams are held, when possible, to share ideas, solve problems and maintain the overall impetus. Links are also facilitated between the work of the teams through the publication of occasional newsletters reporting on developments in each context.

Our experience of setting up initiatives based upon the UNESCO pack in a range of countries indicates that those involved have to be prepared to anticipate and meet difficulties that are likely to occur. This experience confirms the existence of what I have described as periods of 'turbulence', an inevitable feature of attempts to innovate in educational contexts. The nature of this phenomenon varies from place to place, but in general it seems to be as a result of the reactions of individuals within a system to ideas and approaches that disrupt the status quo of their day-to-day lives ('Turbulence' in the context of change is explored in more detail in Chapter 6).

In the light of these likely difficulties it is vital to create a strong infrastructure of team work so that individuals can support one another in dealing with the inevitable pressures of leading the process of change. It is also important that the innovation is conceptualized in ways that allow flexibility for it to accommodate the circumstances in particular contexts.

From our experience in the UNESCO project, five main strategies seem to be powerful in encouraging the implementation of this type of innovation. These are as follows:

The Use of Adaptable Materials

The rationale of the project has led to the preparation of teacher education materials that are intended to encourage reflection and collaboration, consequently, the materials are designed in such a way as to include short pieces of text that will stimulate course participants to draw on their own experience and knowledge. In this way course sessions focus on agendas related to workplace concerns and address problems faced by teachers in their classrooms. Of course, it is also vital that the content of the materials is based upon well developed principles and a cohesive rationale.

Preparation of Personnel

An important key to successful implementation is the careful preparation of those personnel who will be asked to adopt coordinating responsibilities. Within the UNESCO project small teams of coordinators are created in particular settings (e.g. in a college or a school). They are introduced to the thinking and practice of the project through demonstrations, explanations of theory, practice and feedback, following the advice of Joyce and Showers (1988). Members of the teams then collaborate in the process of implementation in their workplace, using the notion of peer coaching within which partners assist one another to experiment with new approaches.

Delegation of Decision Making

In order that local circumstances and needs can be accommodated it is helpful for planning decisions to be made by those near to 'the action'. Consequently, within the project coordinators are asked to take responsibility for formulating their own action plans. In this way appropriate adaptations are made to the materials and, at the same time, coordinators develop a commitment to the success of *their* initiative. Loyalty amongst members of the team adds further to this sense of responsibility for what occurs. We have found that using the idea of action research is a powerful means of encouraging these developments.

Opportunities for Personal Development

Within the project it is recognized that success is often dependent upon the actions of particular individuals. As a result, individuals are invited and encouraged to see their involvement in project activities as a means of developing their own careers. In addition to the recognition they may receive for taking a lead in a significant innovation, they may be offered other opportunities that provide further incentives. For example, they may be invited to contribute to publications or to travel to other districts as resource people assisting in the development of new initiatives.

Support at All Levels

Involvement in innovatory projects can, at times, be stressful, particularly during the early days when there is a strong possibility of turbulence. The implementation strategy must, therefore, place particular emphasis on the establishment of a support system for key individuals. Of course the creation of teams of coordinators is an important factor here but we have found it helpful to encourage people to think strategically about other possible sources of support. It is particularly critical to ensure the goodwill of important individuals and agencies within the community so that, at the very least, their active opposition is prevented. The establishment of networks of communication, both formal and informal, are important means of encouraging a feeling of involvement in project activities.

Observed Outcomes

At the outset of the UNESCO project that forms the basis of the ideas presented in the chapter, a number of colleagues suggested that the idea of one resource pack that could be used in many countries was impossible. Their judgments were that contextual and cultural factors would make the content of such a pack unusable in many countries. In some senses, of course, these colleagues were correct. If we were to develop a pack requiring the rigid acceptance of specific content it would likely only to be relevant in a limited range of contexts. This is why our approach has been to emphasize process rather than content. The content offered in the pack is, therefore, used to stimulate the creation of appropriate responses to specific situations rather than to encourage the adoption of ready-made prescriptions imported from elsewhere.

This is arguably the most significant outcome of the research associated with the project. What we have learned is that improvements in teacher education are most likely to occur when groups of people collaborate together to explore their experiences and understandings. This so often seems to inspire creativity and innovation.

To those readers wishing to develop similar, innovatory projects in education, therefore, the important message is that people matter most. Your best strategy is to create networks of colleagues who are then encouraged to collaborate in making the innovation succeed. They may draw on ideas and even materials from elsewhere, but the basis of improvement is their own combined efforts. In my view, this message applies with respect to national, district and school-based initiatives.

Taking Staff Development into the Classroom

Within the UNESCO project there has been a gradual recognition by colleagues in many countries that the materials and processes involved are most effectively used as part of a school's staff development programme. In such a context the issues that emerge as the focus of activities and the approaches that are generated are much more likely to be feasible and relevant. Furthermore, arrangements can be made in order to support teachers in experimenting with new ways of working in their classrooms. This can help to overcome one of the striking difficulties faced by any attempt to change practices, that of finding time and personal support within the crowded school day. Having said that, it is important to recognize that effective school-based staff development is very difficult to organize.

This style of working has been a feature of particularly successful projects involving groups of schools in England, Ghana, Portugal, Romania and Spain. These initiatives have allowed us to develop deeper understandings of what is involved in trying to move practice forward within a school. Specifically, they address the question of how existing thinking and practice within a school can be used as the basis for creating a more inclusive approach. A detailed account of work over three years in one school will help to throw light on what is involved.

The project is set within 'Southlands', an English 11 to 18 comprehensive secondary school that has established a distinctive approach to the curriculum that emphasizes international experiences. The school serves a diverse community in a large county area. Despite being in competition with a number of selective schools in the district it has a strong reputation for achieving good results in public examinations with all its students. Following the appointment of a completely new senior management team in 1994 it became apparent that the continued success of the school was in danger of being taken for granted. There was, for example, a concern about lack of inter-departmental cooperation and, indeed, relatively little developmental work taking place within many of the departments. Classrooms were seen as largely private domains where teaching was left largely to individuals. In these senses the school bore some of the characteristics of what Hopkins et al. (1994) refer to as a 'promenading' culture.

The new senior management team sensed, however, that the attitude of staff was such that there would be a welcome to some form of developmental stimulus and that this was necessary in order to maintain the school's success. This view was reinforced by an inspection of the school. After spending one week in the school in October 1994 the inspectors concluded that, whilst it was in many ways highly successful, a number of areas warranted further attention. Specifically, the subsequent report highlighted the need to take action in two key areas; i.e.:

1 to observe the need for a greater intellectual challenge and stimulation of pupils in order to realize more fully the considerable potential of the school and its pupils; and
2 to ensure that the delivery of the curriculum is appropriately differentiated so that the learning requirements of all pupils, including the most and least able, are fully met.

The school had, therefore, a formal obligation to develop its capacity for reaching out to all its learners. With this in mind I became involved in discussions with senior staff regarding the possibility of using the UNESCO Resource Pack as the basis of a major review and development project within the school. After preliminary negotiations an outline proposal for a three year initiative to be called 'Successful Learning For All' (SLFA) was then further discussed with the middle managers of the school, and a cross-departmental steering committee was identified. During the initial discussions it was necessary to be clear that successful schools such as this one still have the potential to improve. As my colleague David Hopkins says, 'You don't have to be ill to get better!' This being the case, the action points that had arisen from the inspection process were taken at face value as starting points for what was to be seen as a process of school development.

The aims of the Southlands project were essentially two-fold:

1   To improve the quality of learning for all students and staff; and

2   To provide a supportive framework within the school which colleagues can use to develop professional practice, particularly in the classroom.

In this sense, the project was to be seen as a professional, as well as a school development exercise, and all school departments were to be involved over a three year period. One feature of this was the way in which staff development activities were to be linked directly to the matter of whole-school improvement in the way recommended by available research evidence (e.g. Hopkins et al., 1994). These included workshop sessions based on the UNESCO materials, during which staff were exposed to teaching approaches known to be effective in creating more inclusive classroom arrangements and planned opportunities for colleagues to work in one another's classrooms during periods of experimentation.

In addition, emphasis was placed on locating activities in subject departments, another factor said to be associated with successful school improvement. This involved a simple 'bidding system' whereby departments formulated proposals for the development of aspects of their work . In reality, no bid was turned down, although some were deferred. Bids were assessed against criteria that were developed by the steering committee prior to the start of the project. These criteria indicated that proposals should:

•   arise from departmental discussion;

•   have clear, tangible and specified outcomes;

•   have a clear focus, such as a particular year group or unit of work;

•   involve evaluation and a commitment to reporting back;

•   involve at least two members of a department and extend the concept of 'teacher partnership';

•   encourage a wider range of teaching and learning styles; and

•   reflect whole school priorities and relate directly to declared departmental priorities.

The entire process was supported by the school's staff development budget. Time was created by the use of supply staff, particularly during what were called 'SLFA weeks'. These were recorded in the school calendar in order to encourage staff to focus on their work and raise the profile of the project across the school. Critical friends (i.e. teachers from other subject departments) were used to act as impartial observers for each project and project leaders were coordinated through an *ad hoc* committee. This committee was created at the commencement of the project. It established the nature of the project including the working practices, but eventually it was replaced by a support network that was intended to encourage shared owner-ship of the ideas and, particularly, the findings of the work.

At two staff conferences, held in 1996 and 1997, accounts of the project work undertaken in various departments were presented by members of the teams involved. As will become evident later, these presentations made a big impact on some staff who were present on that occasion. Outlined below are extracts from some of the reports produced by colleagues in three of the departments.

Arts
Our project was chosen in order to address a perceived lack of integration between the subject areas making up the arts faculty (i.e. art, music and drama). If, as is assumed, there is common ground between the subjects, how is this made appar-ent to students studying with us? There was a general feeling that connections were not made explicit and the students regarded each subject as an autonomous area. Therefore, it was decided that a project should be planned and piloted to explore how these connections could be made explicit. All those involved in the decision felt that there were some obvious pitfalls to be avoided; especially the problem of finding a genuinely common approach to the topic, rather than artificially grafting certain subjects onto one another.

The staff involved were chosen by mutual consent, the main criteria being that both had a broad interest in these subjects and were particularly interested in pursuing the ideas involved.

Though the project is not yet complete, a number of points and strategies have been established and research has begun. In parallel to the planning of the main project we have produced a questionnaire for Year 8 students (though in principle it could be extended to other year groups) which enquires about the students' perceptions of the subjects in the faculty and about their attitude to and involve-ment in the arts in general. This should provide us with a clearer picture of how the students themselves view the subjects, and how they connect them with other sub-jects and external cultural activities. We are, obviously, aware that care is needed when drawing conclusions from the students' comments.

The classroom project being piloted in the second half of this Autumn term will be based around a common stimulus and explore issues of exaggeration and distortion as expressive devices in all three of the arts involved. A shared visual starting point will be employed (an image by Picasso). This should help to make concrete the shared nature of the project and allow for more complex or difficult issues of shared practice to be introduced to the students. The nature of the time-tabling in this subject area means that some students will only be involved in two of the three strands of the project. For this reason it is important that the work done in each separate discipline can stand on its own.

Cross-curricular planning of this kind has not been attempted recently in the faculty and this is seen as an opportunity to explore ways in which such activities can be run. Ideally it should allow staff opportunities to develop a greater understanding of the practices involved in the other subjects; knowledge which can be shared across the whole faculty. A perfect outcome would be a set of lessons which can be adapted to fit successfully in the various departmental syllabuses. However, we appreciate that this is not certain to be the case. At the very least we will come out of the project with a better understanding of how students perceive our subjects and how we can encourage them to transfer skills, ideas and concepts between them.

English

Our SLFA bid came about almost by accident. As a result of a departmental meeting on sixth form teaching, it became clear that 'scansion' (the analysis of metre and rhythm in poetry) was a problem area for both staff and students. We decided that we needed to focus on it, and the SLFA project was the perfect medium for such an undertaking. The aim of the project was to introduce the students and staff to the basic elements of scansion using extracts and then look at them in the context of whole poems. The workshop was to provide a confidence boost for staff who felt unsure of this area and a forum for professional discussion.

Deciding who would lead the workshop presented us with a classic 'Catch-22' situation. The leaders would need to be confident in scansion, but the reason for having the workshop was the fact that no one actually felt confident in it. This left us with two options — either (a) enlist outside help, or (b) teach it to ourselves and then to the rest of the department. We could think of no one for (a), and in the ensuing silence, two of us volunteered. The rest of the department would assist where appropriate and attend the workshop itself. A retired member of the department was drafted in to help, as she had a superb knowledge of literature, years of experience behind her, and some time on her hands to hunt out some useful material.

Our first step was to deconstruct our own instinctive approach to scansion. Books on the subject vary considerably in approach and depth, so we were left very much on our own to formulate a system. After many re-writes, the material was distributed to staff before the event so they could familiarize themselves with it. The answers were included in the staff copies, just in case!

Places were limited to 30 students, although there were 60 students studying English in the Lower Sixth. Letters were sent home to parents of participating students, partly to let them know that the event was taking place and to sort out travel arrangements, and partly because we hoped that if the parents were involved, students would be less likely to duck out on the night. We wanted the workshop to be after school as we felt that if it was run during the school day, many students may attend it simply to get out of going to some other lesson. Attending after school would require a level of commitment from the students.

After the staff and students met for coffee in the school dining hall, we moved through to the Lingua block. Staff went to the room where they knew the least number of pupils. Staff worked with a small group of pupils in each room, with the leader introducing each new area and keeping the evening moving along. The two main groups varied slightly in terms of classroom management, but we both roughly kept pace with each other. The rest of the material was to be covered in class time, with the students teaching those who had not attended the evening session.

Afterwards, the staff all met for a meal in the dining room, which gave us the chance to unwind and discuss how the evening went.

We were very daunted by the prospect of leading the workshop, so we were very pleased that it went as well as it did. Remarkably little went wrong. We were a little disappointed that it was so difficult to get enough sixth formers to volunteer, although the 28 who did sign up did attend. Not all the members of the department could attend either, which rather defeated one of the aims of the evening.

Generally, we achieved all we set out to achieve. We created a framework for any future workshops, put together a package of materials, a step-by-step guide to scansion for the department, and we helped raise staff confidence. In the light of the workshop we have re-evaluated how poetry is taught across the whole curriculum and we have been able to make some important changes. We hope to see an improvement in the A level results next year.

Science
Teaching and learning styles formed the backbone of the science department's original SLFA bid, and they remain core to the current initiative, although the methodology has changed. Originally, teams of staff worked together to develop strategies for the introduction of a broader range of teaching and learning styles, and this involved the development of some new course materials. However, whilst this was highly beneficial in terms of staff interaction, production of materials was very time consuming and was not so successful.

Subsequently it was decided to use materials produced by the 'Cognitive Acceleration in Science Education' (CASE) project. The CASE project has been developed over a number of years now, originating at King's College, London University. It draws on many aspects of psychological theory to devise activities which stimulate pupils to alter the way in which they perceive a problem.

The activities rely on the teacher managing the lesson in such a way as to ascertain what the pupils expect from an activity, and then creating 'cognitive conflict' when the outcomes do not fit those expected. The teacher then has to help the pupils to change their ideas to accommodate these new results. The programme has to be regular and long term (once every other cycle for two years) to provide regular environmental stimuli to enable cognitive development to take place.

The activities involve concepts such as identification and control of variables, ratios and proportionality, and correlations. The practicals are all based on scientific activities but are not taught within the context of the Key Stage 3 course, as the 'brain training' lessons are all kept separate. No written records are kept. Results are recorded on wipe-clean laminated sheets to emphasize the fact that it is the process that is important.

In introducing the CASE approach into our department we have set out to achieve the following overall aims:

1   Staff will work together in teams whilst developing and delivering this course. *It is hoped that this will bring the following benefits: Sharing of ideas and experiences should give rise to a more collegiate culture within the science department. According to research this has been linked to improved staff morale and improved effectiveness.*

   Staff will increase their confidence in a wider range of teaching and learning styles, which should make lessons more enjoyable for staff as pupils' interest is more readily maintained. The introduction of this new initiative gives a new direction to courses which have been taught by some staff for many years, and will, hopefully, stimulate renewed interest in lower school science teaching.

2   *As far as the pupils are concerned, the aim is to increase the rate of their cognitive development, and increase the proportion of pupils who are able to operate at the higher order thinking levels (described by Piaget as 'formal operation thought').*

3   *Many of our aims are expressed in terms of the effects on staff and pupils, but it is also the aim of this project to raise awareness of the work of the science department more generally in the school. It has been claimed that the introduction of a CASE programme has benefits in terms of raised GCSE results across all subjects. The aim is improved GCSE results across all subjects.*

It is our hope, therefore, that the value added to pupil outcomes by this project will justify the financial cost of training and special equipment, and will emphasize the importance of practical work in successful learning. It is also hoped that the perception of the use of small group work in science will also become more positive as a result. So, in summary, the outcomes for this project should be measureable in terms of raised KS3 test results (from 1999), and raised GCSE results (from 2001). The outcomes in terms of improved collegiality and working conditions in the science department are hard to measure, but may still be evident.

Examining the Impact

In order to gain impressions of staff views of the SLFA project overall, I interviewed a sample of 12 teachers at Southlands school. Care was taken to gather diverse perspectives. So, the sample included colleagues of different status, age and roles in the school. They included some who had clearly been active in the initiative and others who appeared to be much less involved.

To facilitate the interviews in a way that would create interest and require minimum time, use was made of the 'Timeline of Change', a technique developed by our research team at the University of Cambridge (Ainscow et al. 1995). The aim of the technique is to record how individuals within a school perceive their experience of a particular change over a period of time. In order to stimulate individuals in recollecting their involvement within what occurred, a timeline is used which includes a small number of key events associated with the change. This is presented to the respondents who are invited to annotate it, noting additional events that seem significant to them. They then comment upon the levels of involvement they felt during the period of time represented. These annotated timelines are collated and considered in preparation for a semi-structured interview with each respondent. Data from these interviews are then analysed in order to provide a composite historical account of the change but in a way that illustrates the differences of perspective that exist within the sample.

Two overall issues were addressed through the timeline interviews. These were as follows:

- Has the SLFA project led to any changes in classroom practice?

- What aspects (if any) of the project have been helpful in supporting such changes?

The hope was that feedback on these issues could be used to guide further developments in the school.

The findings of the interviews indicated that for some colleagues, at least, the project had led to tangible changes in their practice. Many of these involved the extension of existing repertoires. For example, one teacher referred to the way his belief in role play had been confirmed by the positive reactions of students to his experimentation. Another very experienced teacher of physical education expressed his amazement in using an approach to the teaching of dance that he would previously never have considered possible for him.

Some teachers' accounts pointed to more subtle changes in their practices. One colleague, for example, referred to the way in which discussions with others in the departments had led her to reflect on her positioning during group work (i.e. '. . . the need to step back and take a look at what the whole group is doing') and the tone of her voice as she addressed the class (i.e. 'I thought, do I really sound like that?').

A particularly encouraging strand in some teachers' comments, given the goals of the project, was their emphasis on using student responses to lessons, particularly those of students experiencing difficulties, as a stimulus for developments in classroom practice. One teacher referred to the way he and his colleagues had been experimenting with information technology as a means of 'reaching more students'. Another talked of the positive reaction of sixth form students to a particular experimental lesson, referring to the way they had talked about it the next day, including how one student had stated how she had felt 'privileged' to take part. The team in another department had emphasized student responses within their staff development programme. The head of department commented:

A strong part of what we have been doing, which I'm particularly keen on, is the emphasis we've placed on trying to involve all the students in lessons, whatever their aptitude, even when they have a disability or a temporary condition that prevents their participation. We've tried to address this in all our INSET and in all the syllabus and materials that we have developed — what are the sorts of barriers that prevent participation in a lesson and how do we overcome them?

In considering the comments of staff to the support provided by the project a number of themes emerged. I will consider each of these in turn.

Finding Time

The majority of teachers interviewed spoke very positively of the staff conferences in connection with the project. Reference was made to how 'we had been ready for something like this'. Some noted that the school had always had a reputation for innovation but that sometimes it had not been successful in putting its good ideas into action in the classroom. The presentations by colleagues during the second of these conferences seemed to have left many with a particularly strong image in their minds:

> I particularly remembered one or two of the staff presentations. That really stayed in my mind, the way they had talked about what they are doing.

Similarly:

> It was particularly interesting the way various colleagues talked enthusiastically about the projects that they had been running . . . It made quite an impact, how enthusiastic they were about their work.

Another colleague talked of how the discussions at the two conferences had challenged his thinking:

> As events they worked because they enabled you to step outside your own kind of habits and ask the question, why am I doing it in this way? . . . That was really very helpful on both occasions.

Having said that, however, many colleagues went on to talk about the problems of finding time to do something practical as a result of the conferences. Some remembered wondering whether there was 'anything in it' for us. Others recalled some feelings of disappointment that nothing else happened. One teacher summed this feeling up when he said:

> There was a dull thud really . . . The problem then, having got that energy, is going back to school, how do you make something happen?

Of course these comments echo experiences elsewhere that indicate that without a clear follow-up strategy even the most successful staff development 'events' have limited longer term impact (e.g. Hopkins et al. 1994; Joyce and Showers, 1988). Much of the problem here does seem to be to do with time. Put simply, how do hard pressed teachers find the time to plan for and implement the good ideas they might have for improving their work in their classrooms?

The school seems to have a particular version of this problem because of its programme of international visits and activities. Staff referred to the problems this creates, especially in the second half of the academic year. One colleague explained what this meant for him:

> The particular rhythm of this school is quite important for us to think about in terms of this or any other innovation. Clearly later on in the year, because of the international visits, really it's very difficult to find time to do things. In fact, you're conscious that you feel less satisfied with your work later on in the year; because there's so much pressure it's difficult even to do much lesson preparation. You're not getting the continuity, children may be missing for a while or you may be missing. And so in terms of any innovation in this school, we really need to think about the question of the yearly timeline.

On a more positive side, some staff argued that for them the success of this initiative was due in part to the way in which time had been built into their working day in order to facilitate development activities. First of all, the policy decision that had been made to reduce the overall school programme of meetings that staff are required to attend had certainly increased the motivation of people to be involved in departmental meetings and activities. But then, more specifically, the way in which some departments had been allocated time in order to implement changes had proved to be very significant. One very experienced teacher said that it was the first time she could ever recall 'being allocated time to sit down and talk about ideas about practice'.

In a similar way, another colleague talked of the impact of being allocated time during the day to discuss the detail of her work with her departmental colleagues. All of this seemed to provide an enormous stimulus for some staff to work together on development tasks. It was in this way that a project, which for some had seemed initially rather vague, if not irrelevant to their day-to-day concerns, finally started to become concrete.

Inventing a Language

Having been allocated some additional time, in some departments the planning activities and opportunities given to colleagues to observe one another's practice seemed to facilitate the creation of a more detailed language in order to discuss aspects of practice. This confirms the argument presented in Chapter 4 suggesting that because of the way in which teachers usually work, each isolated in separate classrooms with little or no opportunity to compare notes on their practice, they often tend to lack a technical language through which they can articulate both to their colleagues and themselves how they currently respond to the situations they meet. They are, consequently, limited in respect to formulating possibilities for extending their working repertoires.

As some of the teachers talked they provided a number of anecdotes which suggested that their activities as part of this project had facilitated the creation of such a language. One department, in particular, had established a staff development programme that creates regular contexts where this can occur. As part of this programme, colleagues take turns in leading workshop sessions after school for members of the team. During these sessions they give demonstrations, using the teachers as students, and provide written lesson plans for their colleagues. One member of this department talked with enthusiasm of the way he had adapted these suggestions for use in his own lessons.

In the same department lessons have been videoed so that the team can discuss examples of practice together. The head of this department explained something of what had occurred:

> We think there is a lot of potential in this idea, but there's been some organizational problems too. So far three staff have been videoed. The system is that first of all individuals take the video home, look at it in their own time and prepare their comments. Then they come back and we all discuss it . . . One recording had been helpful in making me think in more detail about my own teaching, especially when I saw the lesson through the eyes of my colleagues.

She went on to explain that a strong theme in their discussions had been the importance of teachers not doing too much talking during lessons so that the students were encouraged to be more active.

Teachers in the English department described their reactions to the after-school poetry workshop where some of the teachers prepared and carried out a lesson that dealt with the teaching of an aspect of the curriculum that had caused most of them some difficulties. As the lesson proceeded other members of the department observed and, eventually, joined in with the activities. Also present was a retired teacher who had been invited because of her expertise in this aspect of the curriculum. During this lesson she would occasionally interrupt to 'coach' the colleagues leading the lesson. In this way the lesson became a 'workshop' within which students and teachers came together as learners. The event had clearly made a big impression on all involved. Indeed, as one teacher put it, the whole experience had provided a 'template' of how the department should support improvements in the future.

It became clear through the interviews that the creation of a common language was encouraged by the fact that the locus of control for the agenda of the project was in subject departments. This was contrasted with earlier initiatives in the school during which various cross-curricular groupings had been formed. One teacher, reflecting on these earlier activities, commented:

> There was a lot of interesting discussion but really it was just talk and no action. Consequently some people became quite cynical about it, whilst others were quite

indifferent. Sometimes the groups were almost bogus — that was the word that was used. Perhaps the difference about this one is because it's in the department and it's led from the department, it has more of a real feel about it. It connects to the agenda of people's day-to-day work in a sense, and that might be a particular strength. We decide for ourselves what we will pay attention to . . .

Developing a Climate

As teachers talked about the impact of the project it became evident that a factor that had been influential was to do with the climate within particular departments. As Bruce Joyce, the American educational researcher, once commented: 'Innovations in schools are technically simple but socially complex!' So, for example, a colleague in one department noted that during the early stages of the project the atmosphere had not been conducive to 'this sort of thing'. Later, however, following certain changes in personnel in the department, it became possible for colleagues to work together in a more open and relaxed way.

In those departments where significant developments had occurred, these seemed to be associated with noticeable changes in patterns of social relationships. These appeared specifically to be to do with a growing awareness of and sensitivity towards differences of beliefs and perspectives within the departmental team. What seemed to have occurred here was not so much a coming together of views but much more the development of an increased willingness to accept the legitimacy of the views of others. In this way, it would seem, diversity of thought and practice comes to be seen as a source of learning, rather than as a problem that needs to be solved and associated with this maturing of relationships was evidence of practical outcomes, as teachers within a department became more effective in making use of the different traditions, experiences and skills within their teams. An experienced teacher in one large department where there are colleagues with very different expertise and traditions, outlined how this had happened:

> People now seem to appreciate one another's differences more and can communicate better with one another. And we've got to understand each other's work a lot more and personality differences within the team . . . It's as if the north–south divide has been closed; we now feel that we are part of a forward looking department and I contrast that with what I know of similar departments in other schools. There's a strong emphasis on solving problems together, whereas often in the past in this field the subjects have continued to be segregated.

Later she added:

> Recently, for the first time in years, the whole team went out for a social evening together and had a marvellous time, even though the food was awful!

In summary, then, it appears that improved social cohesion can be a means of making more effective use of expertise within a department. However, it also seems that such improvements arise as a result of people working together to overcome common difficulties or address new challenges of a tangible form.

Working across Departments

As we have seen, where the initiative made progress this was fostered within particular departments. This may well be in some senses one of its strengths, however, it also suggests a continuing area of difficulty in respect to innovations in the school. As one teacher put it:

> Although we all get on well together generally, there is a tradition of this not being a collaborative school in any real sense.

Some staff referred to difficulties they had experienced early on in understanding what the project was really about; others said that they had little knowledge of project activities outside of their own departments; whilst a couple of colleagues, including one quite senior member of staff, admitted to having very little knowledge of the project at all.

All of this suggests that the school has some of the characteristics of what Andy Hargreaves describes as a 'Balkanized culture' (Hargreaves, 1995). In other words, individuals carry out their duties mainly within their departments, with limited knowledge of what happens elsewhere in the school. A potential danger in such a scene, of course, is that the so-called Balkanization may lead to situations where the various sub-groups are in direct competition with one another when major decisions or actions are needed. In fairness, there was no evidence here to support such a conclusion. Indeed staff gave the impression that good social links do exist across departments, but that these do not of themselves facilitate professional interactions of a deeper kind.

One teacher suggested that social fragmentation in the school may have been encouraged by the geography of the building, whilst another made reference to the pressures created by the school's breadth of activity. He noted:

> The heavy programme of international study visits and the additional sixth form courses that we offer mean that people are always a bit anxious not to become involved in things that are not directly associated with their main duties.

Certainly as far as this particular initiative is concerned, there may well be a case for exploring ways of strengthening existing strategies for encouraging cooperation between departments, since as one colleague explained:

> I have a real sense that across the school this project has seemed to be on the move; things that are happening in other departments that seem to be positive, although the degree of cross-departmental sharing has been limited.

Providing Leadership

Where the project was active there was strong indication of the importance of leadership. One teacher in referring to his head of department in this connection, described her as 'a real force'. So, what are the features of leadership that can assist in a project like this? The head of department in question, reflecting on what she felt had been her key contributions to what had occurred, suggested the following:

> I've made sure that everybody contributes to the decision-making about what we are going to focus on. It's not been my decision; we've discussed it and everybody has been involved. I suppose I've tried to give a lead on how we should address these things. I've tried to make good use of my knowledge of the strengths of the team, so that I invite people to take a lead in areas where they feel strong. I also try to be sensitive to staff, particularly for example around the use of the video, so that people are not put in a position where they feel awkward or embarrassed. There's a lot of organizing too, to make this happen, like organizing the times, dates and roles . . . And then finally, it's important to set deadlines for people so that things get done.

The emphasis placed here on sensitivity was echoed by others who had taken on leadership tasks within the project. These included some relatively inexperienced staff who had found themselves engaged in activities that required them to have to coordinate activities that involved senior colleagues on some occasions. So, for example, one younger teacher in describing an activity that was partly designed to provide technical support for colleagues who did not have specialized training in the subject they were now having to teach, remarked:

> In setting it up there was obviously a need for a great deal of care so that persons were not made to feel embarrassed amongst their colleagues. So it needed to be planned and introduced diplomatically. The choice of topic was quite important here and the attraction of this particular topic was excellent in that really most of us welcomed some help and attention to that.

It should be added that there was strong evidence that many staff experienced a degree of uncertainty about the exact purpose and rationale of the project during its early phases. In this respect the presence of a number of colleagues who had been centrally involved in its creation proved to be a useful means of overcoming some of these difficulties, particularly by offering guidance to groups within departments as they formulated their proposals. As one teacher remarked, 'It was really useful to have somebody to bounce ideas off'.

Drawing Some Lessons

In reflecting together with senior colleagues in this particular school about what had happened over the three years of the project, we felt that it was possible to draw out some lessons from our experience. These suggested to us a working theory about how to encourage developments in classroom practice that seemed to be relevant to the school in question. It may also be worthy of the consideration of colleagues elsewhere.

Our findings suggest that experimentation with classroom practice is encouraged when certain conditions are created within the departments of a school. Central to this is the provision of quality time during the school day that allows members of a department opportunities to plan together, work in one another's classrooms and reflect upon these experiences. However, for all of this to stimulate a consideration of new teaching approaches it seems to be important to create working relationships within which the differences between colleagues are seen more positively as a stimulus for discussion of alternative ways of working. Where this works well it also seems to encourage the development of a more detailed language of pedagogy that those involved can use to communicate with one another and, presumably, to develop a deeper understanding of their own current practices. Management decisions can help to encourage the climate within which all of this can take place, but the role of subject department heads in providing effective leadership for such efforts seems to be critical. In many cases this may require guidance and support for those taking on this leadership role.

Over the past few years my colleagues and I have worked in many schools, like Southlands, in different countries, as they have used the UNESCO Resource Pack as a basis for initiatives to develop more inclusive practices. Typically, these projects have involved a broadly similar pattern, including the establishment of a small team to coordinate the initiative, workshops for staff in order to encourage classroom experimentation, and the establishment of teams of teachers who support one another as they attempt to develop their teaching repertoires. In this respect the experience of working with schools in Romania and Spain over a period of years has been particularly illuminating for me, not least in throwing light on strategies that can help in moving such initiatives along. It is clear that support strategies have to be designed to fit in with local circumstances and with this in mind, we have found it useful to see schools as being broadly at one of three stages of involvement in their journey towards the development of more inclusive practices. Each stage provides some indication of the forms of support that might be most appropriate.

In schools that might be seen as being broadly at the first stage, there are still staff who need encouragement to become involved. In such contexts we found it necessary for more time to be given to staff meetings and other forms of informal discussions in order to clarify the aims of the initiative, and further demonstrations of interesting classroom practice, where possible, using video material recorded within the specific school. We have found such examples to be particularly power-ful in convincing colleagues within a school of the potential benefits of what is being proposed, as well as assuring them that it is going to be feasible within their working context. In some instances involvement may be obstructed by the presence of what I have referred to as deficit thinking. This usually involves the existence amongst a group of staff of norms that take for granted that certain children, because of their home backgrounds or personal characteristics, cannot be expected to learn successfully. This contributes to a culture that prevents individuals from seeing any realistic value in what the project is trying to achieve. The aim of the project coordinators within such a situation has to be to find ways of opening up minds to new possibilities through discussion and demonstrations that sensitively encourage the consideration of new possibilities.

Where staff interest has been established, the next step involves finding ways of encouraging colleagues to move to a second stage of involvement which is concerned with turning interest into action. The aim now is to encourage teachers to try out alternative teaching techniques in their classrooms in an attempt to create more inclusive conditions. Once again, workshop demonstrations, lesson observations and video recordings are useful, this time as a means of encouraging and guiding classroom experimentations. Examples of lesson plans and teaching materials may also provide tangible support. What is essential at this stage is that teachers who are prepared to experiment with aspects of their practice are given direct assistance by having opportunities to work closely with like-minded colleagues in ways that encourage mutual support. Often this has been a task for one of the school's coordination team, although in some situations other colleagues may be more suitable. The overall aim should be to create small teams of staff who will plan together, support one another and discuss their experiences in trialling different teaching approaches.

We have found that trials of this type usually help to encourage further enthusiasm for the work of the project. Of themselves, however, they are but a step on the journey we are wishing to encourage. In their most limited form they may simply lead to the use of certain 'tricks' of teaching, learnt during a workshop session or as a result of viewing a video, and adopted in a somewhat superficial way. If this is the case the tricks are likely to be gradually rejected since they are not part of the teacher's established repertoire and probably require some degree of additional preparation. Our aim, therefore, is to help colleagues to move to yet another stage, going beyond simply copying techniques picked up from somebody else.

This third stage of involvement is where teachers have understood and adopted the principles of the project and now use these to plan their lessons in a way that is part of their usual approach to teaching. It means that there is an acceptance that the teacher takes responsibility for the participation and learning of all members of their class, seeing the importance of continually adjusting classroom arrangements in response to those children who indicate, by some means, that they are experiencing difficulties. Thus their lessons are designed to maximize support for learning, using all available resources effectively, particularly child-to-child support. They also involve planning in action throughout the lesson as the teacher improvises in response to pupil feedback. Such conditions are evidence of significant movement towards the elusive ideal of an inclusive classroom.

Chapter 6

Moving Schools

Educational policies in many countries seem to be concerned with making schools more effective. All of this can create tensions, however, not least as a result of different perceptions of what effectiveness means and how it can be achieved. And, as Davies (1996) argues:

> Much school improvement is founded on a myth. The myth is that everyone from the government downwards would like school effectiveness, but there are just too many material or attitudinal constraints on its implementation. In fact, governments do not want effective schools in the academic or even vocational sense. The last thing a fragile state wants is too many articulate, well-qualified students. (Davies, 1996; p. 92)

In my own country, the election in 1997 of a new Labour government further highlighted the types of tensions that can occur. Two words seem to stand out from the new government's education agenda: 'standards' and 'inclusion'. For those who are committed to the development of forms of schooling that can reach all learners this emphasis appears to present few problems. Our work is driven by a desire to provide high quality learning opportunities for all children and young people. So, it seems, our moment has come and we have to take the opportunities that all of this seems to provide.

Having said that, it is also important to be realistic. The dominance of a very narrow view of what is valued as being worthwhile educational standards and the continued use of various forms of selection systems still act together in ways that ensure that significant numbers of our young people experience failure in school. There are those within our country who, for a variety of reasons, may not be so enthusiastic to see the deep changes in the education system that will be necessary in order to provide 'excellence for all children', as suggested in government publications (e.g. DfEE, 1997). Some see the existence of a system that ensures prizes for some at the expense of others as being to their advantage. Then, at a more practical level, there are other barriers that are likely to be in the way of progress. Two immediately come to mind.

First of all, there is the major problem of how to redesign a system of education that still bears many of the features of the purpose for which it was originally formulated, that of educating those who will take on élite roles in society. It has been argued, for example, that a surgeon from the nineteenth century dropped into a present day operating theatre would have no idea where he was, whereas a teacher from that period propelled into a modern day classroom would simply pick up the chalk and carry on where she left off! In other words, despite all the reform efforts of the twentieth century we still have forms of schooling that reflect many of the features of a system that was not intended to achieve quality education for all.

The implication is that substantial changes are needed. This leads to a second problem. Put simply it is this: how do we raise the morale and confidence of the one group that is most critical to these profound reforms, the teachers? Having had some ten years of being undermined and ridiculed, it would be hardly surprising if they did not find the idea of yet further proposals for change unpalatable. Certainly those who are arguing for yet further reforms need to remember that ultimately education policies are what happens behind the classroom door. In this sense, as Fulcher (1989) argues, teachers are policy makers. How they choose to interpret external demands as they interact with their classes in the relative privacy of their classrooms is the policy that really matters. This is the deep end of educational reform that is so difficult to reach. It is why Matthew Arnold, reflecting upon earlier attempts to introduce payment by results, concluded, 'The teachers always beat us in the end'.

So, if movement is to occur it needs to be handled in ways that ensure the support of a committed and confident teaching force, and at the same time, deals with contradictory pressures that exist in the overall context within which schools exist. With this in mind this chapter draws on work that I have been involved in with colleagues in this country and overseas in order to explore ways in which 'moving schools' can be developed; i.e. schools that are continually seeking to increase their capacity to respond to pupil diversity. My central question is, how do we create forms of school organization that will encourage the development of practices that seek to 'reach out to all learners'?

The Context of Reform

Every year English schools are required to complete a form for the Department of Education. In it they record the numbers of pupils on role, including those formally categorized as 'having special educational needs'. A few years ago the headteacher of 'Eastside' Primary School experienced a minor problem as she attempted to make her returns using the computer program issued for this purpose. This problem occurred, it seems, as a result of the school's efforts to admit pupils with disabilities of the sort that are more usually educated in special provision. After she had typed the names of most of the pupils falling into this category, the word 'error' started to flash on the screen. On further investigation the headteacher discovered that this was programmed to happen if the names of more than 20 per cent of the total population of a school were entered. Twenty per cent, it seems, represented the maximum number of 'pupils with special educational needs' that an English primary school was expected to enrol.

This story provides a relevant prologue to the account I provide below of how a school that attempts to move towards more inclusive practices experiences contradictory pressures. Staying with the story of Eastside School as an example, I pay particular attention to the ways in which the English reform agenda of the early 1990s had an impact upon the shape and nature of developments. This may be of particular interest to readers in other countries that are being influenced by the ideas that have informed recent English reforms. Before considering the experience of Eastside in detail, however, it is necessary to provide readers with a flavour, at least, of the educational reforms that have so dominated developments in the English context in recent years.

Whilst the great majority of children in England go to their local neighbourhood schools, there is a long tradition of schools fulfilling the role of 'sorting offices', selecting and preparing pupils for their 'future destinations' in life (Hartnett and Naish, 1990). Thus the idea of selecting and grouping children on the basis of their perceived academic potential is well established and has survived despite recent attempts to introduce a more comprehensive orientation. The development of various forms of separate special education provision can be seen as part of this overall pattern of differential educational response. Provision for children with disabilities developed in similar ways to that of many other industrialized countries (Reynolds and Ainscow 1994). So, for example, the first schools for the blind and deaf were founded towards the end of the eighteenth century. Provision for children with physical disabilities was first made in 1851, while before the middle of the nineteenth century so-called mentally defective children were placed in workhouses and infirmaries. Special provision for children with milder forms of disability was to come later.

As with the rest of public education provision, schooling for children with disabilities had begun with individual and charitable enterprise. Only much later was the government to step in, first of all to support voluntary efforts, and eventually to create a national framework in which public and voluntary agencies could act in partnership to see that educational opportunities of some form were made available. Thus the field that came to be known as special education gradually emerged as a response to those children seen as being outside the responsibility of teachers in regular schools. Indeed, over the years, special education came to see itself, and to be seen by others, as a separate service catering for that small population of children perceived as being disabled. Those involved in this work often had little or no contact with the mainstream of education. This tendency to isolation was further encouraged by the growth of separate administrative structures at both the national and local levels; the existence of specialized teacher training arrangements; and the fact that some of the providers of special education were voluntary organizations.

The latter 1960s and early 1970s began to see considerable changes in emphasis in the field. A general concern with equal opportunities contributed to a heightened awareness of children in ordinary schools who were perceived as making unsatisfactory progress and, consequently, there was a growth in the provision of various forms of remedial education, including the establishment of special classes within or attached to mainstream schools. At the same time, new ideas were emerging that were to challenge the basis of existing provision for students now commonly referred to as having special educational needs (Adams, 1986).

As a result of these changes in thinking in the field, the government of the day set up the inquiry that led to the publication of the highly influential Warnock Report in 1978. Barton (1993) describes the report as being 'historically unique', in that it challenged medical notions of handicap and comfirmed that the goals of education should be the same for all children. The report also introduced the term 'special educational needs' and, at the same time, suggested that it was relevant to some 20 per cent of children. On the issue of the participation of these pupils in regular schools, the report's position was somewhat contradictory. Indeed, Fulcher (1989) suggests that the emphasis placed on the notion of 20 per cent of children having special needs at sometime in their school career is, in effect, an argument that has been used to support an expansion in special provision. She argues that the Warnock notion of integration was, in practice, simply a 'new name for special education'.

The Warnock Report was followed by the 1981 Education Act which established a new framework for the education of children seen as requiring special provision. It defined a child with special educational needs as being one whose learning difficulties call for special educational provision to be made. Despite the emphasis placed in the Warnock Report on a relativist position, whereby a child's difficulties are seen in terms of the school context, the 1981 Act retained a traditional discourse on disability, focusing attention on individual child deficits. A major feature of the Act was the introduction of the 'Statement of Special Educational Needs', an extensive reporting procedure used to monitor the progress of individual pupils and, where necessary, to provide them with additional resources. Within this legislation some reference was made to the idea of integration of children said to have special needs. Specifically, it placed a duty on LEAs to ensure that such pupils were educated in their local primary and secondary schools, provided that their parents were in agreement, that it was practicable, that it was educationally efficient, and that it was not unreasonably expensive. What has happened subsequently can only be described as a disappointment from the point of view of those who would wish to see moves towards integrated arrangements. Undoubtedly some children who previously would have been educated in separate provision, particularly those with sensory and physical impairments, are now being dealt with on an integrated basis. On the other hand, there was clear evidence that the overall proportion of children being educated in special schools remained more or less static (Swann, 1991). Meanwhile there was also evidence that, as in other developed countries, the proportion of other students being excluded from mainstream classrooms because of their perceived learning or behaviour difficulties continued to climb at an alarming rate (Department for Education and Employment, 1995). For these reasons Pijl and Meijer (1991) describe the English system as 'two track' in that it has in place parallel, but separate, segregation and integration policies, leading to a range of policy dilemmas.

Dissatisfaction of various forms with the way the provision of the 1981 Act was working led to further government intervention. Specifically, the Education Act (1993) required the Secretary of State for Education to publish guidance on good practice for the identification and assessment of children with special educational needs in the form of a 'Code of Practice' to which all involved must 'have regard'. The code emphasized school-based intervention to begin with. Each school's governing body was required to publish its policy for special needs, to detail its provision for such pupils in its prospectus, to appoint a special needs coordinator, and to report the effectiveness of its policy to parents annually. School inspections were to include a focus on the implementation of these requirements. These changes were intended to prompt schools to give greater attention to the wider range of pupils said to have special needs, i.e. Warnock's 20 per cent.

While the Code of Practice argued for the existence of a range of provision, it also noted that the special educational needs of most children could be met effectively in mainstream schools, with outside help if necessary, but without a statutory assessment or a statement. It went on to recommend that to help match provision to children's needs, schools and LEAs should adopt a five-stage model, the early stages of which should be firmly embedded in the general work of the school. For example, where a child is at stage one of the Code's model, emphasis should be placed on the gathering of information and what is described as increased differentiation within the child's classroom work. This legislation extends the system by which additional funding follows the individual child, perhaps in the form of dedicated additional adult support. Unfortunately, there is some evidence that this tends to reduce a school's capacity to use support creatively in order to encourage pupil participation since it is seen as being attached to individuals rather than as a resource to the school (Sebba and Ainscow, 1996). Indeed, in some instances this may even contribute to children's eventual exclusion since teachers may come to feel that they are unable to teach them when their allocated support assistant is absent. On the other hand, it is fair to say that it is possible to find plenty of examples of more flexible working patterns, not least in the school discussed in this chapter.

These developments aimed at reforming responses to children seen as having special needs were, in themselves, substantial. However, their full significance can only be understood if they are viewed within the context of the wider changes that were going on in the English education system at the same time. The agenda for these changes was increasingly set by national politicians and has been associated with an intensification of interest in how to raise standards of achievement through an emphasis on competition and consumer choice. A widespread public debate on educational standards which first became apparent in the mid-1970s, had become increasingly polarized, resulting in a plethora of government-led reforms. In particular, a variety of legislative efforts to improve schools occurred during the 1980s, culminating in a series of Acts of Parliament of which the 1988 Education Reform Act, known as 'ERA', was the most important. These were consolidated by further legislation in the early 1990s.

Engagement with the details of this radical reform agenda is unnecessary in this context, but it is important to draw attention to the four main fronts on which this attack on the traditional organization of the school system was carried forward. The first of these was *prescription*, of which the prime examples were the National Curriculum and the associated schemes for national testing at 7, 11 and 14. Second was *decentralization*, and here local management of schools (usually known as site-based management in North America), the increased power of school governors and the reduced roles of local education authorities were the main policy initiatives. Third was *competition*, which was to be encouraged by the introduction of grant-maintained status for schools, open enrolment supported by the publication of 'league tables' of school results, and a general emphasis on the use of performance indicators. Finally there was the *privatization* of services to schools, such as cleaning and catering, professional advice and school inspections. This latter reform, involving the full inspection of each school every four years by teams of trained and nationally accredited independent inspectors, acting on behalf of a government agency (The Office of Standards in Education, or OFSTED), proved to be a very significant influence on thinking and attitudes in the school system.

As we moved through the 1990s educational developments in England and Wales continued to be dominated by a concern to implement this reform agenda. The quest for stability, however, was being made against a background of continuing uncertainty and dispute, as expectations for student achievement rose beyond the apparent capacity of the system to deliver. As a result, there were seemingly contradictory pressures for both centralization and decentralization, although it seems unlikely that either approach works by itself (Fullan, 1991).

Those of us in the UK, and particular England and Wales, have been struggling for longer than most with the implications of this centralized–decentralized dichotomy. At the same time as national governments have drawn to themselves more power than ever before, the usual infrastructure of support has been eroded and schools have found themselves increasingly alone in the struggle to take charge of the process of change.

In summary, therefore, it can be seen that in recent years schools in England and Wales have experienced probably the most turbulent times in their histories. Occupational and organizational norms have been challenged, and pre-existing structures swept aside or transformed by central government. It is against the backcloth of this complex and, at times, confusing reform agenda that I will examine the work of one English school that appears to be moving towards more inclusive and enabling practices at a time when it would appear that an increasing number of powerful forces are pushing the system in a different direction (Booth et al., 1998). The account illuminates the tensions and dilemmas that such schools are likely to face. It also throws light on some of the organizational conditions that will be needed in order to overcome these difficulties.

A School for All?

'Eastside' is a primary school in a large English city. Over a number of years, I have visited the school regularly in order to observe the children and teachers at work. My activities during these visits have varied. On some occasions I have 'shadowed' particular children for a morning; occasionally I have stayed in one teaching area to observe the comings and goings of children and staff through a session; always my visits have included lots of discussions, informal and formal, with staff members, children, parents and other visitors to the school. All of these interactions have been driven by a desire to experience and understand the life of a school that has made a commitment to try to become more inclusive. The account presented here is based upon a series of detailed reports that I wrote following each of these visits, the content of which was agreed in each instance with the headteacher and members of staff involved. These reports were seen as contributing to the school's own development strategy.

The school opened in 1992 and was designed to provide 'an inclusive setting' for 420 pupils in the age range 4 to 11, plus the equivalent of 52 nursery places. It serves what the headteacher describes as a multicultural community. Commenting on the children's backgrounds and how these impact on the school, she notes:

> When we analysed the children in Year 6 I don't think there was any child that had a traditional family setting, for example, and something like about two-thirds of our children are on free meals. So there are a number of factors but we don't want to use those factors because we want to have high expectations of the children and not make excuses.

The site and buildings were designed to be fully accessible to children, staff and members of the community, including those with physical disabilities. The stated policy of the local education authority that administers Eastside is to promote the inclusion of pupils with special needs into mainstream primary schools. Eastside itself makes provision for a number of children whose statement of special educational needs describes as having severe learning difficulties, including some who have profound and multiple disabilities. Teaching and non-teaching support staff are available who enhance the various teaching teams in order to address the needs of these children. The aim is to provide all pupils with access to the mainstream curriculum and everyone is regarded as a full member of the school community. With this in mind the school is organized in a way that is intended to promote the integration of special needs provision into the daily life of the school.

The school has four wings: Early Years, Key Stage 1, Key Stage 2A and Key Stage 2B, each of which has its own suite of interconnected, open areas. The wings all have multi-disciplinary teams coordinated by a teacher who is known as the team leader. In the four years since it was established the school has gradually evolved an overall pattern that guides the work of each of these teams. This working pattern is informed by the strong emphasis placed in the school on encouraging pupil autonomy. The school's statement of aims declares that there is 'a shared vision which is one of developing relationships and a curriculum that ensures that everyone feels valued, respected and reaches a high level of achievement'. An account of the operation of one of the wings provides a sense of what the overall working pattern involves.

Key Stage 1 wing caters for some 120 children in the age range 5 to 7, including 15 who have statements of special educational needs. Staffing consists of a team of nine people, five of whom are qualified teachers. The others are support workers with a variety of titles. In addition, the wing is visited on an occasional basis by a number of specialist staff from outside the school.

The process of planning in the wing begins in the summer when the team meets to address the overall curriculum plan for the coming year. Within this plan there are five areas of activity for which the whole team share responsibility. The five areas are reading, writing, maths, finding out and practical work. Each week one member of the team is delegated to take care of each area and the part of the wing where it will take place.

The weekly planning for each area takes account of the overall plan agreed at the start of the school year. Each Friday morning at 8.00am the team meets in order to coordinate the handing over of the particular area to the next member of staff. So, for example, the teacher who looked after the writing room during the previous week will outline what she did and assist one of her colleagues to plan for the subsequent week's activities. The team have developed a common format for this purpose which enables them to plan in a way that takes account of all the children in the wing, 120 of them, each of whom at some stage in the week will work in all the areas. This planner also has to take account of the content of the 'individual curriculum plan' that is prepared for each child. Thus the overall programme for an area has to be for the whole group whilst at the same time having the flexibility to take account of each child's stage of learning.

Beyond this weekly planning process, each day the teacher works out how he or she will organize the day's activities, knowing that any of the children may arrive at any time during the day but not knowing when this will be. In fact, the children are encouraged to choose for themselves the order in which they carry out their assigned tasks, using an individual record sheet to help them plan and report their work.

The visitor to the school is struck by the overall flexibility of the working arrangements that emerge as a result of all this planning. Many children arrive well before the official start of school, making their way to their home base where staff are busy preparing for the day. Once there, the children usually find something to get on with without being prompted. In the Early Years wing parents of the youngest children are encouraged to bring them into the classroom and to help them choose their first activity. They may also help them in choosing books to read. Those who do so generally stay around for no more than five minutes.

Once the morning activities commence the observer is faced with a highly complex evironment. There is almost continual movement as children finish their tasks, complete their individual records and then proceed to their next chosen activity. Having said that, it is also true that a closer scrutiny of what is going on indicates high levels of engagement in the tasks and activities that are set. For example, after a period observing in one area in Key Stage 1 wing I noted that I had seen little or no distraction amongst the children who had taken part. In fact during this one hour period the group size working in the particular area had varied between 13 and 22 children.

In each area a wide variety of possible activities are prepared from which the children can choose. Materials and equipment are arranged in ways that enable children to get at them without assistance. In this way they seem to carry out their tasks with a minimum of teacher attention. This leaves staff free to observe what is happening, intervening as and when they perceive this to be necessary. Within this busy and complex environment the adults are, in fact, to be seen engaged in a continual process of instant decision-making, adapting their existing plans and, indeed, formulating new plans in the light of decisions made by pupils and unforeseen opportunities that arise. This form of what I have called 'planning in action' is, I believe, both vital and demanding. It involves a sophisticated form of improvisation whereby the teachers make what, I assume, are often intuitive judgments about how best to proceed in the light of their observations of their pupils' reactions to classroom tasks and experiences.

The evidence suggests that at Eastside the skills of the teachers in making such judgments are enhanced by the formal planning processes in which they participate. In general these formal processes address two broad areas: (i) the nature of the curriculum experiences that are to be offered to all the pupils; and (ii) the perceived needs of each individual child, including those who are seen as having special needs. It does seem that the understanding, confidence and sensitivities that emerge as a result of these processes provide members of staff with preparation and support as they carry out necessary improvisations during the day.

The emphasis placed on team work is also very evident in the classrooms. This provides many incidental opportunities for staff to assist one another, share ideas and, of course, observe one another's practices. As I have already noted, there is considerable research evidence to support the view that this type of mutual observation in the classroom can be a powerful stimulus for teacher development (e.g. Ainscow, 1994; Hopkins et al., 1994; Joyce and Showers, 1988). However, my observations in the school point to certain pressures that this can also generate. Specifically, these arise from what one teacher describes as a 'goldfish bowl' feeling in which pressure can be generated as a result of staff being under the almost constant scrutiny of their colleagues.

As the work of the children and staff proceeds during a typical day it is often difficult for the interested visitor to pick out those children who are categorized as having special educational needs. In some instances, of course, the disabilities of particular children mean that they eventually can be spotted. What is rarely evident, however, are situations where individuals are being closely tracked or supervised by a particular teacher or support assistant. In fact, a much more sophisticated rationale for learning support is in operation. It is one that seeks to make use of a range of support responses, not least that of the children themselves. For example, Brian, who is aged 8, explained how he sometimes helps Raymond during the lunch hour. He explained:

> It's just to help him with the queue really. He gets angry sometimes and the teachers try to calm him down . . . He lies on the floor sometimes. If you are firm with him, tell him what you mean by get up, he's OK usually. I tell him he has to do the same as the rest.

From an 8 year old this seems to be a sophisticated response to a challenging situation!

It is also evident that considerable efforts are made to sensitize all staff to the types of support that particular children may require at various points during the day. In this way staff are expected to share responsibility for encouraging the participation and learning of all members of the group but without falling into the trap of fostering a dependent relationship that might undermine the overall goal of pupil autonomy. Once again this involves fine judgments that have to be informed by a detailed knowledge of individual children and, indeed, their overall curriculum plans. On one occasion a classroom assistant described how she had been observing David, a 5-year-old boy who she is expected to keep a particular eye on. She explained that she had encouraged David and two other boys to get involved in a sand tray activity. Then, she said, she 'backed off to allow the peer pressure to develop'. Like all the children David has a planning diary (see Figure 6.1) and part of the assistant's job is to help him to use it. Consequently, she explained, her support tasks have to be planned in response to his decisions. Similarly, where she feels it is appropriate, she has to look out for ways of involving other pupils with David. In this particular instance she explained that she had asked one of the teachers to nominate two children who had been working hard and they had been invited to work with David.

Inevitably, visitors to the school with a special education background are somewhat anxious about the vulnerability of certain children in these busy environments. Surely some children get lost, become confused or waste time? My own observations provide little evidence to justify such worries, although I do feel that some children might benefit occasionally from a pressure to achieve more. I have to say, however, that this concern rarely seems to apply to those children seen as having special needs. On the contrary, what is most striking is the way in which the structuring of the environment facilitates responses and forms of learning that might not have been anticipated. An example of this arises from my shadowing of Faheema, a pupil in Key Stage 1 wing. The school record indicates that Faheema is just aged 6, has cerebral palsy and requires a rolator to aid her walking. It also notes that she is able to communicate, to some degree at least, in both English and Punjabi.

I watched Faheema for some 45 minutes as she sat on the floor in a very busy area of the wing doing a shape building task. Her walking frame was just behind her. For much of this period there was little direct adult involvement. However, she did receive some assistance from one of the other pupils. Indeed this particular girl had some difficulties in moving away since when she tried to do so Faheema would call her back, even pulling her arm at one point to persuade her to sit down. In my notes I commented on how I had been struck by the level of engagement sustained by Faheema, even in this context where there were so many potential distractions.

Directly after the lesson one of the teachers mentioned that Faheema had developed her ability to make choices well. Even so, she noted, just over 50 per cent of the child's time is directed by adults. After I explained how I had observed her finish building the shape (a polyhedron) the teacher indicated that the staff

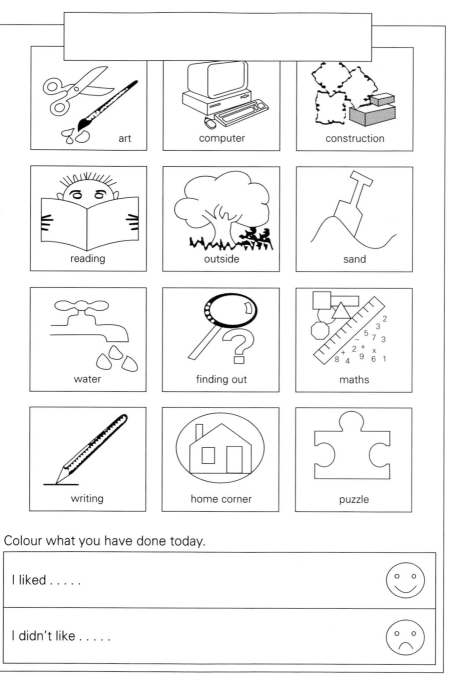

Early Years

Figure 6.1   Pupil planning diary

would probably not have expected this of her. They would have assumed, she explained, that Faheema's fine-motor control was not developed enough and that the task would not 'excite or stimulate her enough'. In this way Faheema had, it seems, overcome the limited expectations of the staff. As the teacher noted:

> There is a good lesson to learn in that and that is why it is important to allow children a level of choice. Out of that has come amazing developments in fine-motor skill and shape discrimination.

This also led her to comment that if planning is, in her words, 'too prescriptive' it may cut off this type of possibility. Commenting on Faheema's persistence and concentration, she remarked:

> If it had been an adult chosen activity, say, at the moment, colour sorting, she would probably done it for about 30 seconds and then had a bit of a 'squawk' for 30 seconds.

Supporting the Process of Inclusion

Ballard (1995) in suggesting that there is no such thing as an inclusive school, goes on to argue that there is, however, 'a process of inclusion that has no limits'. In this sense, what we have seen in a school such as Eastside is an exploration of new forms of practice and organization that are intended to extend the staff's capacity to support the learning of children, whatever their current levels of achievement and perceived difficulties. Consequently, those of us who are interested in the ways in which schools can become more inclusive in this sense can learn much from hearing about and reflecting on schools that have made steps in these directions. In stating that, however, I stress once again that I am not suggesting that our engagement with such a school will help to devise blueprints that can point the way forward for all schools. As I have argued in earlier chapters, what seems to help development in one school may have no impact or even a negative effect in another. So, whilst we can, I believe, learn from vicarious experience, this learning has to be respected for its own qualities. Essentially, it is a form of learning that arises as a result of using new experiences to reflect on current understandings rather than a means of providing prescriptions that can be transposed from one context to another.

What, then, are my reflections on the experiences I have had at Eastside? What do these experiences suggest to me about the ways in which this particular group of teachers are trying to encourage participation and learning? Across the reports that I prepared as a result of my observations and discussions I note, in particular, the ways in which the school is structured in order to facilitate teamwork. Indeed, enormous amounts of time are given over to this process, as we have seen. In addition to the planning processes already described, staff also meet on at least two evenings a week and sometimes more for further planning and inservice activities.

As I have explained, the formal planning processes seem to have two main elements. First of all, there is the planning of the overall learning environment. This involves taking the Progammes of Study outlined in the National Curriculum and, while bearing in mind the principles upon which the school attempts to operate, turning these into appropriate activities, materials and classroom arrangements. The second element is concerned with planning for individuals. This requires the creation of individual curriculum plans for each child based upon the best available knowledge amongst the staff team working with the child. Interestingly, this approach seems to incorporate the notion of individual planning that is so familiar in special education settings but in a way that relates to the needs of all children. In a sense it is an approach that implies that every child is regarded as being special!

As we have seen, this formal planning, carried out in a collaborative way within the teams, provides a basis for yet a third form of planning. Influenced by the ideas of Schon (1987), I have characterized this as 'planning in action'. It is the decision-making that individual teachers and other adults at Eastside make throughout the school day in the light of their interpretations of their observations. It has to take account of the decisions that individual children make as they engage with the opportunities that are provided. It is, I believe, guided by the knowledge, principles and sensitivities that members of staff develop as they take part in the more formal planning procedures that I have described. However, as I have noted, all of this takes place in what can best be described as a 'hothouse' atmosphere within which all staff are subject to the continual scrutiny of their colleagues. In this context, planning in action becomes a demanding requirement on those who work in the school. Fortunately, the evidence indicates that these pressures are, to a degree, alleviated by the heavy emphasis placed on team work and collaboration which, in effect, provides on-going support and encouragement for individual members of staff. As the coordinator of the early years wing noted, 'having to justify yourself to your colleagues helps you to think about what you do in the classroom'.

Beyond the area of planning there are a number of other rather striking features of classroom life at Eastside that seem to facilitate pupil participation and learning. For example, an important feature of the way in which the wings are organized is the emphasis placed on creating flexible and accessible working environments. As I have noted, materials and equipment are made available for the children to help themselves; space is allocated for particular types of activities; and much use is made of concrete materials of various kinds to stimulate activity. Use is made frequently of the floor in order to provide more working space and care is taken to ensure that displays and equipment are at an appropriate eye level for the children. In these ways, considerable overall attention is given to making the classroom areas attractive and stimulating places to be.

The emphasis placed on encouraging pupils to be more autonomous seems to give the teachers more time than in traditional forms of classroom organization. Having said that, it is necessary to remember that staff are having to engage with a large number of children as they move from area to area. On this point one teacher noted that this had now 'become easy' for her and she wonders nowadays what she would do with her time if she had 'an ordinary size class'. In fact, much of the teachers' time is used to move about the classroom, observing, facilitating, questioning, and praising children's efforts. Much emphasis is placed on helping pupils to relate new learning to old, and to connecting the unusual to the known. Helping the children to find purpose and meaning in their experiences seems to be seen as being of particular importance. For example, one teacher noted:

> We all use language like, 'you're learning how to do things carefully' ... I don't think they would understand, 'you're learning how to develop fine motor skills' ...

At the outset of the morning and afternoon sessions, the children usually meet in base groups where the teacher asks questions in order to focus the children's attention, and assigns tasks and arrangements. Later, teachers may occasionally call groups of children together to review activities, reflect on what has happened and plan for further tasks. Here there is a noticeable emphasis on 'reaching out' to individuals, helping them to find meaning in their experiences. Thus, once again, we become aware of how plans are modified during a session through processes of 'trial and error' as teachers 'think on their feet'. It is an example of Huberman's notion of 'tinkering', as referred to in Chapter 4. As a result of this type of tinkering, tasks may be reformulated as required and new materials designed as a need becomes apparent. Similarly, at various moments pupils are encouraged to collaborate in supporting one another's learning. Such groupings of children may have been preplanned or, in other instances, created spontaneously.

As we have seen, the children themselves are given a large degree of independence to shape their programme of activities during much of the school day. However, as we have also noted, this sometimes means that they achieve things that are beyond the expectation of the teacher. Children are required to monitor their own work, reflect upon the meaning of their experiences and keep a record of their achievements. Within this overall pattern those children seen as having special needs are expected to participate equally. As we have seen, in this context such pupils are frequently prepared to be assertive in seeking help, particularly from classmates.

The overall emphasis in the school is on providing support within the classroom, making particular use of what might be described as 'natural' sources of support, particularly the children themselves. Specialist personnel are encouraged to work in the classrooms and, to varying degrees, volunteer helpers, including parents, are involved in a similar style. Within the school the whole issue of how support is used remains one of considerable debate. Teachers worry about the potential dangers of assigning support assistants to particular children, something that tends to be encouraged or even required by the wording of statements. The concern of some staff is that such arrangements may encourage dependence on the assistant and, at the same time, act as a block to child-to-child interactions. One teacher summed up her own position as follows:

> We always try to make sure that equal attention is given to all children ... They are entitled to a carefully planned curriculum which other people can implement at different times. So they all get more adult attention because of our overall curriculum planning.

What has to be stressed, however, is the high levels of task engagement of the pupils, including those seen as having special needs. For me all of this raises questions about how this is achieved. How far is it an outcome of the school's pursuit of inclusion or is it a manifestation of the more general features of teacher effectiveness reported in the research literature (e.g. Porter and Brophy, 1988)?

Impact of National Reforms

What, then, was the impact on this school of the massive reform agenda summarized in the early section of this chapter? Surely a school working in the ways I have described is swimming against the tide in a school system which is being pushed towards policies based on the idea that increased competition between and within schools is the main way of raising educational standards?

The headteacher's response to these issues stresses the sense of vulnerability she feels, particularly with respect to how the school may be perceived from the outside. For me there is an echo here of the words of another headteacher who described to me recently how he felt as though he was living and working in an occupied country! Certainly these feelings of vulnerability mean that the headteacher of Eastside believes that it is essential that great care is taken in presenting the work of the school to the outside world. For example, in explaining her belief that some of the older pupils have missed out on early play experiences and need to be given such opportunities as part of the curriculum, she remained anxious as to how this might be construed elsewhere. She commented:

> I use the word 'play' between you and me. We would use work to anybody else, but to play, to use water, sand, construction equipment, right! But that is their need at the time, so their age is nothing to do with it . . . they need to play, so that is the challenge of inclusion and we are working at it.

In addition to care with language, the headteacher believes it is important to ensure that externally imposed policies are, in her words, 'followed to the letter'. With this in mind she and her deputy spend considerable time carefully checking all documentation that leaves the school or that might be seen by official visitors to the school. Having said that, this is not necessarily seen as being a negative thing to do. Certain of the recent requirements were seen as making a positive contribution to the development of existing practices. For example, the introduction of the special educational needs Code of Practice had, in the words of the headteacher, 'formalized a lot of things we were doing anyway'.

The Statements provided for some children were seen as having a limited value. The head noted that they do direct staff 'towards the kind of areas of learning a child should be working on, so they give us a baseline'. The statement was also seen as being helpful where it provided for some form of additional resources.

A particular area of concern was the impact of the forthcoming inspection of the school. The head's view of this was summed up in the following comment:

> ... we will either do extremely well in an OFSTED or we will do very badly and the reason why we'd do extremely well is because we've got planning structures, we've got documentation, we've got outcomes, you know all those things. But what they (i.e. the inspectors) may not be able to come to terms with is our organization and management, and that's why we have gone through wing files, OK. Your visit has helped to push them on a bit, that we've got the documentation to prove what we are doing.

A further area of concern, also leading to a sense of vulnerability in the school, related to the introduction of the programme of national testing at ages 7 and 11. Nevertheless, even here positive benefits were recognized. The headteacher noted:

> ... testing has been quite an interesting experience for us really, from the point of view that we have recognized that we need to make sure that we can show that the experience of Eastside is a successful one for children. So, therefore, we have to know within the National Curriculum levels where children are at certain times.

Having said that, there remained concern about the limitations of what the test results revealed and staff in the school felt that the results, summarized, as they were, in terms of National Curriculum levels, provided a rather limited description of a child's achievements. Furthermore, they gave no explanation of how the child had got to that level. Concern was also expressed in the school about the potential dangers of classifying children in terms of National Curriculum levels. In this respect the head noted:

> ... you could argue that testing completely undermines inclusion anyway because it separates people out into achievement levels rather than into learning levels.

However, there was once again a recognition of how the testing arrangements had stimulated some useful rethinking. The headteacher commented:

> In terms of Year 6 the results of the tests have opened up quite a few issues for us about the children and their achievements. It's thrown up stuff about all kinds of management issues that involve the children and that's why we've been talking about our emphasis for the coming year in Key Stage 2.

What emerged, therefore, from an exploration of the sense of vulnerability in the school were some interesting contradictions in the argument. Some aspects of the reform agenda were seen as being potential obstacles, while others may well have assisted in strengthening certain practices that are seen as being positive to moves towards greater inclusion. Indeed, the headteacher herself went further in arguing that the overall emphasis on reform had created a climate within which she and her colleagues had come to recognize that staying the same was no longer an option. In this context, change is seen as being inevitable. Indeed she described how she had come to regard a variety of factors, including some of those imposed from outside, as a means of fostering change:

> ... we probably have more intellectual discussions about the nature of education than most institutions because all the time we are constantly challenged. We are constantly challenged by the external factors ... those external factors constantly challenge us, right, and constantly put up barriers to inclusion. So what we have to do is to look at those barriers, look how to get round them, and use them. What we are going to do, for example, is take testing and use it for the very best for our children. We are not going to say, Oh God, it's dreadful. We are going to say OK, what do we have to do to make those children successful in testing, how does it affect us as a whole school and how does that affect our delivery of the curriculum.

Other factors were also seen by the headteacher as a stimulus for change: she mentioned the fact that classrooms are physically open, making more traditional teaching styles almost impossible to use; the deliberate appointment of staff who have had an unusual career pattern and who are, therefore, more comfortable in a constantly changing environment; and the collaborative planning that forces people to talk about what they are doing. This collaborative style is, she argues, encouraged by the high level of responsibility that is delegated to teams and their coordinators.

Leadership in the wing is a critical factor, in her opinion. The coordinators are like headteachers in their own areas of the school. Their skills in creating an appropriate working climate are central to the success of the organization. Indeed, where these skills are absent as, apparently, they were recently in one area of the school, the system readily breaks down. Where this happens the pattern of working means that the difficulties are likely to have a negative impact on the work of all staff and children within a wing.

One final factor was seen by the head as being significant in encouraging change in the school. She argued that the admission to the school of children who in various ways challenge existing teaching arrangements has the effect of encouraging staff to continue 'inventing' new responses.

Possible Implications

It seems, therefore, that the massive reform agenda has had a mixed or even contradictory impact on the development of inclusive practices at Eastside. What then does this suggest that might be of value to others pursuing an inclusive orientation within school systems that are likely to be engaged in similar programmes of reform?

First of all it is clear that much of what we have noted at Eastside is consistent with other evidence about processes that seem to facilitate greater pupil participation in schools (e.g. Ainscow, 1991; 1995). For example, progress seems to be associated with a particular orientation to the task that involves a move away from an emphasis on integration towards a concern with processes of inclusion. That is to say, a move away from an orientation which tends not to challenge or alter the organization, curriculum or forms of teaching offered to the children in general. What I describe as an inclusive orientation, on the other hand, is conceptualized not as how to assimilate individual pupils seen as having special needs into existing arrangements but, instead, as to how schools can be transformed in order to respond positively to all pupils as individuals. In this sense, as Ballard (1995) notes, inclusion values diversity rather than assimilation.

In schools such as Eastside this concern with valuing diversity has a major impact on forms of classroom practice. It seems to encourage the development of practice that places emphasis on building on the children's existing knowledge and experience, helping them to find meaning in the tasks and activities that are set (Ainscow and Tweddle, 1988). According to Udvari-Solner (1996), the 'constructivist' view of learning that informs this approach challenges the assumptions and practices of the reductionism that has pervaded educational practices for generations. In her view reductionism is deficit-driven, suggesting that learning will only occur when tasks are broken down into sequences of steps. Within a constructivist frame, on the other hand, real experiences, discourse with others and personal reflection are all seen as ways of encouraging learning. Thus in classrooms that are informed by constructivism there are no fixed conceptions of the world that pupils must master. Rather the pupil's point of view is sought and serves as the basis for future activities.

In my experience this perspective on teaching and learning tends to be encouraged by certain organizational features. I have noted, for example, that schools that are more responsive to the individuality of pupils tend to be structured in ways that encourage processes of problem solving (Ainscow, 1991). Central to this, as exemplified by Eastside, is collaboration amongst staff. Unfortunately, establishing collaborative working patterns in schools is not an easy task. Weick (1985) suggests that schools are 'loosely coupled systems' consisting of units, processes, actions and individuals that tend to operate in isolation from one another. Loose coupling is also encouraged by the goal ambiguity that characterizes schooling. Despite rhetoric of agreed aims and common missions, schools consist of groups of people who may well have very different values and beliefs about the purposes of schooling. Furthermore, it is important that collaboration does not reduce teacher discretion since, as we have seen at Eastside, responsiveness seems to occur when teachers have sufficient autonomy to make flexible decisions in response to the encounters that occur as the children engage with the tasks and activities that are set. It would seem that what is necessary is a system that is more tightly coupled but without losing the advantage of loose coupling benefits.

In schools such as Eastside that have set out to develop more collaborative ways of working, there is evidence that this tends to have an impact on how teachers perceive themselves and their work (Rosenholtz, 1989). Specifically, greater staff collaboration can lead to changes in the culture of the organization such that teachers view children whose progress is a matter of concern in a new light. Rather than simply presenting problems that have to be overcome or, perhaps, referred elsewhere for separate attention, such pupils may be perceived as providing feed-back on existing classroom arrangements. In this way they may be seen as sources of understanding as to how these arrangements might be developed in ways that could be of benefit to all members of the class.

What happens, then, when attempts are made within schools to introduce structural changes in order to foster more collaborative working patterns? By and large the evidence is that schools find it difficult to cope with change, particularly where this involves modifications in practice (Fullan, 1991). As we have seen, schools in England have had to respond to a plethora of innovations in recent years. This is one of the reasons why a close scrutiny of Eastside School is so fascinating. Here, it seems, is a school where this context of massive reform has been used to facilitate the types of collaboration that appear to be a necessary condition for the development of more inclusive practices.

Just like many other social organizations undergoing significant transforma-tion, the search is for what Fullan (1991) describes as 'order and correctness'. Teachers searching for correctness in a complex school system which is involved in substantial change will inevitably experience ambiguity and a lack of understanding of the direction and purposes of the change. Thus the search for order is a search to determine what actions to take when faced with ambiguous situations. While schools are at the centre of these changes they do not exist in isolation. They are affected by forces which exercise significant power and influence upon the climate of the school in predictable and unpredictable ways. It is in this climate that school staffs construct the realities of their working lives.

Weick (1985) characterizes schools as 'underorganized systems' in that although they tend to be ambiguous and disorderly there is, nevertheless, some order. Furthermore, he argues, anyone who can help to create more order within an underorganized system can bring about change. This may in part, at least, throw some light on what occurs at Eastside. The unusual and challenging factors noted by the headteacher, emanating as they do from both outside and inside the school, create a sense of ambiguity. The structural arrangements introduced by the head-teacher have helped to resolve these, and, as a result, she has managed to draw the staff together behind broadly similar principles. As Weick explains, because ambiguity in organizations increases the extent to which action is guided by values and ideology the values of 'powerful people' (i.e. those who can reduce ambiguity) affect what the organization is and what it can become. Thus, according to Weick, those who resolve ambiguity for themselves and others can implant a new set of values in an organization, which creates a new set of relevancies and competencies, and, in so doing, introduces a source of innovation. Ambiguity sets the scene for organizations to learn about themselves and their environments, allowing them to emerge from their struggles with uncertainty in a different form from that in which they started the confrontation.

It seems, therefore, that the perspective and skills of the headteacher are cen-tral to an understanding of what happens at Eastside. Her vision of the school and her beliefs about how it can foster the learning of all its pupils appear to be key influences, not least because of her insistence on the creation of particular working patterns. All of this means, of course, that replication of these processes in other schools would be difficult, particularly if those in charge were unwilling or unable to make fundamental changes in working patterns.

Improving the Quality of Education for All

The experience of Eastside suggests that moving towards more inclusive ways of working involves a process of growth whereby those within a school develop ways of learning together from and about human diversity. In this sense it has to be seen as a cultural process. As Schein (1985) explains, it is concerned with the development of 'the deeper level of basic assumptions and beliefs that are shared by members of an organization, and that define in a basic "taken-for-granted fashion an organization's view of itself and its environment"' (p. 6). However, it also involves structural factors that bear upon the climate within which such growth may occur. Our work with schools in the IQEA project has thrown some light on what forms of structural change might be necessary in order to encourage the growth of more inclusive ways of working.

IQEA involved a team of university academics based at the University of Cambridge working in partnership with schools to explore ways in which the learning of all members of these communities, including students, parents and staff, can be enhanced (see Ainscow et al., 1994; Hopkins et al., 1994; and Hopkins et al., 1996, for more detailed accounts of the project). As the project developed, we attempted to outline our own version of school improvement by articulating a set of principles that provide starting points for our work. These were as follows:

- School improvement is a process that focuses on enhancing the quality of students' learning.

- The vision of the school should be one that embraces all members of the school community as both learners and contributors.

- The school will see in external pressures for change important opportunities to secure its internal priorities.

- The school will seek to develop structures and create conditions which encourage collaboration and lead to the empowerment of individuals and groups.

- The school will seek to promote the view that enquiry, and the monitoring and evaluation of quality, are responsibilities which all members of staff share.

The intention was that these principles should inform the thinking and practice of teachers during school improvement efforts, providing a touchstone for the strategies they devised.

Our work with schools in the project was based upon a contract which attempted to define the parameters for our involvement, and the obligations those involved owed to each other. In particular, the contract emphasized that all staff be consulted; that an in-school team of coordinators (referred to as 'the cadre') be appointed to carry the work forward; that a 'critical mass' of staff were to be actively involved; and that sufficient time would be made available for necessary classroom and staff development activities. Meanwhile, we committed ourselves to supporting the school's developments, usually in the first place for one year. Often the arrangement continued, however, and in some instances we were involved for periods as long as seven years. We provided training for the school cadre, made regular school visits and contributed to school-based staff development activities. In addition, we attempted to work with the schools in recording and analysing their experiences in a way that also provided data relevant to our own on-going research agendas (West et al., 1997).

The commitment to work with the schools in these ways presented us with a number of difficulties and dilemmas. In a more traditional project we might well have chosen to introduce to the school an established model of development based upon research carried out elsewhere. Then, having set the initiative going, our task would have been to stand back and record the process and outcomes of the intervention. In IQEA, we deliberately chose to adopt a very different approach, based upon an alternative perspective of how change can be understood and facilitated. Rather than seeking to impose externally validated models of improvement we were seeking to support schools in creating their own models. Our assumption was that such an approach, that builds upon the biographies and circumstances of particular organizations, is much more likely to bring about and help sustain significant improvements in the quality of schooling.

It follows, therefore, that we did not view school improvement as a 'quick-fix' business. In attempting to work with schools in this way, we found ourselves confronted with staggering complexity, and by a bewildering array of policy and strategy options. It was our belief that only through a regular engagement with these complexities can a greater understanding of school improvement be achieved.

As a result of such engagements with schools involved in the IQEA project we evolved a style of collaboration that we referred to as 'working with rather than working on'. This phrase attempted to sum up an approach that deliberately allows each project school considerable autonomy to determine its own priorities for development and, indeed, its methods for achieving these priorities.

The experience of working with these and other schools leads me to suggest certain ingredients that seem to assist in developing schools that can be more effective for all pupils. It is important here to note my use of the word 'ingredients' in order to make it clear that what I am outlining is not a recipe! Unfortunately the fields of school effectiveness and school improvement have been prone to the formulation of lists of characteristics that appear to offer deceptively simple technical solutions to what are in essence complex social issues. Such lists are particularly attractive to those who seek quick-fix solutions, not least those politicians who see educational improvement as a means of ensuring their popularity. Lists are guaranteed to lead to eventual disappointment. School improvement is a highly complex process requiring a much more sophisticated approach that has the sensitivity to address these complexities. Our own work illustrates the fact that schools are idiosyncratic communities, within which many competing views are held, particularly when it comes down to the fundamental beliefs that guide teachers' interactions with their classes. This being the case, each school has to develop its own way forward and, whilst outsiders can and must be involved, there is strong evidence to suggest that improvement has to be driven from the inside (Barth, 1990; Fullan, 1991; Hopkins et al., 1994).

In this respect, evidence from school effectiveness research can be useful as a starting point for a process of internal review, leading to the setting of priorities that can be used to guide improvement efforts. It is important to stress, however, that its use is as a stimulus for the development of internally driven improvement strategies, not as an imposed blueprint as to how improvement can be achieved. For example, Figure 6.2 is an activity that I have used to stimulate such a process in many schools in this country and overseas. As can be seen, it uses evidence from a review of school effectiveness research by Louise Stoll to engage staff within a school in thinking together about their own contexts in order to develop their own improvement plans.

Recognizing that school improvement will not be achieved through the use of recipes, in what follows, I outline some ingredients that provide 'possibilities' for those who are interested in the development of schools that can be more effective in reaching out to all learners.

The work of individual teachers is much influenced by the overall organization of a school. Where the school is well managed by leaders who support the staff it is much easier for teachers to do their best work. The overall atmosphere of the school is particularly important. Schools that are more successful are places where teachers, pupils and parents show good relationships and share common goals. It is important, therefore, to review existing school arrangements in order to decide upon areas that should be improved.

This activity will help you and your colleagues to review your school's organization. It will focus on areas such as:

- relationships between staff, pupils and parents;

- use of available resources to support learning;

- the ways in which difficulties are addressed;

- policies for guiding practice; and

- staff development.

Step 1
Working with a group of colleagues (e.g. five or six people), discuss the attached diagram. It summarizes research from certain countries about what seem to be some of the characteristics of effective schools. It suggests three overall features of schools that are successful in teaching all children. These are: a common mission, an emphasis on learning and a climate conducive to learning. Around the outside of the diagram is a summary of the evidence that points towards these features.

As you discuss the diagram you should consider the following questions:

- Are these the features of an effective school in our country?
- Are there any elements that are missing from the diagram?

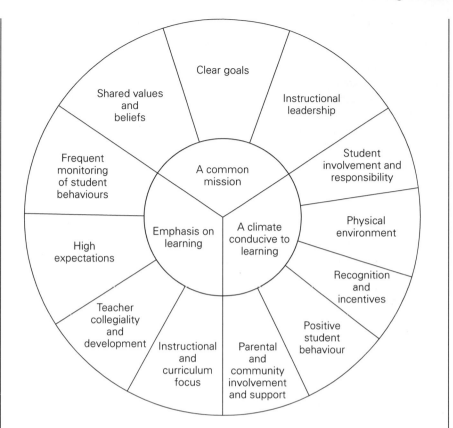

The characteristics of effective schools (Stoll, 1991)

Step 2
In the same groups you should now review your own school in relation to the ideas you have discussed. In particular: what are the strengths of this school? what areas of the school need to be developed further?

Step 3
Design an action plan for developing the school. It should include:

1   Targets
The changes we want to make over the next year.

2   Strategies
The methods we will use in order to bring about these changes.

3   Success criteria
The means by which the implementation of the action plan will be evaluated.

Step 4
Each group should present its action plan to the rest of the staff. These should be discussed in order to agree a way forward that makes good use of all of the suggestions.

Figure 6.2   Reviewing school organization

Creating Conditions that Support Risk-taking

Much of my research over the last few years convinces me of the importance of the school context in creating a climate within which inclusive practices can be fostered. The nature of such positive contexts can take many forms and, as I have already stressed, generalizations are very difficult. Nevertheless, the monitoring of developments in particular schools over time suggests certain patterns that are at least worthy of consideration. These suggest a series of organizational conditions that seem to facilitate the risk-taking that seems to be associated with movements towards more inclusive practices. More specifically they indicate that such movement is not about making marginal adjustments to existing arrangements, but rather about asking fundamental questions about the way the organization is currently structured, focusing on aspects such as patterns of leadership, processes of planning and policies for staff development. In this way the development of inclusive schooling comes to be seen as a process of school improvement (Ainscow, 1995b).

By and large, schools find it difficult to cope with change (Fullan, 1991). In this respect they face a double problem: they cannot remain as they now are if they are to respond to new challenges, but at the same time they also need to maintain some continuity between their present and their previous practices. There is, therefore, a tension between *development and maintenance*. The problem is that schools tend to generate organizational structures that predispose them towards one or the other. Schools (or parts of schools) at the development extreme may be so over-confident of their innovative capacities that they take on too much too quickly, thus damaging the quality of what already exists. On the other hand, schools at the maintenance extreme may either see little purpose in change or have a poor history of managing innovation.

In working with schools that were faced with this inevitable maintenance–development dilemma during the recent period of English educational reforms, my colleagues and I have found it useful to ask staff to carry out some form of review in order to generate possible areas for development. Often this generates too many possibilities such that decisions have to be made about what will be the priorities, moving from the separate, perhaps even conflicting concerns of individuals or groups, to an agreed set of issues which represent the most important concerns of the whole school community. A school's priorities for development usually relate to aspects of curriculum, assessment or classroom practice within the context of interpretations of the requirements of the overall reform agenda.

In attempting to achieve a consensus about priorities for action we encourage colleagues in schools to bear in mind the following criteria:

- *Manageability*: how much can we realistically hope to achieve?

- *Coherence*: is there a sequence that will ease implementation of these changes?

- *Consonance*: do these priorities coincide or overlap with external requirements for reform?

Careful monitoring of English schools in our project during recent years indicates very strongly that those that take account of these concerns have had much greater success in bringing about improvements in their work. In particular, we have found that schools which pay attention to the matter of consonance and, therefore, see externally imposed changes as providing opportunities as well as (or, indeed, instead of) problems, are better able to respond to these demands. We have also found that it is important to be clear about what is *not* a priority — otherwise, it is possible to dissipate staff efforts and enthusiasm across too many initiatives for which they may have neither the means nor the inclination to support.

The IQEA schools were, therefore, encouraged to review, and in some cases to reconsider, their development priorities on a regular basis. In this way we were keen to ensure that colleagues within each had:

- defined the area or issue to be tackled;
- ensured that this was a 'real' issue, concerned with aspects of the school's life that was widely recognized as being significant;
- considered how this could be tackled in a way that contributed to the development of the whole school whilst, at the same time, helping it to respond to external requirements for quality assurance faced by all schools; and
- communicated this to all stakeholder groups (e.g. staff, pupils, parents and governors).

Moving practice forward necessitates a sensitive engagement with processes of change in order to strike a careful balance of maintenance and development. In working with schools I find it helpful sometimes to bring the issue of how to manage change on to the agenda for staff discussion. Here I find it useful to get colleagues to reflect upon their previous experiences of change in order to develop guidelines that can be used to support their future efforts. Figure 6.3 is an example of an activity that I find useful in this respect.

Attempting to move practice forward also leads to a further area of difficulty which is experienced at both an individual and organizational level. This involves forms of turbulence that arise as attempts are made to change the status quo. Turbulence may take a number of different forms, involving organizational, psychological, technical or micro-political dimensions. At its heart, however, it is frequently about the dissonance that occurs as people struggle to make sense of new ideas. It is interesting to note that there is evidence to suggest that without a period of turbulence, successful, long-lasting change is unlikely to occur (Hopkins et al., 1994). In this sense turbulence can be seen as a useful indication that the school is on the move. The question is, how can teachers be supported in coping with such periods of difficulty? What organizational arrangements are helpful in encouraging the development of practice?

From our experience of a range of schools that have made tangible progress towards more inclusive policies we note the existence of certain arrangements that seem to be helpful in dealing with periods of turbulence. These provide structures for supporting teachers in exploring their ideas and ways of working whilst, at the

Having reviewed aspects of classroom practice and school organization you will have decided upon some areas that need to change. Unfortunately changing arrangements and practices in schools is often difficult, not least because everybody is so busy with their existing work. This means that you and your colleagues will have to be smart in handling change. This activity will help you to think about what is involved in change. It will focus on:

- planning strategies;

- facing difficulties;

- supporting everybody involved; and

- monitoring progress.

Step 1
Spend a few minutes writing some notes about a change that you experienced in your work. It might have been a change in organization (e.g. a new timetable); a change in the curriculum (e.g. the introduction of a new scheme of work or new text books); or a change in teaching style (e.g. the introduction of cooperative group work). It might have been a successful or an unsuccessful change. Try to answer the following questions:

- Who proposed the change?

- What was the intention?

- What actually happened?

Step 2
Form groups of four or five and tell the stories you have written about. Then prepare a group report listing advice you would make to teachers wishing to change or develop some aspects of their practice.

Step 3
Report to the rest of your colleagues and discuss the implications together.

Figure 6.3 Managing change

same time, ensuring that maintenance arrangements are not sacrificed. More specifically they seek to support the creation of a climate of risk-taking within which these explorations can take place. In attempting to make sense of such arrangements my colleagues and I formulated a typology of six 'conditions' that seem to be a feature of moving schools. These are:

- **effective leadership**, not only by the headteacher but spread throughout the school;
- **involvement** of staff, students and community in school policies and decisions;
- a commitment to **collaborative planning**;
- **coordination** strategies, particularly in relation to the use of time;
- attention to the potential benefits of **enquiry and reflection**; and
- a policy for **staff development** that focuses on classroom practice.

In working with schools on their improvement projects we ask them to carry out a review of these organizational conditions to see whether it might be helpful to make adjustments in ways that will provide greater support to staff as they face the inevitable periods of turbulence. With this in mind we developed a series of instruments that can be used by staff to carry out such a review (i.e. Ainscow et al., 1994; Ainscow et al., 1995; Hopkins et al., 1997). For example, Figure 6.4 is a rating scale that is completed by individual staff and then used to facilitate discussion of the situation in the school in relation to the six conditions.

Using our typology of six conditions as a guide, it is possible to draw out some important messages about the restructuring that may be necessary within a school if it is to provide the context within which teachers will be prepared to consider new possibilities for reaching out to all learners. I will consider each of these in turn.

Leadership

In schools that I have observed moving successfully towards more inclusive ways of working, I see evidence of what is currently seen as a shift in thinking about leadership. This shift involves an emphasis on 'transformational' approaches, which are intended to distribute and empower, rather than 'transactional' approaches, which sustain traditional concepts of hierarchy and control (e.g. Sergiovanni, 1992) Typically, this leads the headteacher to seek to establish a clear overall vision of the school that encourages a recognition that individuality is something to be respected and, indeed, celebrated. Such a vision is usually created through an emphasis on group processes that are also used to facilitate a problem-solving climate. All of

---

Discussion exercise

Improving the quality of education for all

Exploring conditions that support school development

Experience in the project schools over the last year has led us to reconstruct our typology of conditions for school improvement. Our current thinking is summed up by the following six rather general headings:

- Staff development
- Involvement
- Leadership
- Coordination
- Enquiry and reflection
- Planning

The following sheets suggest extreme positions with respect to other areas of school life.

Tasks:
1 Indicate on each line your perception of your own school, (a) at the start of the year; and (b) currently.
2 Where you believe there has been movement make some notes as to what factors may have had an influence.

IQEA Condition 1: Staff development

Staff development activities make little impact on classroom practice.		Staff development activities are leading to improvements in classroom practice.

. . . .
. . . .
. . . .
. . . .
. . . .
. . . .

IQEA Condition 2: Involvement

Pupils and parents feel that they have little opportunity to influence policy.		Pupils and parents are fully involved in policy discussions.

. . . .
. . . .
. . . .
. . . .
. . . .
. . . .

IQEA Condition 3: Leadership

Very few members of staff feel able to take a lead in school development activities.		All staff feel able to take a lead in school development activities.

. . . .
. . . .
. . . .
. . . .
. . . .
. . . .

IQEA Condition 4: Coordination

| Staff are uncertain about priorities and plans, and how decisions are made. | | Policies, plans and decision making procedures are understood by all staff. |

. . . .
. . . .
. . . .
. . . .
. . . .
. . . .

IQEA Condition 5: Enquiry and reflection

| Little use is made of data (e.g. classroom observations, test results) to inform planning and monitor progress. | | Data are used to inform planning and monitor progress. |

. . . .
. . . .
. . . .
. . . .
. . . .
. . . .

IQEA Condition 6: Planning

| Staff are rarely involved in school planning processes. | | Staff are fully involved in school planning processes. |

. . . .
. . . .
. . . .
. . . .
. . . .
. . . .

Figure 6.4 IQEA rating scale for collecting data on conditions for supporting school improvement (from Ainscow et al., 1994)

this helps to create a context within which leadership functions can be spread throughout the staff group. This means accepting that leadership is a function to which many staff contribute, rather than a set of responsibilities vested in a small number of individuals. It also seems to involve approaches to working with colleagues that make use of teachers' existing knowledge of how learning can be encouraged derived from their work with pupils (Ainscow and Southworth, 1996).

My experience is that as staff become more involved in development activities they become increasingly aware that they can take a broader view of their work. Overview becomes possible and longer term plans are made legitimate. In itself this becomes a feature of staff development and management training for all colleagues. At this stage it is crucial for the senior management team to take the risks inherent in devolving responsibility in order to foster this staff development process. It is also important that certain individuals take on specific coordination tasks.

Within the IQEA project we recommended that schools should appoint at least two coordinators, one of whom, at least, being a member of the senior management team. These coordinators, referred to as 'the cadre', were asked to take responsibility for leading the day-to-day activities of the project in the school. Watching the ways in which different coordinators operated confirmed our belief in the importance of the tasks they perform if school improvement initiatives are to be sustained.

In the following account Les, who was deputy headteacher of a large urban secondary school, reflects upon the way he carried out his coordination roles (Hopkins et al., 1994). The school's work within IQEA involved a fundamental rethink of the use of staff task groups which at times led to some 'turbulence' as the staff became more involved in policy development. In particular the emergence of new, more widely representative staff groups had implications for the responsibilities of existing structures such as the senior management team and heads of faculty group. Les and his two coordinator colleagues were particularly successful in supporting this restructuring process.

The school became involved in the IQEA project in June 1991. It was decided to involve three members of staff as the coordinating group, one of whom was to be a deputy head to give authority and management expertise to the school's involvement. I was keen to get involved personally as I felt that the processes envisaged by the project could be of benefit to the management of the school in general, not just with respect to making learning more effective. In particular, the emphasis on staff involvement in both planning and implementation of change was especially attractive.

In general my task was:

1   *to act as a link person between senior management and the project, and to facilitate similar linking between the project and the staff in general.*

2   *to provide for direct access to the management structure of the school for the project (e.g. for resourcing, meeting times)*

3 to lead a cadre of three and to provide with the other two members, initial frameworks for both the management of the project and the issues to be focused upon.

4 to help facilitate amendments to the school management and development structure which would enable the outcomes of the school's involvement in the project to be more effective and which would also be of benefit in making the planning process in the school more effective, open and accessible to all staff in general.

With regard to the first three points **above** a decision was made very early on with the two other initial staff representatives at the first IQEA session to set up a specific structure for managing our involvement in the project. It was at this stage that the need for a larger staff group (known as 'the expanded cadre') was felt to be required. Such a group would allow for wider staff representation, but would also help deal with two problems of perception which had arisen early with the staff: concern that participation would mean extra work at a time when initiatives were mounting, that the project was a back door way to introduce appraisal and that the involvement of the school had taken place with insufficient staff consultation.

In the early phases, the expanded cadre was quite tightly directed. Working with the two cadre members, precise schedules were drawn up for each term, targets were set prior to each meeting of the expanded cadre. To play down the role of senior management in the expanded cadre, the meetings were chaired by the staff member of the cadre, although items for the agenda were discussed fully, prior to each session by the cadre. As part of this initial schedule interviewing was suggested by myself and adopted by the expanded cadre for the first area of involvement. This allowed for a precise, initial initiative to be used which was already on the school agenda and enabled a process of staff INSET, focused on small groups, to be first implemented. Later, developing effective learning strategies was adopted by all the staff after a prioritization session.

To help make the above more effective, through my working with the headteacher and senior management, training days were set aside for staff to work on IQEA related issues, a residential weekend was resourced for the expanded cadre to help develop a group identity and regular meeting time was allocated on the school calendar for meetings, both of the expanded cadre and for staff in general working on project related issues.

However, it was clear to me from the start that the main value of involvement in the project lay in what it had to offer to the management structures of the school in general, in particular, with regard to perceptions amongst some of the staff concerning a lack of involvement and openness in connection with decision making and planning. Consequently, in discussions with the headteacher, it was decided to discuss with the school policy group ways of reforming its composition to more fully reflect staff and to enhance its role within planning. This resulted in the formation of the school development group which now meets on alternative Wednesdays and focuses its attention on issues of planning. Working through this group I *also drew attention to the need for greater formal whole-school involvement in the school development plan and its role in setting targets and structures for future effective planning and implementation of policy. A training day is now set aside each year for development planning to be discussed by all staff and the drafting and planning from and with reference to, the development plan is now established within the school management structure.*

With regard to the project directly, the interviewing process was well received by staff as a consequence of the process used based upon IQEA ideas. Its introduction has been more effective as a consequence. The expanded cadre has become much more confident, especially following the residential weekend, and there is good, positive discussion at meetings of the expanded cadre. This was seen most clearly during the session in which the individuals spoke of their involvement before receiving the CFPS award.

From anecdotal evidence, the changes to the policy group and development planning process have led to staff in general feeling more involved and able to participate in planning and decision making than in the past.

However a number of aspects need to be considered at this stage:

- *With regard to the second phase of the project (focused on the development of effective learning strategies for all students), momentum has been harder to maintain. Partly as a consequence of general staff concern that National Curriculum assessment is now the priority which should be tackled above all else, staff have not seen the need to work so urgently on effective strategies. The original schedule which I drew up with the cadre was extended. With hindsight, the tighter timing should have been retained to keep staff working at a brisk pace. Matters concerning this were brought to a head in quite a vocal expanded cadre meeting, and amendments were made to the programme and initial plan as a consequence.*

- *Much time has been devoted to ensuring that staff were involved in what was taking place to ensure as much openness as possible. However, in the first year of the project, I should perhaps have taken more care to allay concerns of fellow deputies about the work of the project and to keep them fully appraised of what was taking place, especially with regard to the changes to the management and planning structure.*

- *At the end of the first year, a number of issues combined to provide a significant episode for the project and school. The structural changes were now taking effect within the management structure and the position of the School Development Group was now beginning to be established. However, this was now resulting in changes to other groups which traditionally were predominantly involved in planning and decision making such as the senior management team of deputies and senior teachers. Eventually a working relationship between the two has been established, both with defined roles, which is proving both productive and effective for both. This, though, came after considerable discussion and it was at this stage that the problem outlined in the previous point also came to a head. The outcome has been positive, with greater communication and a good structural, supportive relationship having developed between senior staff and the school development group. This has been crucial for the future progress of the school.*

- *As pressure on staff has mounted with regard to SAT assessment, NC changes, there has been an increase in staff demands for time to be allocated to the administration of education. I feel that our established involvement in the project should now be used to protect time for staff to be able to plan ahead and to work on effective learning methods. Without our present involvement and staff expectations of it, such time would be harder to conserve from staff and for staff.*

From my involvement in all of this I feel that I have learnt the following:

1 *The need to work with a supportive team who get on with each other personally as well as professionally. The cadre was made up of staff who knew each other socially and who had already worked together on school visits. This made the management of the project much easier and allowed each cadre member to be that much more supportive of the others.*

2 *Staff scepticism can be overcome but only through involvement and trying to present as much professional integrity as possible. This means taking time to communicate and interact with staff, informally as well as formally.*

3 *It has reinforced the need for long-term planning, especially where different groups of staff are concerned. There needs to be some concept of where you are going eventually.*

4 *There is a need to communicate fully with everyone involved. One cannot rely on assumptions or perceptions being shared implicitly. Time needs to be spent cultivating staff at all levels.*

5 *The importance to the project of having the support of senior staff, both in a personal and structural sense, to help ensure the effectiveness of what is being implemented and for what is being done to be seen as a whole-school programme.*

As we see from this account, a coordinator needs to have clear views, but also be able to listen to, and accommodate, the views of others. This flexibility enables the coordinator to judge when to move things on, when to be willing to change the agenda and when to provide time and space for staff to explore ways forward. All of this implies that the coordinators have a strong sense of personal security. Their function ought not to be that of control, but rather to be a guide to staff as they seek to participate in constructive developmental activity. To be effective, this guidance should be based upon their:

- perspective of the overall aims and plans which exist in the school;

- knowledge of areas of developmental activity and expertise already in existence in the school;

- awareness of, and contact with, individuals and agencies that can provide external support and expertise.

A sensitive use of influence can often move people in directions which they would not themselves have chosen, but in directions which can be of greater benefit both to the school and to the individuals concerned. Above all, coordinators need to be involved in the activities of the group in order that empathy exists, so that they can show encouragement, and generate self-confidence within each member of the group. At its most effective, their work in facilitating, enabling and encouraging others may not be readily apparent in the outcome of the activity. This may be a source of some threat to a coordinator who feels the need to be seen to be effective.

As I have noted, with the appointment of coordinators who are expected to provide leadership for a school development initiative there is likely to be a significant change in the degree of delegation of power from senior management to the staff. This is particularly the case when a group of people are drawn around the coordinators to act in an advisory and planning capacity. A range of issues relating to staff development and curriculum development is likely to form the remit of such a group. The group may identify issues to address which have traditionally been the responsibility of members of senior management teams. The effective functioning of the coordinator in this situation would appear to be crucially dependent upon the quality of delegation from the headteacher, who needs to create a climate in which staff as a whole are able to respect and relate to the coordinator. It appears that this can best be achieved when:

- there is positive support for, and effective definition of, the limits of responsibility of both the coordinator and any groups which may be established;

- all relevant matters are communicated to, or channelled through the coordinator;

- the coordinator is able to feel supported by the whole of the senior management team;

- the coordinator's role is clearly understood by all of the staff; and

- the staff are able to relate to them on a personal level.

The coordinators' effectiveness is likely also to depend upon the quality of the support that they are offered. In this respect the provision of advice and support for coordinators is a key element, a theme to which I return in more detail in Chapter 8.

Involvement

Apparent in what I call 'moving schools' is an emphasis on involvement that usually extends beyond the teaching staff to include pupils, parents and members of the community. Interestingly this style of working is similar to the 'incorporative approach' noted by Reynolds (1991) to be a characteristic of highly successful schools. Arguably the critical group to which involvement needs to be extended is the pupils themselves. In this respect the crucial issue is that teachers plan their lessons and organize their classrooms in ways that encourage involvement in the tasks and activities that are set. Here an emphasis on cooperative learning activities of the sort referred to in Chapter 4 is particularly important. In effect group work is a way of setting tasks that encourage involvement.

However, it is also important to recognize the ways in which pupils can contribute to our understandings of a school's efforts to become more inclusive. Their involvement in discussions about such moves allows us to see things in a way that may challenge our assumptions. For example, in working with one large urban secondary school that has made great efforts to develop a more inclusive approach, my colleagues and I decided to hold discussions with groups of pupils (Ainscow, Booth and Dyson, 1999). Their perspectives helped us and, indeed, members of the staff to view the school in a new way. They also helped us to determine further possibilities for development.

We found that the students tended to evaluate their experiences of the school mainly in terms of relationships. Fortunately relationships in the school were generally positive and this led us to conclude that this explained, in part at least, why it seemed to 'get away with' what we saw as a considerable range of exclusionary tactics, such as withdrawal from class, temporary suspensions and the creation of so-called 'bottom set' classes. Such responses tend to be met with negative student reactions in other schools, but it is possible that it is not just relationships that are influential here since in our discussions we also sensed an acceptance of differences amongst the students and, indeed, a concern with the rights of individuals that is generally rather unusual in English society. This carried with it echoes of debates that tend to be more apparent in other countries, e.g. in Australia, where it is common to hear that everyone has a right to a 'fair go'.

This sense of acceptance manifested itself in a variety of forms. It was noticeable, for example, in the relaxed relationships that seemed to exist between girls and boys. Similarly, we could find little or no evidence of racism amongst the students we met. But, given our professional backgrounds in special education, the most striking thing was the way in which students with disabilities were accepted as being just part of the 'normal' school community. Students' disabilities, including category labels such as 'Downs', were frequently mentioned in a noticeably matter-of-fact manner during our discussions. For example, a blind student talked openly about her own disability and, indeed, referred to the disability of others in a 'taken for granted' tone. She explained how she travels to school by taxi with two other students, commenting, 'They're both special needs, Down's!'. Similarly, in introducing one of her friends, Elaine, she remarked, 'She's special needs, not

Down's!' (The distinctions made here are in themselves fascinating). When one group was asked about students in their classes who experienced learning difficulties, discussion focused on the reading difficulties of one of the individuals present. It was only much later in the conversation that the students thought to draw attention to the fact that two members of their class have Down's Syndrome.

Most of the students seemed very positive about the presence of students with disabilities in their classes. One student commented, 'I don't see why they shouldn't be in the school because they're just normal, just people same as all of us. They should all have the same chance as anyone else should have'. This theme of seeing people with disabilities as being part of what is normal was echoed by many of the students. For example, one student explained that 'we have a laugh with them, treat them as normal people', whilst another student commented, 'Sometimes they're teased but it's only normal joking. They don't do it seriously; they don't take offence'.

Some of the students were keen to promote the advantages that occur because of the presence of those with disabilities in the school. One argued:

> It's a good thing bringing them into the mainstream. It helps them cope a bit more. I've seen people who are at special school and they are so different to how the kids are here who are in the mainstream. I went to an athletics meeting with a special needs group. Ours were so well balanced but the kids from the special school had the same disabilities but were so different. Ours, because they've been with mainstream kids and are made to do things that they wouldn't do in a special school, it makes them realize that if they're asked to sit down they've got to sit down. Their kids were getting up and running all over the place and it was really dangerous . . .

One older student argued that all students had a right to attend their neighbourhood school. When pressed about those whose bizarre behaviour might disrupt classes, or those who might be a danger to others, he argued that at least they had 'a right to try!' In accepting the right of all students to be in their school, the students were also quick to point to the responsibilities that must go along with this. Here they were particularly critical of the fact that some of those with disabilities were at times given different treatment. For example:

> Students with disabilities get away with everything. We were stood at the can machine the other day and there were three of them from the disability unit downstairs and they just came over and pushed us out of the way and they were only small. She pressed it, put her money in, and they were pressing all the buttons . . . If we did that to them, like push them out of the way, we'd get done, but they didn't get done.

Another student felt that it was inappropriate that sometimes those with disabilities were allowed to get away with arriving late for lessons. Similarly, another student felt it was wrong that a blind classmate was allowed to swear in class. In a sense these feelings that everybody should have equal treatment can be seen as yet further evidence of the acceptance that everybody has a right to be present.

Many of the students talked about the occasional help they give to disabled classmates. One person talked about how he assisted a visually impaired student in his class. A clear look of joy was apparent in his face as he gave this account. Having said that, however, some still felt that sometimes too much adult assistance was provided for certain students, e.g. '. . . they could find their own way round school but they still get taken around'.

Collaborative Planning

In order to support staff in exploring alternative ways of working, considerable emphasis should be placed on collaborative planning. This needs to be guided by an ongoing search for what will work locally rather than what seems to work elsewhere (Huberman, 1993). Here it is the process of planning, rather than plans in themselves, that seems to be crucial. In particular, the active involvement of staff encourages the creation of common purposes, the resolution of differences and the basis for action by individuals. Consequently, the benefits of any planning activity often outlast the currency of the plan itself, offering a level of shared understanding which is a prerequisite for widespread empowerment.

In my work with schools I place considerable emphasis on encouraging staff to become more effective in planning together. An example will illustrate what this might involve. For some years staff in an urban secondary school had expressed their concern about the reading skills of a large proportion of students and how this was holding back overall progress. It was decided that an initiative would be carried out to involve staff in an intensive effort to address this issue with Year 9 students. The aim was to improve reading skills amongst **all** students by adopting a coordinated whole-school approach. The project was supported by members of the IQEA team who also took responsibility for carrying out a thorough evaluation of what occurred. The intention was that the project should benefit the particular cohort of students throughout their school careers, whilst, at the same time, assisting all staff in developing powerful intervention responses that would be available to subsequent groups of students.

In designing the project, attention was given to building upon expertise that already existed within the school. The approaches used also took account of existing policies, in particular the school's language policy. This policy, which had been agreed some years earlier but never really implemented, was based upon the following beliefs:

- all teachers are teachers of reading;

- reading in a student's parent tongue should be valued;

- reading should be purposeful, engaging and enjoyable;

- reading should provide opportunities to enhance real literacy (i.e. to enable a reader to distinguish between fact and opinion and to recognize bias and stereotyping; glean relevant information — using appropriate reading and information retrieval skills; develop understanding and empathy; come to terms with graphicacy and number as a means of communication; and come into contact with alternative views of the world.)

The central strategy was that within the four core faculties, maths, English, humanities and science, small teams of staff would collaborate in a process of designing and trialling experimental lesson plans. The fundamental question that staff were to explore was, how can a focus on reading during the planning of lessons lead to more successful learning and higher standards of achievement? Hence the title of the project was, *Effective Reading for Effective Learning*.

The various staff teams used a common format for planning (see Figure 6.5) that was prepared in the light of the best available knowledge about how subject teachers can enhance reading within their lessons (e.g. Lunzer and Gardner, 1984). They were assisted in trialling and evaluating materials and teaching strategies by colleagues from the school's learning support team. This process was replicated throughout the school year with the intention that an emphasis on achieving effective reading would become a usual aspect of teaching throughout the school.

Further support material was made available to the staff teams to assist them in following the six steps in the format for planning.

Over a period of some months many of the staff began to recognize the power and, indeed, the pleasure of planning together with their departmental colleagues, and there was strong evidence that this stimulated the development of some very creative approaches to enhancing literacy across the curriculum.

Coordination

As noted earlier, schools can be seen as 'loosely coupled systems'. This loose-coupling occurs because schools consist of units, processes, actions and individuals that tend to operate in isolation from one another. Loose-coupling is also encouraged by the goal ambiguity that characterizes schooling. Despite the rhetoric of curriculum aims and objectives during recent years, schools consist of groups of people who may have very different perspectives, values and beliefs about the purposes of schooling. What we see in moving schools are various forms of communication that are intended to coordinate the actions of teachers and others behind agreed policies. However, these have to work in ways that do not reduce the discretion of individual teachers to practise according to their own preferences. Teaching is a complex and often unpredictable business that requires a degree of improvisation. Indeed, as I have already noted, it might be argued that a significant hallmark of a more inclusive school is the degree to which the teachers in it are prepared to 'tinker' with their usual practices in the light of the feedback they receive from members of their classes. Consequently, teachers must have sufficient autonomy to make instant decisions that take account of the individuality of their pupils and the uniqueness of every encounter that occurs. What is needed,

Step 1: **What do we want to achieve in this unit/series of lessons?**
Step 2: **What printed materials are available?**
Step 3: **How can reading be used to help students' learning in this unit?**
Step 4: **What strategies can be used to help all students to engage with the printed material?**
Step 5: **What support do we need to try out these strategies?**
Step 6: **How can we assess the impact on the students?**

Figure 6.5   Effective reading for effective learning: A format for teachers' planning

therefore, seems to be a well coordinated, cooperative style of working that gives individual teachers the confidence to improvise in a search for the most appropriate responses to the pupils in their classes; in other words, a more tightly coupled system without losing loose-coupling benefits.

How, then, can such an organization be coordinated in order that those involved can work in a more efficient way? It does seem that relationships are the key to establishing greater coordination. It has been suggested that school relationships may be structured in one of three ways: individualistically, competitively or cooperatively (Johnson and Johnson, 1994). In schools with an individualistic form of organization teachers tend to work alone to achieve goals unrelated to the goals of their colleagues. In consequence, there is little sense of common purpose, no sharing of expertise and limited support for individuals. Furthermore, such schools often move towards a more competitive form of organization.

In a competitive system teachers strive to do better than their colleagues, recognizing that their fates are negatively linked. Here the career of one teacher is likely to be enhanced by the failure of others within the school. In this win–lose struggle to succeed it is almost inevitable that individuals will celebrate difficulties experienced by their colleagues since they are likely to increase their own chances of success.

Clearly, therefore, the organizational approach, which is most likely to create a positive working atmosphere, is one that emphasizes cooperation. The aim must be to encourage a more lightly coupled system within which the efforts of individuals are coordinated in order to maximize their impact. In such a school individuals are more likely to strive for mutual benefit, recognizing that they all share a common purpose and, indeed, a common fate. They know that their performance can be influenced positively by the performance of others. This being the case, individuals feel proud when a colleague succeeds and is recognized for professional competence.

A school that is based upon a cooperative structure is likely to make good use of the expertise of all its personnel, provide sources of stimulation and enrichment that will foster their professional development, and encourage positive attitudes to the introduction of new ways of working.

Ultimately, the success of a school depends upon the success teachers have in working with their classes. There is little doubt that teachers teach better when they experience support from their peers, yet in many schools little emphasis is placed on developing the coordination mechanisms that will encourage such support. As a result, teachers may feel threatened, isolated and alienated. Establishing various kinds of staff working groups is a way of providing teachers with the opportunity to share ideas and support each other's efforts to improve the quality of education provided for all pupils. Working groups can provide the basis for coordination and support throughout a school: more specifically they can:

- provide help, assistance, support and encouragement as colleagues seek to improve their practice;
- act as an informal support group for sharing, letting off steam, and discussing problems;

- serve as a forum in which more experienced colleagues can help others as they plan developments; and
- create a setting in which camaraderie and shared success occur and are celebrated.

Working groups of this type succeed when they are carefully structured to ensure active participation by members and, where possible, concrete products (e.g. lesson plans or teaching materials) that can be used later. The structure of meetings should point members towards increasing each other's expertise in order that they do not generate into gripe sessions, destructive criticism of each other, or amateur therapy. Members need to believe that they sink or swim together, ensure considerable face-to-face discussion and assistance takes place, hold each other accountable to implement personal action plans between meetings, and periodically initiate discussion of how effective the group is in carrying out its mission (Johnson and Johnson, 1989). Task-orientated discussion, planning and problem solving, as well as mutual support, should dominate the meetings.

Andy Hargreaves (1995) has pointed to some possible difficulties that may occur when a school attempts to improve coordination by means of increased collaboration. He notes the existence of four types of school culture: fragmented individualism, Balkanization, contrived collegiality and true collaboration. Too often schools are characterized by two of these types: fragmented individualism, whereby teachers work in isolation or, in larger schools, Balkanization in which sub-groups of staff may be in competition when major decisions or actions are necessary. However, Hargreaves also points to the potential dangers of contrived collegiality involving a proliferation of unwanted contacts among teachers that consume scarce time with little to show for it. Rather what we should seek is true collaborative cultures that are 'deep, personal and enduring' — neither are they strings of one-shot deals — rather a culture of collaboration is central to the day-to-day work of teachers.

Some staff working groups may be set up for more formal, policy purposes. Of course, some policy decisions can be made by governors or management team alone and other decisions may be made in a staff meeting after a few minutes of discussion. However, there are decisions that require much longer consideration before a recommendation can be formulated. In particular, schoolwide issues call for careful review and planning involving the whole staff. In such situations a useful strategy is to appoint a task group representing the whole school that is given responsibility for considering the issues and planning the actions that the staff might take. For such a group to be successful it needs to be given clear goals, a time scale and the resources required for it to function. Membership of such a group may be on a voluntary basis, but sometimes teachers are asked and expected to serve.

Some useful practical guidelines for setting up task groups are provided in Johnson and Johnson's book, *Leading the Cooperative School*. Our experience is that many schools are using various types of staff groups but that too often these become rather aimless talking shops, consuming time and, sometimes, reducing morale. What is proposed here is meant to be purposeful and cost-effective.

From our work with schools in IQEA we have seen many examples of schools that encourage a high level of coordination through the use of staff working groups (Hopkins et al., 1994). One particular primary school seemed to have developed this style in a very effective way. The deputy headteacher, Monica, explained their approach, as follows:

We are a large primary school with 24 staff. The use of staff groups has developed as an effective way of enabling staff to focus on planning and be engaged in the development of specific curriculum areas while maintaining their involvement in the development of the whole curriculum and whole school issues.

There are three parallel, mixed ability classes in each year group. Each Year Team of teachers is released for one half day towards the end of the summer term so that they can make an overall plan of work for the coming year. Our school curriculum framework outlines the content for their plans. The Year Team decide how to group the subject content and in which order to teach it. This enables each team to work in the most effective way, making use of their expertise. They can also ask other subject coordinators for advice.

At the end of each term they are also released to make detailed plans for the coming term. One hour per week is included in the time budget for Year Team meetings. This enables them to refine and adjust their plans as well as to discuss any problems. The strength of the Year Team is in mutual support and inspiration.

The time spent on planning is valued as enabling the more efficient use of time and resources during the term. It is also seen as helping to raise the standard of work produced in the classroom.

Monday is our regular staff meeting time. There is a sequence of staff meetings, middle management meetings (year coordinators and senior staff), staff INSET and curriculum groups.

All staff are members of curriculum groups. Each year coordinator is also a subject coordinator. Our present curriculum groups are 'PSE', 'Humanities' and 'Aesthetic and Creative'. These groups change according to our priorities for development. The mathematics, science and language coordinators continue to develop their subject areas and these curriculum groups will be reconvened when necessary.

In the current climate of change, staff are working to implement and monitor National Curriculum requirements. The use of groups means that a few staff can concentrate on developing one subject area and construct policy statements and school guidelines to ensure continuity and progression.

All policies and documents produced by any group must be discussed by the whole staff and amended if necessary before being passed to the governors for approval.

We were concerned with the time gap which was occurring between groups producing draft policies or guidelines and there being staff meeting time for dis-cussion. Also, with a large staff, we could not be sure that all staff felt able to contribute to the discussion through pressure of time and items on the agenda. We therefore started giving draft copies of the policies to the year coordinator for discussion within their Year Team. Each team can then scribble their comments on the draft version, either during a team meeting or individually, at a convenient time.

This has proved to be a most effective way of getting useful responses from all members of staff. The revised draft is again given to Year Teams for comments. The senior staff approve the final version before submitting it to the governors.

This process emphasizes the management role of year coordinators and ensures that all staff are fully involved in the decision making process.

All staff are involved in producing the school development plan. The curriculum groups and subject coordinators produce their own plans for the coming year. Whole school issues can be raised by any member of staff.

All staff discuss all aspects of the development plan. We regard this as essential if all staff are going to be committed to implementing the plan. After the whole staff discussion, the plans are discussed by the senior management team and the middle management team so that the advantages and disadvantages of each element can be discussed and prioritized.

Our school development plan is organized on a financial year basis as many of the aspects will be dependent on money. Each coordinator is then allocated a budget to support their subject area.

The use of staff groups enables our staff to work more efficiently and effectively, to maximize the expertise available within the school and to develop their own professional skills.

The effective use of teacher time is further enhanced by the support of non-teaching staff. A secretary does all the reprographic work; any duplicating handed in before school is ready by lunchtime. Teachers do not handle dinner money, they only count the numbers for school dinners, packed lunch or going home. A librarian is responsible for the children's library and the staff library. Any books or other resources purchased are catalogued by the librarian who will also help staff with the preparation of material — labelling, covering etc.

Our staff room is also a resource base. All new resources are displayed there before going onto the shelves so that staff are aware of what is available. There is frequently informal INSET taking place through discussion of problems and strategies. Staff are quite happy to ask for help from whoever has the relevant expertise, regardless of the 'allowance hierarchy'.

This format is not static but developing. Each year refinements or changes are made, either in response to staff requests or in anticipation of future needs. Our aim is to improve the quality of the education for all our children. In order to achieve this we need all of our staff working together to provide a stimulating and cohesive curriculum with a happy and structured environment.

Monica's account is an excellent example of how effective working groups can be as a means of coordinating improvement efforts when they are well thought through. Particular features that should be noted are:

- the way in which groups are constructed to ensure that all staff are involved;

- the allocation of time to support staff as they take on additional responsibilities;
- attention to ensuring good communication between the various groups;
- accountability of individuals who are designated to take on coordination tasks.

As we see, the issue of communication is a vital component of overall school coordination. In order to organize itself to accomplish its goals, maintain itself in good working order, and, at the same time, adapt to changing circumstances, sound procedures for communication are essential. Meetings must be scheduled; reports from task groups distributed; departmental meetings organized; summaries of various activities need to be written and sent round to all staff. All of these responses are structured communication opportunities. The communication network thus created determines the amount and type of information a member of staff will receive from colleagues.

In the IQEA project we emphasized the importance of creating an effective communication network within schools. In particular we have stressed the importance of all staff being aware of progress related to project activities and decisions that require them to take particular actions. Fullan (1991) stresses the importance of effective communication within a school during improvement initiatives. He notes that no amount of good thinking by itself will address the ubiquitous problem of faulty communication. Since change is a highly personal experience, and since schools consist of numerous individuals and groups undergoing different (to them) experiences, no single communication is going to reassure or clarify the meaning of change for people. A cardinal fact of social change is that people will always misinterpret and misunderstand some aspect of the purpose or practice of something that is new to them.

To be successful in coordinating developments in school, therefore, it is necessary to work at communication. A study of the theory of change indicates the importance of frequent, personal interactions as a key to success. Indeed, Fullan argues that two-way communication about specific innovations that are being attempted is a requirement of success. To the extent that the information flow is accurate, the problems get identified, which means that each person's perceptions and concerns get aired.

Enquiry and Reflection

In our engagement with what I am calling moving schools my colleagues and I have observed that those schools which recognize that enquiry and reflection are important processes find it easier to sustain their momentum and are better placed to monitor the extent to which policies actually bring about desired changes. A particularly important aspect of enquiry and reflection relates to classroom practice. From our monitoring of schools within the IQEA project we have strong indications that where teachers are encouraged to help one another to explore dimensions of their work through mutual observation, leading them to talk about detailed aspects of their practice, this can have a significant impact upon their actions. An emphasis on the creation of teacher partnerships is a good example of how a commitment to this idea has to be matched by organizational arrangements that make it happen in practice (Ainscow et al., 1998).

Recently I spent a delightful afternoon with two colleagues, Pam and Rosie, who had been exploring the benefits of such a partnership in an inner city secondary school for girls. The bulk of our discussions were built around an analysis of videos they had made of their lessons. They had previously looked at these together. Both talked specifically about the way that looking at themselves had made them more aware of things they do as they teach. Pam noted the way she walks around holding her hands behind her back, whilst Rosie observed that she tends to keep saying 'right'.

Pam's video was of her lesson with a 'top set', Year 9 geography class. The class were seated, some girls in rows but with two sets of tables pointing towards the centre of the room. Rosie mentioned that seeing Pam's room arrangement was leading her to think about the set up in her own classroom. Pam has been working on the development of 'teaching through questions' in her lessons, using questions to encourage the students to think more deeply about the content and to link the ideas to their day-to-day experiences (e.g. 'Why does it rain?'; 'What difference does the rain make?'). Having read a play, the students were set a series of writing tasks. As they worked Pam moved around the room, appearing to think aloud, posing more and more questions. Her style at this point struck me as being relaxed and conversational. It was noticeable that students were not put on the spot to respond and Pam suggested that she was trying to avoid an atmosphere of them feeling under pressure to always find 'the correct answer'. Rather, she wanted the girls to feel free to think creatively. They were asked to write down what the sun does for us and Pam wrote on the blackboard, 'What does the sun do?'

Pam explained that she had worked in a similar way with the lower sets, possibly placing less emphasis on writing. She noted that in fact some of the most interesting responses had come from girls in the middle set. It struck me that this relates to an article by Keddie (1971) in which she explains how students who are perceived as being less able may give unusual responses, but that sometimes teachers may reject these because they are seen as being 'incorrect'. Pam's approach led me to reflect that perhaps a way to raise expectations is to learn how to use questioning more effectively and to value diversity of responses.

We discussed the forms of lesson preparation necessary for this way of working. Pam felt that you had to 'know your stuff'. Certainly a deep understanding of the content would seem to be important in order to formulate probing questions, both before and during the lesson, and to use student responses to further stimulate their thinking. Timing also seems to be important and Pam felt that this came with experience.

Rosie is in her second year of teaching and her video showed her working with a potentially difficult, 'lower set' Year 11 English class. She worked on 'figures of speech' using a mnemonics technique which she had seen demonstrated during a workshop. During the early part of the lesson this clearly worked well and the girls appeared in the main to be engaged in what was a rather abstract set of ideas. It was interesting for me to see the different ways in which the girls responded, given that many of them appeared to have lost confidence in themselves as learners. Some girls were clearly reluctant to be seen failing and they used different ploys to ensure that they did not take any risks in front of their peers. This seemed to be one of the advantages of Rosie's approach in that, as in Pam's lesson, nobody was put on the spot!

Midway through the lesson Rosie felt that she was losing the interest of some students. She explained how she decided to try something that she had been thinking about but had not done before. This involved a singing/chanting approach to the various figures of speech, with everybody finger-snapping the rhythm. The impact of this was very striking. The more confident girls clearly enjoyed all of this, joining in very enthusiastically. Even more impressive, however, was the way in which the fun of the activity appeared to give confidence to certain girls who had previously seemed reluctant to participate.

Our discussion of this lesson became interlinked with our analysis of what had occurred in the lesson taught by Pam. In particular the three of us reflected together on ways of drawing out the learning potential of students who have lost confidence and/or interest and, as a result, become marginalized within school. It occurred to us that in order to reach these students, teachers had to be prepared to 'take risks' in trying out ways of working that they had not previously used. Of course, this was exactly what Rosie had done here!

For me this experience confirmed the value of teachers having time and opportunity to reflect together on the details of their practice. However, this would be difficult without the shared experience (in this case, viewing the videos) that facilitates the creation of a common language of technique and the type of supportive relationship that Pam and Rosie clearly enjoy.

Staff Development

The presence of these first five conditions seems to provide the basis for a climate that supports teacher development and, in so doing, encourages teachers to explore new responses to pupils in their classes. To this end, schools also need to have a well thought out policy for staff development. This has to go well beyond the traditional patterns by which teachers attend external courses or, more recently, the use of one-shot school-based events. More than anything it seems that if staff development is to have a significant impact upon thinking and practice it needs to be linked to school development (Fullan, 1991). As such it should be concerned with the development of the staff as a team, whilst not ignoring the learning of individuals.

It is helpful to think of two elements of staff development: 'the workshop and the workplace' (Joyce, 1991). The workshop is where understanding is developed, demonstrations provided and there are opportunities for practice. However, as we have seen, for transfer of ideas and skills that the workshop has introduced back into the workplace (i.e. the classroom and school), attending a workshop is insufficient. Our experience suggests that ability to transfer into everyday classroom practice requires 'on-the-job' support. This implies changes to the workplace and the way in which we organize staff development in schools. In particular, it means there must be opportunity for immediate and sustained practice, collaboration and peer coaching, and conditions that support experimentation. We cannot achieve these changes in the workplace without, in most cases, drastic alterations in the ways in which we organize our schools. In particular, it requires that time is set aside for teachers to support one another within teams and partnerships established in order to explore and develop aspects of their practice.

I can quote many examples of schools that have used staff development as a central strategy for supporting staff as they have attempted to develop aspects of their practice. All of them work from an assumption that attention to teacher learning is likely to have direct spin-offs in terms of the pupils' learning. All of them demonstrate the benefits of investment of time and resources in staff development.

An excellent example is that of 'Sunnyside' Infants School. There, over a period of years, a sophisticated strategy was developed that helped to create the conditions for effective staff learning. At the outset there was a concern with how to find time to observe children in the classroom for the purposes of carrying out new assessment requirements. With this in mind a staff development day was led by an external consultant, focusing on the theme of making children independent learners. This event had an enormous impact on the thinking of the staff. Specifically, the consultant led the staff through a series of problem-solving processes looking at how one of their classrooms might be reorganized in order to encourage greater autonomy amongst the pupils. Gradually the teachers worked together to rearrange the furniture and resources and subsequently they carried out similar activities in other classrooms. It does seem that part of the impact of this approach was to do with the context within which it took place (i.e. the classrooms), the tangible nature of the task (i.e. re-arranging equipment, etc.), and, of course, the fact that it encouraged considerable discussion about personal theories of teaching and learning.

Following on from the day, the staff continued to meet on a regular basis to explore classroom management issues. Eventually this led to the formulation of a 'house-style' involving the use of learning centres in which pupils carry out assignments. After one year there was clear evidence that this was encouraging much more independence amongst the children.

During the following year staff began to question the quality of learning going on in the learning centres. Their concern was that pupils might simply be completing tasks without any significant learning taking place. With this in mind they decided to work in small teams to observe one another's classrooms. Observations focused on the quality of engagement in the learning centres. To facilitate these observations the headteacher covered classes to free teachers. She asked them to plan the observations together and also allocated time so that they could debrief what occurred.

The evidence indicated that this strategy had a significant impact. Specific changes in teaching style were evident in all classrooms; there was clear evidence of increased pupil autonomy in learning, even with the very youngest children; and the quality of dialogue about teaching and learning was very striking to the visitor. Indeed it was reasonable to surmise that a significant change had occurred in the culture of the school.

A crucial element of the Sunnyside strategy was the importance placed on locating staff development activities inside the classroom. So much inservice education occurs away from the usual context where teaching takes place and, indeed, is led by people who have not even visited the specific contexts in which their participants have to operate. Eisner suggests that this is 'akin to a basketball coach providing advice to a team he has never seen play' (1990, p. 102).

Conclusion

As we have seen, the ingredients for supporting the development of moving schools are overlapping and interconnected in a number of ways. More than anything they are connected by the idea that attempts to reach out to all learners within a school have to include the adults as well as the pupils. It seems that schools that do make progress in this respect do so by developing conditions within which every member of the school community is encouraged to be a learner. In this way, responding to those who are experiencing barriers to learning provides a means of achieving overall school improvement.

Of course, none of this is easy. As I have argued, deep changes are needed if we are to transform schools that were designed to serve a minority of the population in such a way that they can achieve excellence with all children and young people.

Chapter 7

Developing Schools for All

The idea of inclusive education is gaining ground in many parts of the world. It was given further impetus by the UNESCO World Conference on Special Needs Education, held in Salamanca, Spain, in 1994. The conference considered the future direction of the special needs field in the light of international efforts to ensure the rights of all children to receive basic education. It examined how far special needs is part of this 'Education for All' movement. In other words, is the aim to move towards a unified system of schooling that is capable of responding to all children as individuals, or to continue with the tradition of parallel systems whereby some children receive separate forms of education?

In many countries 'The Salamanca Statement and Framework for Action' (UNESCO, 1994) is being used to formulate strategies that will support movements towards inclusive schooling (Sebba and Ainscow, 1996). Until recently progress in the United Kingdom has been limited, apart from pockets of excellence in a few local authorities and schools. In an attempt to find ways of encouraging schools to move towards more inclusive ways of working, my colleagues and I in the Centre for Educational Needs at the University of Manchester (CEN) have developed a programme of research in this country and overseas. This includes a project that is currently being carried out in partnership with the Centre for Studies on Inclusive Education (CSIE), the aim of which is to develop, evaluate and disseminate an index that can be used to review and improve current practice with respect to inclusion in schools. The 'Index of Inclusive Schooling' sets out to build on existing good practice within a school in order to encourage ways of working that will facilitate the learning of all pupils; minimize the need for exclusions; and support a school's efforts to widen its capacity for responding to diversity. In these senses it is clearly based on the principles and ideas set out in this book as to how more inclusive practices can be developed.

In this chapter I outline the rationale for the Index project, showing how it attempts to operationalize these principles and ideas in ways that are feasible within the contexts of schools. The account also provides another illustration, therefore, of how the development of inclusive schools can be encouraged by the use of forms of collaborative inquiry.

Existing Work

The Index project builds on earlier work carried out by teams of researchers in Australia and North America. Following a programme of research at Macquarie University an 'Integration Index' was developed (Centre, Ward and Ferguson, 1991). This has three separate aspects; (i) an index of academic integration; (ii) an index of social integration; and (iii) a total integration index (combining the first two indices). Using a predetermined cut-off point for evaluating the mainstream placement of a particular child, the researchers found that 63 per cent of pupils in stage one of their study were successfully integrated in terms of academic and social outcomes. They went on to interpret the implications of their data for the development of practice. In their conclusions they suggest that the new indices permit 'a more objective grounding of otherwise relatively subjective judgments' of these educational experiences of children with disabilities in mainstream settings.

Clearly this Australian work provides an excellent starting point for the current project. However, it is important to note that since it was carried out, thinking in the field has moved on. In particular, there has been a move away from the notion of integration towards inclusion. As I have explained, the word 'integration' tends to be used to describe a process of *assimilation* within which individual children are supported in order that they can participate in the existing (and largely unchanged) programme of the school; whereas 'inclusion' suggests a process of *transformation* such that schools are developed in response to the diversity of pupils who attend.

This emphasis on inclusion as a process can also be linked to the need to scrutinize the way schools exclude pupils in various ways (e.g. Booth, 1995). There is, for example, evidence that even schools that are seen as being apparently successful in including pupils with particular disabilities may, at the same time, be developing organizational or curriculum responses that have the effect of excluding or marginalizing other groups (Booth and Ainscow, 1998).

In seeking to develop the Index of Inclusive Schooling all these arguments have been addressed. In particular they have encouraged a move away from a scrutiny of individual children, defined as being in some ways special, towards a wider and deeper investigation of the processes by which particular schools include and exclude all pupils. Such an orientation is nearer to that adopted within another project carried out more recently in the USA.

This work had been undertaken by a team of American researchers from a number of universities, coordinated by Luanna Meyer at Syracuse (Eichinger et al., 1996). Their concern is with helping to provide schools with a clearer picture of the components of what they call 'quality inclusive schooling for students with severe disabilities'. With this in mind they have worked with schools in New York to develop and evaluate 'Program Quality Indicators' (PQI). These take the form of a checklist that can be used by school district personnel, families, consumer groups and evaluators interested in establishing how closely a particular programme mirrors what is known about quality inclusive schooling. Completing the checklist is seen as a form of 'needs assessment' that can facilitate further developments.

The authors suggest that the quality indicators are based upon certain basic principles that are intended to guide developments. These principles are: (i) inclusion is a basic value that extends to all children: everyone belongs and everyone is welcome; (ii) inclusion is not conditional, and programmes must fit the child rather than children fitting the programme; (iii) special education must become an integral part of general education and the two separate systems must become unified in their efforts to meet the needs of children; and (iv) children with disabilities must be full and active participants in school and community, occupying socially valued roles.

The quality indicators are listed under four levels, concerned with the assessment of a particular context in relation to local district factors, overall school arrangements, educational placement and responses to particular children. Like the Australian initiative, this work provides valuable starting points for the development of a British Index. It is clearly more widely focused than the Australian Index and is geared to the development of policy within a school district. It is specifically concerned with children who have disabilities but also pays some attention to other groups that may be marginalized or excluded. In all of this it works from a strong value position and this draws attention to a potentially difficult area, i.e. whose values will be used as a basis for the Index?

All of the American indicators focus on observable features but, inevitably, some of these are very difficult to evaluate, requiring an engagement with complex data and, in some cases, value judgments to be made. Indeed it can be argued that some of the most significant indicators are the ones that are most difficult to appraise. In developing an Index that can be used with confidence and authority it is necessary to provide detailed explanations of what types of data are necessary and how these are to be used as evidence in respect to indicators.

Developing the Index

During 1996 and 1997 an 'expert group' of teachers, parents, representatives of disability groups with wide experience of attempts to develop more inclusive ways of working, and researchers from three universities (i.e. Cambridge, Manchester and the Open University) worked together in order to produce a pilot version of the Index. This was then piloted in a small number of English primary and secondary schools. The evidence was that these schools found the Index to be helpful in raising awareness of issues to do with inclusion within their communities and, at the same time, they reported that it enabled them to focus on developmental issues that might otherwise have been overlooked. The next stage in the project involves more detailed research that is being carried out in schools in four English school districts during the school year 1998–99.

The Index is based upon a theoretical framework that draws on evidence from two main bodies of knowledge. First of all, it uses existing research evidence regarding processes that are known to facilitate the participation of students who might previously have been excluded or marginalized (e.g. Ainscow, 1995a and 1996; Booth and Ainscow, 1998; Wang and Reynolds, 1996). Secondly, it draws on

---

Dimension 3: Classroom experiences
Indicators:

3.1 Pupils are entitled to take part in all subjects and activities
3.2 Teaching and learning are planned with all pupils in mind
3.3 The curriculum develops understanding of and respect for differences
3.4 During lessons all pupils participate
3.5 A variety of teaching styles and strategies are used
3.6 Pupils experience success in their learning
3.7 The curriculum seeks to develop understanding of the different cultures in society
3.8 Pupils take part in the assessment and accreditation systems
3.9 Difficulties in learning are seen as opportunities for the development of practice

---

Figure 7.1   Extract from the 'Index of Inclusive Schooling' (pilot version, 1997)

recent evidence regarding effective processes of school improvement (e.g. Elmore, Peterson and McCarthy, 1996; Hopkins et al., 1994; Louis and Miles, 1990; MacBeith, Boyd, Rand and Bell, 1996). Using these knowledge bases the Index aims to encourage all members of a school community to collaborate in reviewing and developing areas of policy and practice with respect to a series of 'dimensions and indicators' (see Figure 7.1).

Unlike the American indices, which focus on specific students seen as having special needs, the concern is with the involvement of all members of the school's community. The dimensions and indicators are different too, in that they focus specifically on processes that are known to facilitate participation, whereas the American materials are mainly concerned with the measurement of participation *per se*. The procedures for using the Index are also different from the Australian and American versions in that all decisions about the focus and strategies for carrying out review and development are made within the school. This approach is supported by the evidence about effective school development referred to in the previous chapter.

Thus the aim of the Index is to help schools to determine where they are in terms of inclusion and exclusion, in order to move thinking and practice forward. In this sense it is concerned with processes of school and teacher development. It also takes account of wider contextual factors that are likely to have an impact upon the work of schools.

Using the Index

The Index uses 'best available knowledge' in the fields of school improvement and inclusive schooling in order to provide an effective means of reviewing and developing practice within a school. The recommendations for using the Index draw on experiences and research described in the school improvement literature, not least the work I have carried out with my colleagues in the IQEA project. It involves a cycle of activities that are used to review and develop existing policies and practices. The scope and duration of such a developmental process will vary from school to school. Furthermore, each school may elect to go through the cycle on more than one occasion and a cycle usually involves six stages. In what follows I summarize what is involved during each phase of a cycle. These suggestions are based on the initial pilot work in five schools and experiences of other successful school development initiatives.

Phase 1: Negotiation

Before specific planning decisions are made, members of the wider school community are informed about the Index and consulted on how it might be used. It is suggested, therefore, that various measures be carried out to achieve this purpose. As far as is possible briefing meetings should be held with the various stakeholder groups (i.e. staff, pupils, parents and governors). These should include a presentation of and engagement with the principles upon which the Index is based. These are:

- all pupils have a right to the same range of educational choices;
- schools should value all pupils equally and celebrate diversity;
- schools should be developed to facilitate the learning of all pupils;
- effective development requires the involvement of all members of the school community.

Consideration is also given to 'what's in it' for the school; the commitments that are necessary in order to use the Index successfully; and the implications for those who are to take on the role of coordinators. As a result of these initial discussions agreement is sought as to whether or not to go ahead. Ideally this decision should involve the whole school community.

Evidence from other similar innovations indicates that this initial phase of negotiation is crucial to successful implementation and that it is particularly important that it should involve the active participation of the headteacher and other senior colleagues. Consequently, it is recommended that meetings may usefully be supplemented by other forms of communication, such as visual displays, written notes and letters, and contributions in existing school publications. It is important to stress, however, that such approaches are likely to be much less convincing than well managed face-to-face interactions.

Phase 2: Coordination

Schools are advised to form a coordinating group that is reasonably representative of the different stakeholder groups. As far as possible this should include staff, pupils, parents and governors. Membership should also include the headteacher or a deputy head. The role of this group is to act on behalf of the whole school community in designing, steering and evaluating the use of the Index, working in ways that continually seek to encourage participation and respect for different points of view.

Throughout their work they are encouraged to place an emphasis on creating an ethos that encourages participation. Clearly, therefore, it is important to select persons who are likely to have skill and credibility with others in the school community. For example, research on leadership in school development (see Chapters 6 and 8 of this book; and Ainscow and Southworth, 1996) suggests that the following skills are important when working with groups of colleagues:

• developing a clear purpose for activities;
• establishing rapport with colleagues;
• leading meetings and other group activities;
• maintaining interest and enthusiasm;
• solving problems, including difficulties over relationships;
• encouraging collaboration;
• providing support;
• keeping people informed.

In addition, it is recommended that the coordinating group should include at least one external facilitator who will act as a 'critical friend'. This involves attending planning meetings, assisting in the collection of evaluation data and being prepared to question taken-for-granted assumptions that may be leading 'insiders' to overlook barriers to and possibilities for development in the school. Here a local inspector or adviser, or a colleague from a higher education institute, might well be an appropriate choice.

Phase 3: Initial Audit

This involves collecting evidence about the 'dimensions and indicators'. Suggested techniques and instruments for collecting evidence related to these are provided but coordinating groups are free to go beyond these examples. The aim is to collect evidence that will assist in determining 'where the school is' and, in the light of this, making decisions as to which aspects of the school may need to be developed. Emphasis is placed on the use of participatory methods of enquiry in order to ensure that different perspectives and opinions are taken into account.

The audit is carried out in two stages as follows:

1 *Survey*: this involves collecting opinions about the dimensions and indicators from as many members of the school community as possible, using a series of rating scales designed for this purpose. Various scales are provided and coordinators will need to decide which of these should be used and with which populations. One of the scales attempts to survey opinion as to the current situation in the school and is intended for use with adults (staff, parents and governors). Another gathers views on what respondents would like the school to be like. It is recommended that these should be issued and completed at a meeting where their purpose can be fully explained. Further scales are completed by different age groups of pupils (see, for example Figure 7.2, which is meant for use with primary

Rating scale 3
For pupils

a Primary Pupil Rating Scale

We want to know what you think about this school so that we can try to make some improvements. Read these sentences and tick one of the three boxes to show what you think.

	Yes ☺	I'm not sure 😐	No ☹
1a The teachers think every lesson is important			
1b Sometimes there are two teachers in my classroom			
1c People in this school are always helping each other			
1d There are other adults that help me with my work in class sometimes			
1e My teacher asks me to say what I think about school			
1f Someone checks if pupils are away from school			
1g The teachers do their best to keep pupils who get into trouble in school			
1h The teachers are helpful when someone's bullied			
1i Disabled people would find it easy to get around this school			
2a People in school listen to what I have to say			
2b My family know about what we do in school			
2c People where I live think this is a really good school			
2d I can take part in lots of things in school			
2e I like my lessons in school			
3a In school I learn to think about people who are different			
3b I am kept busy doing all sorts of things in the classroom			
3c We do lots of different kinds of things in our lessons			
3d I think I am learning a lot of new things in school			
3e We learn about people from different parts of the world			
3f If I need some help with my work my teachers show me lots of different ways			
3g I was made very welcome when I first came to school			
3h People make me feel important here			
3i Sometimes the teachers tell us to work together in the classroom			

Figure 7.2 'Index of Inclusive Schooling': extract from a rating scale for use with primary school children

---

Indicator 3.2   'Teaching and learning are planned with all pupils in mind'

Evidence:
Plans have built in strategies for responding to diversity. Lessons are flexible enough to enable modifications to be made in reaction to pupil responses. Planning is monitored to ensure it is taking account of the learning of all pupils. Homework is set in ways that all pupils will be able to complete some aspects of the task. Opportunities are provided for pupils to clarify homework instructions.

Methods:
Examination of department policies and lesson plans; observation of lessons; observation of planning meetings; examination of pupil homework planners; interviews with pupils and staff.

Questions:

- Do planning documents record strategies for responding to diversity?

- Are modifications and adjustments made during lessons in response to pupil reactions?

- Is teaching monitored in order to see how well it responds to pupil diversity?

- Is homework planned in order that all pupils will be able to complete some aspect of the tasks set?

- Are pupils given opportunities to clarify the requirements of homework tasks?

Figure 7.3   Suggestions for collecting data in relation to Indicator 3.2

age pupils). Again it is best if these are completed in a group or class context, possibly with an adult reading each item as it is completed.

2   *Scrutiny*: Having carried out the survey the coordinating group need to analyse and examine their findings. Patterns are noted and contradictions considered, drawing on the perceptions of different members of the group. As a result of this process a small number of indicators are chosen for much closer scrutiny. In essence these are likely to represent aspects of the school that may need attention in order to foster a more inclusive way of working. Quite how many indicators to address at this stage is difficult to know, but clearly it is important that the decision is made by the co-ordinating group, taking into account the time available for carrying out the investigations. Having chosen the items for consideration it is necessary to plan what kinds of evidence will be needed to inform the group's discussions of what actions might be taken. Detailed advice is provided about the types of evidence that should be collected for each indicator, the methods that might be used and questions that need to be considered as the evidence is analysed. For example, in Figure 7.3 are the suggestions for collecting evidence related to indicator 3.2. Of particular note here is the list of questions, which is intended to challenge those within a school and to encourage a sense of critique. We feel that this is a particularly vital

ingredient given the tendency for self-review processes in schools to be carried out in a somewhat superficial manner.

Once again these suggestions are reviewed by coordinating groups in order to come up with approaches that will be appropriate to the particular context.

Phase 4: Development

Having scrutinized the information collected, the coordinating group then needs to recommend priorities for development. It is important that these become an integral part of the school's overall development procedures. In considering development priorities we have found it useful to bear in mind the following questions, adapted from MacBeith et al. (1996):

- why are we doing this?
- what is important in this school?
- how can we involve everybody who has an interest?

Quality of planning is a central factor in the successful implementation of any innovation. All who are involved in a particular venture need to have a sense of direction for the 'journey' they have embarked upon. However, as explained in Chapter 6, our research suggests that a number of more specific aspects of planning seem to be important if innovations are to succeed. First of all, plans need to be strongly linked to a clear vision of what the particular innovation intends to achieve. In this sense it is important that the proposed change is congruent with the overall beliefs and values of those who are directly implicated. In the case of a school, for example, this means that its core mission should be explicitly related to plans for development. Then the school can grow in ways that are compatible with its values, and any changes that are adopted will develop practice and simultaneously strengthen educational beliefs.

Secondly, the process of planning is at least as important as having a plan. Indeed some would argue that what is essential is planning, not plans. On the other hand, others might say that the plan should be a by-product of the planning process. Whatever the emphasis, the message is very clear: the means by which plans are produced is absolutely vital. Specifically, it is imperative that all potential contributors are involved, differences shared and action steps identified and agreed. This latter point is especially significant. A development plan needs to move into action. Plans should be judged not so much in terms of their articulation of destinations to be reached, but rather in terms of how far they are leading to movement. Plans and planning should make things happen.

Thirdly, plans need to be known by all who are likely to be involved in their implementation. In part, this point relates to what has just been noted. If the process of planning is cooperative and participative then it is more likely that stakeholders will know what is going on, as well as why and how.

If communication is important, so too is it necessary to keep everyone aware of progress that is made. Not only do people need to know what the plan is, but also how well they are doing in working towards the agreed goals. For this reason progress checks of various kinds will be needed in order to gauge the pace of implementation and the success of the plan. Experience suggests that it is helpful if progress checks involve:

- giving somebody responsibility for ensuring that these take place;
- reviewing progress at team meetings, especially when taking the next step forward or making decisions about future directions;
- deciding what will count as evidence of progress in relation to success criteria;
- finding quick methods of collecting evidence from different sources; and
- recording the evidence and conclusions for later use.

Finally, it is important to recognize that no plan is able to anticipate all eventualities at the outset. As progress checks are conducted, therefore, adjustments will be needed to ensure that headway is maintained. Plans will need updating to keep them in tune with the present — if not, the plans may become outdated and irrelevant. In this sense the plan has to continue evolving, hence planning is an on-going process not a one-off event. Planning keeps the innovation going.

In summary, then, development needs to be seen as a process which involves all interested people, keeps everybody informed of intentions and actions, and is on-going, because initial plans have to be reshaped in response to new circumstances.

Phase 5: Second Audit

After an agreed period of time a further audit is carried out in order to evaluate progress. Once again evidence related to the 'dimensions and indicators' is collected in order to allow comparisons to be made, using the same rating scales as in Phase 3. Here it is important that the findings of this evaluation process be disseminated as widely as possible within the school community. As I explained in the previous chapter, our studies of successful school innovations emphasize the importance of having effective communication networks. In particular, they point to the importance of all staff being aware of progress related to project activities and decisions that require them to take particular actions. It does seem that no amount of good ideas alone, will solve the ubiquitous problem of poor communication within the busy environment of schools. Since change is by its nature a highly personal experience, and since schools consist of numerous individuals and groups undergoing different (to them) experiences, no single communication is going to reassure or clarify the meaning of the innovation to people. A cardinal fact of social change is that people will almost always misinterpret and misunderstand some aspect, at least, of the purpose or practice of something that is new to them.

To be successful in coordinating innovations in educational contexts, therefore, it is essential to work hard at communication. Studies of the theory of change indicate the importance of frequent, personal interactions as a key to success. It seems that two-way communication about the specifics of the innovation that is being attempted is a requirement of success. To the extent that the information is accurate, the problems get identified. In this way each person's perceptions and concerns get aired.

Phase 6: Future Plans

The cycle is completed by a consideration of what further actions (if any) need to be taken. These may, of course, include a further cycle of development using the Index. Throughout the whole process the issue of timing has to be monitored carefully. Significant change takes time and implementation plans have to be sensitive to the pace at which development occurs, attempting to keep everybody fully involved. With this in mind, coordinators need to have clear views of the purposes of the innovation, whilst at the same time being willing and able to listen to, and accommodate, the views of others. This flexibility of approach enables the coordinators to judge when to move things on, when to be willing to change the agenda, and when to provide time and space for colleagues to explore ways forward. This implies that the coordinator will have a strong sense of personal security. Thus the function is not that of control, but rather that of providing guidance to staff as they seek to participate and contribute to the development activity. Such guidance should be based upon the coordinators' perspectives on the overall aims and plans; knowledge of expertise available within the context of the innovation; and awareness of external support that might be mobilized.

Accounts from Pilot Schools

During the second year of the Index project (i.e. 1997–98) five schools in three LEAs explored the use of the pilot materials. The accounts that follow are based on comments made by school representatives at a meeting held in May 1998. Work in these schools is continuing into a second year.

A Primary School in the North-west

In this urban school for 450 boys and girls aged 4–11, one third are eligible for free school meals; 70 pupils are seen as having special educational needs requiring extra support; and 13 have statements. A significant number of families live in socially and economically disadvantaged conditions. About 10 per cent speak English as a second language (mainly of Bengali origin). The Index very quickly became a catalyst for the school to focus on bilingual aspects of the school in order to try and measure how inclusive a school it was.

The first stage was the completion of the Index's Pupil Rating Scale by the same numbers of bilingual and non-bilingual children from all year groups (Year 3–Year 6) in Key Stage 2, with a generally positive response by all children involved, although it became obvious that for junior aged pupils there were too many variables in the scale and they responded too literally to some phrases; for example: 'I take part in all the school tests' and 'When there are activities after school anybody can join in'. There was no significant difference in the responses of bilingual and non-bilingual learners.

This part of the Index process led the staff to focus on literacy (devising their own 24 point questionnaire) in order to probe more deeply into inclusive practices in the school, with findings such as: bilingual pupils were also fluent in two other languages (Bengali and Arabic); they felt good speaking their own language in class but not in the playground; and they wanted notices around the school to be in other languages as well as English.

Finally, the staff decided that if things were to be more inclusive within school, they needed to know more about children's experiences out of school and they drew up another questionnaire covering outside interests of bilingual and non-bilingual learners. Bilingual girls, it turned out, had fewer hobbies than non-bilingual; they looked after siblings, learnt to cook, played with friends in each others' houses and did more at home than their brothers. Non-bilingual boys and girls had more hobbies and after school activities.

This school, like others in the pilot study, was only able to use part of the Index to explore aspects of its structures and practices and is committed now to exploring other parts. The school's management team in this school has started to discuss the range of issues and findings revealed by the Index exercise and will address them in the near future. One conclusion was that the Index's questionnaires and dimensions 'proved useful at a very early stage and helped staff and pupils think about "inclusiveness" in a very general sense'. However, some of the questions raised were 'too general for the staff' and 'age inappropriate' for a proportion of the pupils.

A Primary School and Nursery in the Midlands

This school has 500 boys and girls aged 5–11, plus 78 half-time nursery places in a predominantly white, working class urban area with significant housing problems. It is located very close to an airport with accompanying noise disturbance. Many children are on the at-risk register and there is a high mobility of pupils, with a 56 per cent turnover of children each year. There is also a high turnover of staff. The headteacher described her school as 'in at the bottom with inclusion — we want to learn and change'.

As a result of two separate exercises using first the Index's Rating Scale for staff and then the Pupil Rating Scale for Year 4 children, it was reported that the awareness of inclusion among the school's staff has increased significantly and for the better. Two key targets were identified for urgent action. The first is to create a new approach to the induction of new children into the school after responses from the pupils revealed their concern about friends and classmates arriving and leaving with such high rapidity. For example, 58 per cent of pupils in Year 6 did not start in the school's reception class.

The second target for action concerns the use of learning support assistants (LSAs). For example, children's responses to the questionnaires showed many of them did not know why the LSAs were in the classroom. The school is now looking at how to use the LSAs to the maximum advantage, rather than simply just being an extra body in the classroom. The children's response rate was high, better than expected, and they enjoyed doing the exercise. It was found also that there was a real benefit for the headteacher to work with them on this rather than the class teachers.

The school has found that while the Index project was laborious at the beginning of the pilot study period and seemed as if it was not getting very far, it now feels that good foundations have been laid for future work on developing inclusion. The 'improved awareness about inclusivity' has prompted the school to focus more clearly, including on an already planned new building and issues raised by inclusion, such as physical access.

As a result of the work with the Index the school has established an 'Inclusion Committee', comprised of a group of the school's governors and the key teacher responsible for the Index (the manager of the nursery). The two key targets mentioned above have now gone into the school development plan. The school feels it is now well past the first stage of the 'laborious process of informing people' and gathering data, and wants to use the information alongside other data reflecting different aspects of the school. 'With hindsight, it would have been better to start the Index study with a specific project', said one of the teachers who is coordinating the initiative.

A Coeducational Comprehensive Community High School in the North-west

There are 1 000 students at this school, which has an excellent reputation for its policy of including learners with varying disabilities and learning difficulties. Fifty-two students are on the special needs register and have statements. The school is specially resourced to cater for students with visual impairment, moderate learning difficulties, specific learning difficulties, hearing impairment, emotional and behavioural difficulties, and motor impairment. To get themselves started with the Index process in school, staff decided on a specific project — to investigate the experiences of the students with motor impairment and, in particular, to examine how included or excluded they were.

Conveniently, there were students with motor impairment in every year group, thereby permitting the involvement of all non-disabled students who were in the same form as a disabled learner. As well as the Index's Pupil Rating Scale being issued to 178 students, the school issued the same number of the Index's Initial Rating Scale 2 to parents and 69 of the Initial Rating Scale 1 to staff. Fifteen questionnaires were also issued to the school's governors. Staff had assistance from the LEA and an MSc student from a nearby university helped to analyse the data. The main finding revealed how well included the motor impaired students were in the school and staff felt they could confidently move on to discover more data about inclusive practices within the school to do with other disabled and non-disabled students. 'Although we knew a lot about these motor impaired students, it surprised how well they were included.'

Of disappointment, however, was the low rate of return of the parent questionnaire, but it was felt that part of the explanation was the 'inappropriateness of some of the questions for parents'. In future, the school wants questionnaires to be more specific about the inclusion of students with different disabilities or learning difficulties, confidently predicting they will 'come up with some very good answers'. These and other findings are being put into the school's development plan.

A County High School in the North-west

This mixed school for 1 090 students aged 11–16 years is in an urban area, near to a large city. The school began using the Index's questionnaires for pupils at the beginning of the pilot study period and then moved on to those for staff. The whole process was led by the deputy headteacher who said that the most important outcome showed that the Index was 'a management tool to find out where a school is at any point in time'. Because the Index touched on so many areas it alerted the school to the areas to be worked on. As the deputy head noted, 'The scale of the Index process is enormous. It touches on every single aspect of school life'.

The data that was collected led the senior management to 'tinker with school policy in response to findings', whether these were from staff, parents, governors or pupils. Not least it showed significant gaps between what was desired by staff in school and what was actually being achieved.

Students were involved via the school council and their responses were both valuable and vital to the evaluation process. At a meeting some 60 students, representing different age groups, took part in a group exercise during which they were asked to rate their school against the various indicators in the Index. On a number of points staff thought something was being done in the school but the students' answers suggested that it was not. It was noted, 'There's no power like the views of pupils to move a school forward'.

Another finding from using the questionnaires, which this school always followed up with discussion and debate, was the high number of initiatives already running in school which the Index instantly touched upon. It was noted, 'The Index shows you that some things will take a short input to fix, others are huge and will be done in a year or more'. For example, 'peer-counselling' and 'differentiation' both came out of follow-up discussions and are now on the agenda of things being tackled by the school as a result of the Index work.

A County First School in an Outer London Borough

This mixed school is popular and over-subscribed and has within the last three years embarked on an active policy of attempting to include more children with disabilities or learning difficulties. It is situated in a comfortable part of outer London with little or no social or economic disadvantage in the neighbourhood and has 350 pupils aged 5–8 years.

The use of questionnaires with reception class pupils showed that a set of different questions were needed for such an age-group; the results from responses from the remainder of the 72 pupils randomly picked across the three year groups were, however, valuable and informative. The headteacher carried out this part of the Index exercise and found it time consuming, but extremely valuable and felt the pupils were probably more honest with her than they might have been with their class teacher. This school suggested that a series of Index questionnaires would be useful for different age groups e.g. nursery and reception; infant; junior; secondary.

The highest number of negative responses for any one dimension from the Index was 7 out of 65; overall the pupils were 'very positive' in their responses. The school found it difficult to identify areas for development from the raw data; far more meaningful were the subsequent discussions which will feed into the school development plan review.

The main conclusion from the questionnaires returned by parents was that they did not see themselves as equal partners with teachers and, indeed, did not want to be treated as equal as they recognized the extensive decision-making regarding the curriculum was 'taken by the school'. Parents' views were requested via the school newsletter and responses collected were 'all extremely positive'.

The key area identified for development as a result of this first Index exercise was the induction of children during the academic year. Broad agreement was the main finding from the staff questionnaire on their perceptions of the current situation in the school relating to the five dimensions in the Initial Rating Scale.

Some Thoughts

These accounts are very encouraging, not least in that they illustrate the creative ways in which the Index materials and processes have been adapted in order to fit with local 'cultures'. There is also evidence that they have stimulated considerable discussion of how to move towards more inclusive practices and the beginnings, at least, of significant developments. As a result of these experiences it was felt that future efforts might usefully take account of the following points:

1   The initial process of setting up the use of the Index in a school takes time. Indeed the whole process will clearly spread over two years, at least, as it feeds into and becomes part of normal school development activities. Schools needed more specific directions at the start since some seemed uncertain during the early stages. In some cases the coordinating group had limited representatives of the various stakeholder groups.

2   We need to find ways of encouraging schools to engage with 'deeper' aspects of their thinking and practice. There was a tendency to focus on what might be seen as more peripheral aspects of the Index agenda. Pupil data were very encouraging in this respect in that they tended to present staff with challenging feedback on school life. However, more use needs to be made of the more probing questions related to the indicators.

3   Similarly, the idea of the 'outsider' acting as 'critical friend' needs to be given much more emphasis. This should help to push things along in the early stages as well as providing a means of encouraging a more probing approach.

The Index project is still developing, with further research going on to refine the materials and to demonstrate the effectiveness of the approaches that are being recommended. Following the completion of this research, which is funded by the Teacher Training Agency, it is intended that the materials will be published by the Centre for Studies on Inclusive Education (address: CSIE, 1 Redland Close, Bristol BS6 6UE). In the meantime, the impact of the materials in the pilot schools has confirmed my commitment to the arguments I have made for the importance of reconstructing the special needs task as a process of improvement aimed at the development of more inclusive practices. This leads me to argue once again that a detailed consideration of the barriers experienced by some pupils can help us to develop forms of schooling that will be more effective for *all* pupils.

Chapter 8

Supporting School and Teacher Development

The proposals outlined in this book for developing more inclusive schools assume significant changes in thinking and practice amongst many teachers. They also necessitate a major rethink of the roles of specialist support staff, such as learning support teachers, special educational needs coordinators, LEA advisers and educational psychologists, all of whom will need to focus much more on the issue of how schools can be developed in order to create inclusive arrangements.

This chapter looks at what these new roles might involve. It also provides a detailed explanation of the skills and expertise that are required amongst those who lead and coordinate development work within schools and, indeed, those from outside schools who also are involved in providing support.

Rethinking Roles

As we have seen, developing inclusive practices in schools is far from easy. Whilst the analysis I have provided suggests certain conditions that seem to support such development, these are not readily established in organizations where they are currently absent. What is required, it seems, is a fairly significant redirection of resources and effort in order to shift organizations that are structured to facilitate maintenance of the status quo, towards ways of working that will encourage growth. The creation of arrangements that encourage development provide opportunities for staff to become clearer about purposes and priorities, leading to a greater sense of confidence and empowerment, and an increased willingness to experiment with alternative responses to problems experienced in the classroom. For this reason I have argued that the special needs task has to be reconstructed as a process of school and teacher development. Put simply, this means that by improving overall conditions a school supports staff in overcoming barriers to participation and in developing a wider range of responses to pupils who experience difficulties in their learning. In so doing, it adopts a way of working that is essentially about the 'reformation of ordinary education, to make it more comprehensive' (Vislie, 1995). Such moves are likely to be to the benefit of all children in a school.

What, therefore, are the roles of specialists in this reconceptualized special needs world? In general terms, three options seem to be possible:

- Maintenance roles — where they respond directly to those pupils who struggle within existing arrangements, and perhaps, in so doing, unintentionally assist in the retention of the status quo.

- Modifying roles — where they respond to those pupils who struggle within existing arrangements by seeking to adapt existing arrangements.

- Developmental roles — where they respond to those pupils who struggle within existing arrangements by working with colleagues to make new arrangements that may facilitate the learning of all pupils.

I am well aware, of course, that the pressures on schools in many countries, resulting from ill-conceived central reforms and underfunding, create many dilemmas with respect to which of these roles might be most appropriate. In addition, many of those who are given the special needs task may feel that they lack the expertise and support to negotiate with colleagues in order to take on a much more developmental role.

The approaches I am proposing demand that those whose task is to support movement towards more inclusive ways of working must focus their gaze on the context of schooling. More specifically they have to be skilful in working with their school colleagues in reviewing current arrangements, analysing barriers to participation, formulating problem-solving strategies and managing change. In this way they have opportunities to contribute to the overall task of school improvement. Indeed, it may well be that they become involved in the leadership of such initiatives.

Within the IQEA project there were a number of striking examples of how support staff, particularly learning support teachers, took on key developmental roles within their school's improvement strategies. Mary Cohen, who was Learning Support Coordinator in one of the project schools, has written an excellent account of how she led the introduction of a new policy that involved 'problem-solving partnerships between teachers to face the uncertain work of providing effective learning for all' (Cohen, 1997). Central to this new policy was the creation of a specific teaching area within the school which was spacious enough for groups of teachers to work alongside one another in experimenting with new approaches. Relating the strategy to the work of Bruce Joyce on effective staff development, she suggests that this context provides a 'workshop in the workplace'. It also provided Mary with opportunities to provide leadership to her colleagues in their attempts to develop more inclusive ways of working through greater collaboration.

Management and Leadership

Changes in legislation in many countries have significantly altered the role of management in schools (West and Ainscow, 1991). As a result, many more schools seem to pay greater attention to management structures, processes and roles. There is, however, the worry that this focus on management as a technical process can lead to an over-reliance on 'systems' and a corresponding decrease in the amount of attention given to those aspects of school life which can unite and inspire human effort. Such aspects can be usefully grouped together under the term *leadership* in a way that refers to processes used to influence groups of staff towards the achievement of common purposes.

There is considerable evidence in studies of school effectiveness to suggest that leadership is a key element in determining school success (e.g. Stoll, 1991). More recently, studies of leadership have tended to move away from the identification of this function exclusively with the headteacher, and have begun to address how leadership can be made available throughout the management structure and at all levels within a school community (Hopkins et al., 1994). As noted in Chapter 6, this shift in emphasis has been accompanied by changes in thinking about leadership itself, with an increasing call for 'transformational' approaches which seek to empower, rather than 'transactional' approaches which tend to sustain traditional concepts of hierarchy and control (Sergiovanni, 1992).

One consequence of this shift in thinking is the realization in many schools that management arrangements may need to be modified or revised so that leadership can be more widely exercised. So, whilst leadership and management remain inextricably linked, in times of change it is necessary to have positive strategies within a school for developing leadership approaches and reflecting these in management structures.

It will be recalled that our engagements with schools involved in the IQEA project led to a style of collaboration that we referred to as 'working with rather than working on'. This phrase was our attempt to sum up an approach that deliberately allowed each project school considerable autonomy to determine its own priorities for development and, indeed, its methods for achieving these priorities. This way of working places considerable responsibility on those teachers within a school — the so-called project cadre — for the implementation and success of development work. Thus the tasks taken on by these individuals were crucial to the success of such developments. What is it, then, that such teachers do when school improvement is successful?

To explore this issue two members of our team conducted a series of semi-structured interviews with teachers in certain of the project schools where there were clear signs that developments were occurring (Ainscow and Southworth, 1996). Their replies were surprisingly consistent, suggesting some general patterns that are worthy of attention amongst others asked to take on coordination or leadership roles in their schools. In addition, as part of the process of data analysis, presentations were made of the initial findings at three meetings attended by around 100 IQEA coordinators in all. This enabled us to test out our interpretations and, to some degree at least, validate our findings. The teachers' ideas about how they exercise leadership in their schools fell into five categories. These categories overlap with one another and several interrelate and interpenetrate. So saying, it is nevertheless helpful for the sake of description to present them as distinguishable areas of activity. They are (in no specific order):

Dealing with people
Taking a whole school view
Keeping up the momentum
Monitoring developments
Establishing a climate

Dealing with people

The teachers made it abundantly clear that they were aware of the importance of creating and sustaining positive working relationships with their colleagues. In many cases this meant that they first needed to develop stronger links with their partners in the cadres. At the same time these teachers appreciated that they needed simultaneously to involve others. One spoke about trying 'to widen the group of people involved by selecting people who had been on the fringe' of committees and previous working parties in the school.

Mixed in with this attention to others was another strand. Intuitively these teachers were concerned with the dynamics of the existing work groups in their schools. They wanted to ensure not only that there was a reasonable working atmosphere amongst themselves and their colleagues, but also to enhance the effectiveness of the various staff groups. This meant that there was a duality to their awareness; they wanted both positive and productive relationships to develop. Hence they sought to 'draw together the staff' and make strong links with other formal groups in their schools, especially senior management teams and school development planning groups.

Tied up with all of this seemed to be one other dimension. Several of these teachers quickly came to realize that in being concerned to encourage staff collaboration they were themselves learning more about working with adults. For some this was recognized as new learning since, by tradition, teachers are trained to work with children and not adults. For others, involvement with IQEA meant that they had to refine their skills in this area. Yet all of them, by virtue of their involvement in the cadre, were now leaders of adults as well as teachers of children, and all needed to develop their own skills in dealing with people.

Taking a whole school view

All of the teachers interviewed seemed to appreciate that if the improvement initiatives on which they were embarked were to have any chance of success then they, individually and collectively, needed to have the 'big picture' of both their projects and their schools. Many of the teachers realized the importance of collecting information about their schools, both formally and informally. They also felt that it was vital to share information with one another and to develop common understandings about the school as a whole. Indeed, from their mutual awareness they identified what needed to be done, how and by whom. They also carefully orchestrated involvement both of colleagues inside and outside their schools.

In addition, attention was paid to resources. Three types of resource in particular were mentioned during the interviews. The first of these was people as resources to one another, hence the desire to involve many other colleagues. The second resource was time. Here it was generally recognized that if the process of improvement was to have any chance of success then time had to be devoted to it. This meant that individuals needed to be released from some of their existing commitments and that time was needed for meetings, planning and staff development activities. Third, there needed to be some financial support. Money was needed to buy time and to pay for the various staff development activities.

It was recognized in all of these schools that if certain changes were to happen then the organization itself needed to change and in each school important shifts had already taken place in organizational structures. So, for example, in one school there had been a concerted effort 'to get rid of the hierarchical structure'. Also, in the same school, new roles were developed for some staff and 'quality time' for meetings was created by reorganizing the timetable. The improvement process was further integrated into the work of the school through links being established with the school development planning routine.

Keeping up momentum

All the teachers were aware both that they needed to implement their school improvement projects, and, having got things started, to keep the momentum going. Getting things started seemed to be less of an issue than keeping things moving. The teachers attempted to maintain the impetus by making use of formal and informal communication systems in their schools. In terms of the formal means they generally relied on two events: they used staff meetings for brief progress reports and senior management team meetings to share concerns and to enlist additional help and support. Informally, they used more varied means. For example, some spent a lot of time after school talking informally with colleagues individually or in groups. Throughout all this talking the aim was to try to be positive about the developments and 'to explain why we are doing it'. According to the teachers all this talk was beneficial because it was appreciated by colleagues that they were being supported and that an interest was being taken in their work. These conversations also helped to develop professional dialogue and to establish a common language in each of the schools. One of the teachers (who was very consciously using talk to shape developments in the school) believed professional discussion was very important because 'I think that unless you can articulate it, you actually don't know that you are doing it'. In other words, talking was a process of project realization. At the same time this teacher was aware that in creating a vocabulary for school development she was also, simultaneously, helping to change the nature of professional discourse in her school.

Monitoring developments

Many of the teachers we interviewed recognized the importance of monitoring what was happening in the school and how projects were being implemented. They spoke of 'reviewing progress', of writing progress reports for other groups in the school and of 'evaluating' how their respective projects were going. In particular, they focused on whether there was too much or too little pressure on staff. One teacher recognized that she was very 'visible around the school' and that this in itself was a form of pressure on colleagues to make things happen. Another spoke about 'consciously watching' to see whether there were too many advisory people working in one area of the school. In effect she was checking to see that involvements and resources were balanced out and not over-burdening her colleagues.

All the teachers accepted that managing change involved overcoming difficulties and encountering setbacks, since they accepted that change creates periods of turbulence. Many of the interviewees spoke about interpersonal tensions and strains. For example, one said: 'You get your discords and falling out and all that'. Whilst another said, 'not everybody gets on with everybody, it isn't possible, but we professionally aspire to work together'.

These teachers observed the organizational and interpersonal tensions that arose from their projects. They negotiated with individuals and groups, bargaining with some and striking deals with others. For these teachers monitoring the change process was not a passive activity, rather it was active and, indeed, interactive and, moreover, at times it required them to become active in the micro-political process of the school.

Establishing a climate

So far I have described what these teachers said they did, but not how, now I want to identify briefly the ways in which they work. Four strategies were particularly noticeable. First, in all these schools careful use was made of staff development activities to promote the project, to involve colleagues and to equip staff to implement the necessary changes in practice. Second, the quality of talk in the schools was regarded as important because much relies on the capacity of the staff to exchange ideas, share problems and find common solutions. Third, a great deal of negotiation took place between members of the cadre and between them and their colleagues. Discussion and debates occurred to explain and promote the projects and, as a consequence of this, dialogue deals were struck and plans agreed. Fourth, at particular points in the development process there came a time when problems or issues needed to be confronted, when allowances could no longer be made for certain individuals or groups, and when frankness and resolution were needed.

Overall, then, these processes and the other points I have noted about these teachers' leadership behaviour helped to establish a climate that seemed to be supportive of school development activities. In particular, they were seeking to assuage their colleagues' doubts and concerns about managing change or coping with yet another development. From this sense of reassurance came confidence.

The interviewed teachers themselves grew in stature in their own eyes and, it seems, in the eyes of their colleagues.

Perhaps the most notable feature of their comments was the sense of openness they saw developing in their schools. According to these teachers' reports, their schools were becoming less shuttered and sealed, and more receptive to ideas. Their schools had begun to change as organizations; they were becoming more permeable from the outside and more susceptible to innovation. Indeed they were establishing some of the characteristics associated with what Senge (1989) refers to as 'learning organizations'.

Some Implications

In one sense the findings of this study were encouraging in that they seem to be consistent with other recent studies in this area. Specifically, they echo the summaries of research reported by Fullan (1991). For example, across the five categories described we can see that these teachers believed in what Fullan refers to as the 'primacy of personal contact'; used a blend of 'pressure and support'; acknowledged that implementation was a 'process of clarification'; and were confronting the cultures of their schools in an attempt to encourage greater collaboration.

In addition to confirming these earlier findings, these data are helpful in drawing our attention to some of the issues involved. Too often in the school improvement literature findings conclude with typologies or lists of recommendations, that seem to imply that what is needed is the application of a series of recipe-like responses that will readily fit any context. Our detailed knowledge, built up over time, of the schools in this study helped us to recognize that the unique biography of each organization means that those leading improvement activities have to devise their own ways forward. In doing so, they have to be sensitive to the sorts of structural, cultural and micro-political factors reported here, and the ways in which these impact upon their colleagues' perceptions of any changes that are proposed.

If this begins to sketch out the deeper meaning of what these teachers were trying to accomplish, it does not really explain why they chose to do so. At this stage I can suggest two possible reasons that may throw some light on this issue. First of all, it seemed that these teachers were keen to develop a climate of learning in their schools because they were 'teacher-leaders'. That is to say, they brought to their leadership tasks what their professional experience had taught them about influencing and developing others; they wanted to change their colleagues by establishing processes in their workplaces which were inherently educative. Just as they knew from their teaching that it is necessary to create in the classroom a positive atmosphere that encourages the risk-taking associated with learning, they also applied a similar orientation to their new responsibilities to improve the quality of practice in their schools. Thus it can be argued that they were 'educative leaders', who were using their knowledge of professional development to create a particular kind of organizational culture in their schools. These teachers had a fundamental belief in the power of professional learning and, indeed, tended to see themselves as the leading learners in respect to their school projects.

Secondly, all of them seemed to understand that it is far from easy to create such a learning environment or, indeed, a collaborative culture. They needed help and support every bit as much as their colleagues. In particular, they needed to understand more about how adults learn, since many were aware that they could not always apply their knowledge of classrooms and child development directly to the staffroom and to their colleagues' learning. This, in part at least, is what they valued in the support they received from the members of the IQEA team who acted as consultants to their schools. They explained how they consciously and unconsciously noted specifically how we dealt with groups of adults and took from us such ways of working that seemed relevant to their situations. They used this knowledge to give confidence to their colleagues and themselves. Importantly, they also noted the emphasis we placed on working in pairs and as a team, and tried to deploy similar ways of working themselves. Thus their involvement in IQEA was for them yet another source of support for learning. In this sense when they worked with us they were aware of our attempts to create a climate of learning which they, in turn, attempted to transport into their schools. It seems, therefore, that in many ways the medium of IQEA was its most important message.

Consultancy

The other important agenda for our discussions with these teachers focused on our work as consultants attached to their schools as part of IQEA. Here our concern was with which of our activities (if any) had had an impact upon their work in coordinating school development activities. This agenda raised a rather obvious methodological issue in that we were asking the teachers to comment directly upon the work of ourselves and our fellow IQEA team members and, consequently, we had to recognize that the nature of the data gathered was influenced by this factor in ways that are impossible to determine. Nevertheless, the discussions did, at times, take on a critical edge which suggests that the teachers were prepared to delve into areas of our activities about which they had some reservations. Certainly the discussions provided a fascinating 'mirror' on our practices, reflecting back to us a series of images about what it is we were perceived to do.

Once again our scrutiny of the data led us to identify five over-lapping categories of activity which help to summarize the teachers' views about what they had noted us doing in IQEA. Specifically they point to those of our responses that were seen as having some impact upon the work of those teachers taking on leadership roles in school. The five categories were:

Pushing thinking forward
Framing the issues
Encouraging partnerships
Providing incentives
Modelling ways of working

It will become clear from the analysis that the teachers experienced some difficulty in articulating quite which elements of IQEA had had an impact on their thinking and practice. Indeed, most had some problems in recalling any tangible aspects of the project. As one teacher put it, 'The project is kind of amorphous — it's been a general atmosphere'. After a little prompting, however, all the teachers were able to describe particular events or ideas that had been introduced as a result of project activities, and as the discussions developed more and more attention was focused on matters of process. This emphasis is reflected in the five themes discussed below.

Pushing thinking forward

Although much of the emphasis in the discussions was on process issues, the teachers did make reference to certain types of specific input from the IQEA team. These can be seen in relation to two contexts. The first of these concerned inputs provided during out-of-school meetings, when cadre members from different schools came together; and, the second, related to inputs provided by team members during meetings or staff development events held in their schools.

The out-of-school gathering usually took the form of whole day sessions involving training activities and planning discussions. Leading these sessions presented a number of dilemmas for the project team, not least that of trying to focus on topics that would be relevant at a given time for each of the various school groups. Our interviews led to some encouraging feedback on this issue. Whilst some of the teachers made reference to 'sometimes switching off' during discussions that seemed irrelevant, the majority did not see this as a problem. Indeed, a couple of the teachers felt that we seemed to have an uncanny knack of hitting the current issues in their schools. One noted, 'almost by magic IQEA sessions always seem to be where we are at'. It may be that the overall style adopted during these sessions, that of framing the various activities and discussions around a series of questions to be explored, was helpful in allowing participants to construct their own working agendas directly connected to their current concerns in school. Certainly a number of the teachers referred to the project sessions encouraging them to look at issues from different perspectives, thus forcing them to consider new possibilities for addressing their development strategies.

Some of the teachers recalled more specific inputs that had impacted upon their work. For example, one referred to a session that had addressed the theme of 'involvement' that had led to significant developments with respect to how his school utilized the energies of pupils and parents in order to support their school development efforts.

Overall, references to IQEA sessions focused mainly on more general statements about their success in pushing thinking forward. One teacher's comments were indicative of this theme. She noted that the sessions 'influence my thinking, direct me towards reading, in fact do my reading for me!' She went on to say, 'I thrive on that. I go home and I'm still thinking about it'. In a similar vein another teacher remarked, 'It's not as if we go away from each meeting and spend hours reading either, it's self-contained'.

It seemed, too, that the stimulus to thinking reported here was also encouraged by the fact that the teachers attended the sessions with colleagues from their schools. This meant that they could debrief the experience of the day together, often in the car going back, or during subsequent days. Our suggestion that they should take responsibility for sharing ideas from the session with the rest of the staff also seemed to encourage a deeper engagement with the topics under discussion.

The teachers were all positive about the involvement of members of our IQEA team in their schools. Reference was made to ways in which these visits had helped the school in connection with specific developments, such as the introduction of a teacher appraisal scheme in one school. On other occasions the impact might have been on the way in which such developments were implemented. For example, in one school an IQEA team member had impressed on staff the idea that 'decisions should be made at the lowest level possible'.

Once again, however, these inputs were seen most significantly in terms of their impact upon the thinking of the teachers. As one put it, 'You guys have infected our ways of thinking'. However, 'infecting' other people's thinking can also lead to certain negative effects. In a number of the schools the development of the ideas of cadre members seemed to have created tensions between them and their colleagues, who, it appeared, found the use of unfamiliar terminology rather irritating or even threatening.

Another important dimension of the work of the IQEA team in the project schools related to staff development. Emphasis was placed on the importance of work in classrooms. This was seen as a very positive aspect of the initiative, not least its capacity to 'stimulate creative discussion' about aspects of practice. One teacher compared all of this to a previous experience of attending a masters degree course which, she argued, had been much less influential because 'it didn't have any involvement with the organization'. Again, however, the introduction of this emphasis on school-based staff development did create a degree of turbulence when it was seen by some colleagues as being in conflict with existing practices. In one school, staff development had been seen as an 'entitlement' to go out of school in order to attend short courses. The IQEA approach, with its heavy emphasis on within-school staff development processes, was seen by some as a potential threat to this well-established avenue for spending time away from school.

Framing the issues

In our interactions with teachers in the IQEA schools we tried to resist any temptation to impose ways of working from elsewhere. At times this created further dilemmas for us. In particular, the fact that the schools were paying for our involvement in their improvement programmes meant that we were keen to be seen to provide them with the best available knowledge, but on the other hand, we were committed to enabling each school to develop its own capacity for managing change. This being the case, we attempted to work in ways that maintained the locus of control regarding all aspects of the project firmly within each participating school. It was interesting, therefore, to hear the teachers make so many references to our ways of working. Undoubtedly these had had far more impact than the actual content of our inputs.

Where our work had been particularly influential it seemed to have involved us in a process of helping teachers to frame their problems and to consider a range of possible ways forward. One teacher referred to this as 'chanelling our thoughts'. The data also provided some useful pointers to what are the key factors in this framing approach to working with teachers involved in leading improvement activities. The first factor seemed to involve the 'mapping' of possibilities. Teachers reported that during IQEA meetings they found it helpful when we asked them to analyse what currently happens in their schools through some form of auditing. Then, having carried out this analysis, they found it valuable to be involved in various types of group activity designed to establish new possibilities for action. The important dimension seemed to be that these activities encouraged the teachers to view their own school through 'fresh eyes'. In this way the outcomes of the initial analysis could be reconsidered, leading sometimes to the recognition of an appropriate way forward.

Associated with the process of mapping of possibilities was a second key factor, that of talk. Many of the teachers drew attention to what they saw as the value of having 'quality time' to discuss their work; from their accounts it seemed that the typical day in an English school provides little or no time for such talk to take place. The visit of a member of the IQEA team, or a trip out of school with a colleague to attend a project meeting, provided firm boundaries within which such discussions could take place. On some occasions, also, the way in which activities were framed during the IQEA meetings facilitated talk by providing terminology and creating a structured context that colleagues could use to open up sensitive areas for discussion that might be impossible to address within a normal working day.

Many examples were cited of when IQEA team members had assisted groups of staff to resolve issues within their school by asking probing questions or by challenging colleagues to address matters that were being overlooked or, indeed, tactically avoided. One teacher described how a team member had confronted a school group that he felt had achieved a false consensus by ignoring differences of opinion that existed between them. Reference was made to how he had 'bollocked' the group and that subsequently this had led to a 'clearing of the air'. As a result, much more open discussion of different possibilities for action became possible.

Whilst what I have referred to as a 'framing' approach to the interventions in the project schools seemed to have been generally welcomed, it also had the potential to create conflict. In particular, the emphasis on staff participation in defining problems and debating possible solutions appeared to have engendered some turbulence in those organizations where there existed a tradition of top-down decision making. This feature was particularly apparent in two of the schools. In one, for example, a teacher observed that 'the style of the project said that development comes from staff needs and by staff identifying a way forward for themselves'. She explained that this had created some tension in her school, where this had not been the tradition, and, significantly, she felt that she 'was in the middle of it'.

Encouraging partnerships

As we have seen, the work of teachers who act as leaders of school improvement activities can create a number of difficulties for them. In a sense they enter a kind of 'no man's land' between their colleagues in the staff room and the senior management team. In acting in the interests of the whole school they may, on the one hand, be seen as agents of authority; whilst on the other hand, they want to be perceived as acting on behalf of the staff. This may be experienced in different ways from school to school, but it is undoubtedly a source of pressure.

This being the case, it was encouraging to hear the teachers describe their positive feelings about their work, many of them talking with obvious delight and pride about what they and their colleagues had achieved. They also spoke in some detail about the impact of all of this on their own thinking and practice. One teacher seemed to sum up these feelings when she said, 'It's a lovely feeling to be deeply involved in something'.

Important to this overall feeling of confidence about what had happened seemed to be the concept of partnerships. Whilst these teachers frequently found themselves having to face difficult and, at times, stressful situations, the existence of various partnership arrangements seemed to be an enormous source of strength to them. In particular, they seemed to value the partnerships they felt they had with various members of the IQEA team. As one teacher put it, 'I don't know if I would have been so confident if we hadn't got such support . . .' At times of turbulence within the school the presence of an 'outside' partner had proved to be particularly valuable. In one school, for example, it was reported that a member of the IQEA team had 'had to come in and really hold our hands and reassure us that this is actually all right'.

Through their involvement in the project the teachers felt that they had become more skilful in establishing partnerships with colleagues in their own schools. A number also referred to having become more skilful at working with outside agencies such as LEA advisers. Perhaps more than anything else, however, the various types of partnerships encouraged by IQEA seemed to have the effect of confirming people in what they were doing and, at the same time, making them feel valued. One teacher referred to the feeling that it was now recognized that there was 'a proper job to be done' in order to support staff in carrying out improvement efforts. Partnerships also seemed to have supported people in doing this 'proper job' by creating closer working relationships within which colleagues could share ideas, solve problems together and, as we have seen, assist one another during times of discomfort.

Providing incentives

Keeping school improvement initiatives going over time presents a number of difficulties, made even worse during times when schools are bombarded by new national requirements. Circumstances change, new priorities arise and, inevitably, sooner or later key personnel move on. In addition, the schools in this sample had been grappling during the early 1990s with the requirements of an extensive range of externally driven innovations arising from the then government's reform agenda. As they sought to bring about improvements in the work of their schools they had to respond to all of these new requirements that had involved radical changes in policies for curriculum, assessment and finance. As a consequence, it was easy for them to be distracted from their overall purposes. We had observed that the schools in the sample had, in fact, been particularly successful in keeping their impetus going, despite the difficulties they faced, and we were particularly interested to know if any of our actions had been of assistance in this respect.

Most of the teachers described how our visits to their schools had created deadlines. The fact that they knew we were about to visit often seemed to act as a spur to their actions. Some reported how on occasions the momentum had been lost and that they had faced our visits with a certain amount of anxiety. More positively, however, many felt that the visits provided an incentive to get on with their work.

The teachers suggested that discussions with the IQEA team were often helpful in defining ways forward and, therefore, in giving a much clearer sense of direction to their work. It was also good to report on what had happened to an outside audience and, in so doing, to recognize achievements that might otherwise have gone unnoticed. In these ways meetings with the IQEA team sometimes became celebrations that enhanced feelings of motivation. In a similar way it was felt that opportunities to meet with teachers from other project schools provided further incentives, including sometimes, as a result of a certain amount of competition between them. As one teacher noted, 'listening to other schools made us realize that we're further down the road in terms of development than we thought'.

Modelling ways of working

As I have explained, the discussions with these teachers focused much more on the process of our involvement in their work than on the actual content of our interactions. It seems that it had been the way the IQEA team had carried out its work that had had the most noticeable impact. Central to this seemed to be a process of modelling how groups of adults can learn how to be more effective in working together in order to solve problems and get tasks completed successfully.

A number of the teachers explained in very specific terms how team members had become tacit 'role models', who they had followed in carrying out their work with colleagues in schools. For example, one teacher noted, 'It was quite interesting watching, especially at the start, how pairs of you would work together and with us. Sometimes you would talk things through in front of us when you had a dilemma . . . In fact, watching you talking through conflicting views was quite important'. She went on to explain how she and her two colleagues had carefully planned and rehearsed how they would replicate this approach as they worked with a team of staff in their school. She noted, 'some of the actual strategies you used to get us to work together . . . we would use with our colleagues'.

Another teacher reported that working with members of the IQEA team had helped her to recognize that 'staff teams weren't managed as they should be'. She described how she had 'tried to copy the way (we had) worked, back with my department'. Apparently, the particular features she had tried to incorporate were sharing responsibility with group members and making people feel valued. Others described how our deliberate system of working mainly in pairs had encouraged them to explore the development of partnerships in a much more conscious way. As one teacher saw it, the basic rationale of this is that 'nobody has all the answers'. Where this had been successful people were very enthusiastic about its impact upon improvement activities. This was summed up by the remark, 'Suddenly it was a group of people trying to work together, not trying to score points'.

The modelling of ways of working with colleagues was also commented upon in connection with a further issue, that of creating 'openness' within which colleagues would be prepared to explore alternative perspectives and ways forward. At its best this provided a supportive climate within which colleagues felt able to explore aspects of one another's classroom practice. For one teacher this was the most significant contribution of the project, confirming her belief in the idea of classrooms as 'centres of inquiry'.

Drawing Some Conclusions

These findings confirm evidence from elsewhere about the key tasks necessary for external consultants to have an impact during school improvement interventions. They mirror, for example, the findings of Saxl, Lieberman and Miles, (1987) who found that certain core skills pervade the work of those who are successful in assisting teachers during staff development initiatives. Like ours, their findings point to the importance of certain processes such as 'open communication, clarifying expectations, legitimizing the role and addressing resistance'.

All of this further confirms a theme that keeps reappearing through the pages of this book, that of growth within schools through what is essentially a social process of helping those involved to learn *how* to learn from difference in order to develop new possibilities for action. It seems to me that it is in this way that the cultural change that is needed within an organization in order to create more inclusive ways of working can be achieved.

As I have suggested, for this to happen we need educative leaders. Such leaders recognize that school growth hinges on the capacity of colleagues to develop. Moreover they understand that professional development is about both individuals and collegiality; it is to do with each teacher increasing his or her confidence and competence, and the staff increasing their capacity to work together as a team. Educative leadership has been shown to be a key element in creating more collaborative school cultures because leaders are instrumental in establishing certain beliefs upon which such cultures are founded (Nias, Southworth an Yeomans, 1989). This means that individuals have to be valued and, because they are inseparable from the groups of which they are a part, so too should groups. It also seems that the most effective way of promoting these values are through ways of working that encourage openness and a sense of mutual security. These beliefs, it now seems, are also central to the establishment and sustenance of schools that are seeking to become more inclusive. Perhaps, then, it is no accident that leaders in such schools are essentially teachers who base their actions on principles of professional learning rather than on the practices of military, business and commercial leaders, which are sometimes held up as models for those involved in educational change.

As we have seen, however, educational change is not easy or straightforward. It involves a complex weave of individual and micro-political strands that take on idiosyncratic forms within each school context. Consequently, it involves much negotiation, arbitration and coalition-building, as well as sensitivity to colleagues' professional views and personal feelings. It is about changing attitudes and actions; beliefs and behaviour. How long all of this will take depends upon so many factors, since the interpersonal dynamics are unpredictable and, of course, context specific. Leaders and consultants alike need to be able to examine the circumstances they face in each school and be able to respond to the personal and political dramas they meet.

It follows that providing leadership in schools that are attempting to become more inclusive is not for the faint-hearted. Nor is it comfortable for any other colleagues in these schools. To be a teacher in such a school means that you need to be able to accept and deal with questions being asked of your beliefs, ideas, plans and teaching practices. In such a context interprofessional challenge will be common. Therefore, those who provide leadership must model not only a willingness to participate in discussions and debates, but also a readiness to answer questions and challenges from staff members. Furthermore, they need to enable staff to feel sufficiently confident about their practice to cope with the challenges they will meet.

I assume that some, at least, of those who read this chapter are themselves taking on leadership roles in respect to development activities in schools. For these readers, in particular, I believe that the ideas reported above will provide much food for thought, always bearing in mind the points I have stressed about the need for individuals to 'devise their own ways forward' and take account of the 'unique biographies' of their organizations. Having said that, it is also important to recognize the importance of developing leadership skills, particularly in the area of working with adults in ways that facilitate their professional development. With this in mind, I conclude the chapter with a suggested activity that can be used by a group of colleagues who are interested in supporting one another in developing these skills (Figure 8.1).

This activity will be particularly relevant to those inside and outside of schools who have the task of coordinating the development of more inclusive practices. It will help you to consider the skills that are needed in order to support such development effectively.

The approach that is described attempts to build on existing practice within a school, using staff cooperation as a means of developing new responses. It is, therefore, an approach to development that emphasizes the idea of 'growth', with outsiders seeing themselves as 'gardeners' who are seeking to assist the process.

All of this means that coordinators have to be skilful in encouraging involvement, co-operation and creativity.

Step 1

Work alone to complete the questionnaire below. It requires you to think about your own experience of coordinating development in schools and write about your skills.

Research suggests that the following skills seem to be important to success in coordinating groups of adults in the development of practice. Make some notes about your own skills in these areas.

Leadership skills

1 Developing a clear purpose for activities

2 Establishing rapport with colleagues

3 Leading meetings and other group activities

4 Maintaining interest and enthusiasm

5 Solving problems, including difficulties over relationships

6 Encouraging collaboration

7 Providing support

8 Keeping people informed

Step 2

Compare your ideas with two other colleagues. Each person should explain what they have written. The colleagues should listen carefully and actively. They should only interrupt to ask questions that might help the individual to clarify their ideas. *No* advice should be given. The aim is to support each member of the trio to develop their own ideas.

Step 3

Each of you should now develop an action plan that can be used to guide you in acquiring further skills. The action plan should address the following questions:

1 What skills do I need to develop?

2 How can I develop these skills?

3 Who can support me in this work?

Figure 8.1 Leading development in schools

Chapter 9

The Development of Inclusive Education Systems

The proposals developed in this book are based very evidently on experiences in the field. Nevertheless, they are in many ways radical, not least in that they challenge many existing beliefs and practices, both in regard to general education policies and, indeed, the contributions of the field of special education. As we have seen, too, those who choose to follow the road towards greater inclusion are likely to experience many barriers to their progress and, regrettably, too often they face these barriers in relative isolation.

In this chapter I move the focus away from individual schools in order to consider the issue of inclusion in relation to the wider contexts of education systems as a whole. With this in mind, I begin by reviewing international trends in thinking in the field in order to map out policy options. Then, using evidence from a recent study in my own country, I consider possible ways forward for encouraging the development of more inclusive education policies at the national or district levels.

International Trends

The field of special education has developed relatively recently and unevenly in different parts of the world (Reynolds and Ainscow, 1994). Its development has involved a series of stages during which education systems have explored different ways of responding to children with disabilities and others who experience difficulties in learning. As a result, special education has sometimes been provided as a supplement to general education provision; whereas in other cases it may be totally separate.

For a number of reasons, attempting to define the numbers of children who receive special forms of education presents considerable difficulties. In particular, care has to be taken in considering any data that are presented since terminology and categorization systems vary considerably from country to country, while in some countries it is very difficult, even impossible, to obtain reliable and recent data. To illustrate these difficulties, figures reported in the same year with regard to children with disabilities in so-called developing countries range from 31 million (Mittler, 1993), through 117 million (Brouillette, 1993) to 160 million (Hegarty, 1993). What is beyond doubt is that across the world many children do not receive any form of conventional schooling, including large numbers who have disabilities. Considerable concern also exists about the poor quality of teaching offered to children in many schools, particularly in developing countries (e.g. Levin and Lockheed, 1993); whilst in the developed world, although sufficient school places are usually available, the problem still exists of finding forms of schooling that will enable all children to experience success in their learning. Sadly, for too many children their attendance at school is a largely unsatisfying experience, leaving them despondent about their own capabilities and disillusioned about the value of education to their lives (Glasser, 1990; Smith and Tomlinson, 1989). Indeed it has been argued that in some countries such circumstances are the major cause of children becoming categorized as 'having special educational needs' and, as a result, being marginalized in or even excluded from general education (Booth and Ainscow, 1998; Fulcher, 1989). These realities exist despite the fact that it is now more than 50 years since the nations of the world, speaking through the Universal Declaration of Human Rights, asserted that 'everyone has a right to education'.

A helpful source of data with respect to patterns of special education provision internationally arises out of a survey of 63 countries carried out recently (UNESCO, 1995), although, again, great care needs to be taken in interpreting the findings because of the way in which data were collected. Overall the evidence from many of the countries in the sample implies that integration is a key policy idea, although only a small number spelled out their guiding principles explicitly. The report suggests that there is a case for 'guarded optimism' in that, since UNESCO's previous survey in 1986, special educational provision has become much more firmly located within regular education at both the school and administrative levels. However, the pattern of provision varies from country to country. In 96 per cent of countries the national ministry of education holds sole or shared responsibility for the administration and organization of services for children with disabilities. Other ministries sharing responsibility are mostly those of health and social welfare. State funding is the predominant source of finance, whilst other funding comes from voluntary bodies, non-government organizations and parents. Most countries acknowledge the importance of parents in matters relating to special educational provision, and some give them a central role in the processes of assessment and decision making. There was also evidence of a substantial increase in inservice training of staff related to special needs issues. Having said that, the report also warns against complacency in that many countries face fiscal and personnel constraints such that even maintaining the existing level of investment may not be easy. Add to this the pressures created by more general school reforms in many countries could, it is argued, reduce the priority given to provision for children seen as having special needs.

An analysis of the history of special education provision in many Western countries suggests certain patterns (Reynolds and Ainscow, 1994). Initial provision frequently took the form of separate special schools set up by religious or philanthropic organizations. This was then, eventually, adopted and extended as part of national education arrangements, often leading to a separate, parallel school system for those pupils seen as being in need of special attention. There is also some evidence of similar trends in developing countries (see, for example, various chapters in Mittler et al., 1993).

In recent years, however, the appropriateness of having such a separate system has been challenged both from a human rights perspective and, indeed, from the point of view of effectiveness. This has led to an increased emphasis in many countries, in both the developed and developing countries, on the notion of integration (Ainscow, 1990; Hegarty, 1990; O'Hanlon, 1995; Pijl and Meijer, 1991; UNESCO, 1995). As an idea this can take many forms and in itself remains a topic of considerable debate (see for example, Fuchs and Fuchs, 1994 and Norwich, 1990).

Such an emphasis, involving attempts to increase flexibility of response within neighbourhood schools, seems sensible for economically poorer countries given the extent of the need and the limitations of resources (UNESCO, 1988). It is also important to recognize that in many developing countries substantial 'casual' integration of children with disabilities in local schools already occurs, particularly in rural districts (Miles, 1989).

In considering the current scene internationally with respect to integration we immediately come up against differences of definition. For example, Pijl and Meijer (1991) use the term 'integration' as a collective noun for all attempts to avoid a segregated and isolated education for pupils with disabilities. As a result of their survey of policies for integration in eight Western countries they suggest that its scope can range from the actual integration of regular and special schools (or classes), to measures for reducing the outflow from general education to special education provision which results in it becoming very difficult to quantify the numbers of pupils with special needs who receive their schooling in integrated settings, particularly if the important distinction is made between locational integration ('being present'), social integration ('mixing with the other pupils') and curricular integration ('learning together with the other pupils').

The existence of well-established separate provision in special schools and classes creates complex policy dilemmas, leading many countries to operate what Pijl and Meijer (1991) refer to as 'two tracks'. In other words, these countries have parallel, but separate segregation and integration policies. A rather obvious problem here, of course, is the costing implications of maintaining such parallel arrangements.

In some countries integration still largely represents an aspiration for the future. In Germany, for example, while some pilot initiatives based on the idea of integration are underway, students who are declared eligible for special education must be placed in a special school, while in the Netherlands it is reported that almost 4 per cent of all pupils aged 4 to 18 attend full-time special schools, although the exact proportion varies with age. So, for example, 7.4 per cent of 11-year-olds are in special schools (Reezight and Pijl, 1998). Recent national policy developments are attempting to change this emphasis. Similar developments in other countries, such as Austria, England and New Zealand, have led to major discussions of what might be the future roles of special education facilities and support services within a system driven by a greater emphasis on integration.

Some countries (for example, Australia, Canada, Denmark, Italy, Norway, Portugal and Spain) have shown considerable progress in implementing the integration principle universally. Here the local community school is often seen as the normal setting for pupils seen as having special needs, although even in these contexts the situation often exhibits variation from place to place (Booth and Ainscow, 1998; Daunt, 1993; Mordal and Stromstad, 1998; Pijl and Meijer, 1991).

A problem reported from a number of industrialized countries is that despite national policies emphasizing integration, paradoxically there is evidence of a significant increase in the proportions of pupils being categorized in order that their schools can earn additional resources (Ainscow, 1991). As a result of her analysis of policies in Australia, England, Scandinavia and the United States, Fulcher (1989) suggests that the increased bureaucracy that is often associated with special education legislation, and the inevitable struggles that go on for additional resources, have the effect of escalating the proportion of children who come to be labelled as disabled. As an illustration she describes how in Victoria, Australia during the 1980s, some pupils in regular schools came to be described as 'integration children'. She notes that over 3 000 children came to be seen as being in this category, which had not existed prior to 1984, and that often schools would argue that these pupils could not be taught unless extra resources were made available. It is because of situations such as this, of course, that changes over time in the numbers of children with special needs said to be integrated must be treated with caution.

Dissatisfaction with progress toward integration has caused demands for more radical changes in many countries (e.g. Ainscow, 1991; Ballard, 1995; Skrtic, 1991; Slee, 1996). One of the concerns of those who adopt this view is with the way in which pupils come to be designated as having special needs. They see this as a social process that needs to be continually challenged. More specifically they argue that the continued use of what is sometimes referred to as a 'medical model' of assessment, within which educational difficulties are explained solely in terms of child deficits, prevents progress in the field, not least in that it distracts attention from questions about why schools fail to teach so many children successfully. Such arguments lead to proposals for a reconceptualization of the special needs task. This suggests that progress will be much more likely when it is recognized that difficulties experienced by pupils come about as a result of the ways in which schools are currently organized and the forms of teaching that are provided. In other words, as Skrtic (1991) puts it, pupils with special needs are 'artefacts of the traditional curriculum'. Consequently, it is argued, the way forward must be to reform schools and improve pedagogy in ways that will lead them to respond positively to pupil diversity, seeing individual differences not as problems to be fixed but as opportunities for enriching learning. Within such a conceptualization, a consideration of difficulties experienced by pupils and, indeed, teachers, can provide an agenda for reforms and insights as to how these might be brought about. However, it has been argued that this kind of approach is probably only possible in contexts where there exists a respect for individuality, and a culture of collaboration that encourages and supports problem-solving (Ainscow, 1991; Skrtic, 1991).

All of this has helped to encourage an interest in the orientation discussed in this book, that of **inclusive education**. This adds yet further complications and disputes to those that already exist. Driven, in part at least, by ideological considerations, the idea of inclusive education challenges much of existing thinking in the special needs field, whilst, at the same time, offering a critique of the practices of general education. Put simply, many of those who are supporting the idea are raising the question, why is it that schools throughout the world fail to teach so many pupils successfully?

As I explained in Chapter 5, this new, inclusive orientation is a strong feature of The Salamanca Statement on Principles, Policy and Practice in Special Needs Education, agreed by representatives of 92 governments and 25 international organizations in June 1994 (UNESCO, 1994). Moves towards inclusion are also endorsed by the UN Convention on the Rights of the Child. Specifically, the adoption of the Convention by the UN General Assembly and its subsequent ratification by 187 countries imposes a requirement for radical changes to traditional approaches to provision made for children with disabilities. The Convention contains a number of articles which require governments to undertake a systematic analysis of their laws, policies and practices in order to assess the extent to which they currently comply with the obligations they impose in respect to such children.

Article 28 of the Convention asserts the basic right of every child to education and requires that this should be provided on the basis of equality of opportunity. In other words, the Convention allows no discrimination in relation to access to education on grounds of disability. Furthermore, the continued justification of the types of segregated provision made in many countries needs to be tested against the child's rights not to be discriminated against, not least in that Articles 28 and 29, together with Articles 2, 3 and 23, seem to imply that all children have a right to inclusive education, irrespective of disability.

Advancing towards the implementation of this new orientation is far from easy, however, and evidence of progress is limited in most countries. Moreover, it must not be assumed that there is full acceptance of the inclusive philosophy (e.g. Fuchs and Fuchs, 1994; Brantlinger, 1997). There are those who argue that small specialist units located in the standard school environment can provide the specialist knowledge, equipment and support for which the mainstream classroom and teacher can never provide a full substitute. On this view, such units may be the only way to provide feasible and effective access to education for certain groups of children.

In summary, then, as we consider the way forward for developing educational systems that encourage and support the development of schools that are effective in reaching all children in the community it is necessary to recognize that the field itself is riddled with uncertainties, disputes and contradictions. However, what can be said is that throughout the world attempts are being made to provide more effective educational responses to such children, and that encouraged by the lead given by the Salamanca Statement, the overall trend is towards making these responses, as far as possible, within the context of general educational provision. This is leading to a reconsideration of the future roles and purposes of specialists and facilities in the special needs field.

Developing Policies for Inclusion

How then can school systems encourage the development of inclusive practices? What approaches to policy development are helpful? Recently the Department for Education and Employment in England published a consultation document called 'Excellence for All Children: Meeting Special Educational Needs' (DfEE, 1997b). The document places the issue of inclusion at the centre of discussions regarding the development of policy and practice for pupils categorized as having special needs. This could have major implications throughout the education system and, as a result, local education authorities (LEAs) would need to review existing arrangements as a basis for their development plans.

In this context, my colleagues, Peter Farrell and Dave Tweddle, and I recently carried out an exploratory study for the DfEE (Ainscow et al., 1998). The study involved an initial engagement with a small number of key issues in order to map out conceptual, strategic and methodological agendas that could be used to guide subsequent research and national policy development. Specifically, it set out to describe and evaluate arrangements in a number of LEAs, and to provide illustrative examples of good practice in relation to the following themes:

- the inclusion of pupils with special needs in mainstream schools; and

- collaboration between special and mainstream schools.

More specifically, the study explored factors that may help to foster such developments as well as possible barriers to progress. Following the emphasis on collaborative inquiry that has been made throughout this book, we decided to carry out the research in a way that involved a partnership between academics and practitioners in order to ensure direct links between research and development.

Data were collected in 12 LEAs nominated by the DfEE. These varied in size, geography and experience in relation to notions of inclusive education. For example, they varied from, at one extreme, having 2.36 per cent of pupils in special schools to, at the other, 0.61 per cent (Norwich, 1997).

The methodology for the study involved the development of an evaluation instrument (i.e. the LEA Review Framework) that was used by the LEAs in the study to review their existing arrangements with regard to inclusive education. Its use also facilitated the collection of data related to the overall research agenda of the study. Here it was important to recognize that the field is rich with different perspectives, definitions and competing positions. It was necessary, therefore, that the information gathered should be sensitive to these differences.

The LEA Review Framework was based on a series of indicators that attempted to define operationally the features of an inclusive policy. It also outlined the types of evidence required and the questions to be addressed in scrutinizing this evidence in order to make evaluative judgments. It was necessary to collect diverse information in order to probe deeply into what occurs within a local authority, including both quantitative and qualitative data, from pupils, school staff, parents, officers and members of the local community. For the purposes of this initial study, however, emphasis was placed on drawing together and supplementing existing material within the sample LEAs.

The review in each LEA was undertaken by teams of coordinators. For strategic purposes two persons in each LEA were designated as the coordinators (a senior officer and one other colleague). They attended meetings with the research team to facilitate the planning of the study, received training in the use of the LEA Review Framework and, later, participated in the drawing of conclusions prior to the production of the final report. The coordinators were encouraged to form larger, more representative teams within their authorities to assist in the review process.

The research team maintained regular telephone contact with the coordinators throughout this process and, where necessary, team members visited some of the LEAs to help in the data gathering and reporting processes. LEA reviews were reported within a common format, and these were then analysed by members of the research team in a way that deliberately set out to draw on their wide experience and diverse perspectives. This emphasis on collaborative data analysis and mutual critique continued after the completion of the draft report, when the LEA representatives met once again in order to discuss and comment on the findings of the study, and to share common experiences and problems. These findings were supplemented by evidence from a review of existing projects, LEA reviews elsewhere in the country, and recent and relevant research evidence regarding the development of inclusive practices.

As I have noted in previous chapters, within the field there are varied and sometimes competing definitions of inclusive education. Indeed the findings of this particular study helped to throw further light on these differences. In the meantime, a rather broad approach was taken in developing the LEA Review Framework. Following the emphasis in the government's consultation paper, within the study inclusion was taken to be a 'process of developing ways of facilitating the participation and learning of pupils with special needs in the mainstream'. In this sense it could be assumed that all the LEAs had some interesting experiences upon which to build. Whilst the specific focus was on the participation of those pupils defined as having special educational needs, in order to find ways of moving practice forward we argued that it was necessary to scrutinize the ways in which schools respond to the diversity of all learners. Similarly, we decided that the process of increasing participation in mainstream schooling required an engagement with processes that may be associated with the exclusion of some pupils.

Keeping these concepts in mind, the LEA Review Framework focuses on the following **indicators**:

1 LEA policies encourage inclusive schooling;

2 pupils attend a local mainstream school;

3 schools are organized to respond to pupil diversity; and

4 agencies work together to support the development of inclusive practices.

Clearly these indicators represent ideals and, in that sense, it could be assumed that no LEAs have these features fully in place.

In the context of the study, the indicators provided 'standards' against which existing arrangements could be considered in order to gather information that might be used to inform planning. To facilitate this process a series of questions were developed which mapped out the aspects of LEA policy and practice that needed to be scrutinized (see Figure 9.1). These questions also suggested the types of information required.

The Framework was used within the twelve participating LEAs to carry out a process of review. The research team was anxious to recommend a process to the LEA coordinators that would be realistic in the time available and that would be effective in engaging representatives of all groups that might influence progress towards inclusive practices (e.g. headteachers, teachers, LEA officers, parents, pupils, support staff). It was felt that this would be best achieved by organizing conferences to which approximately 30 to 40 representatives would be invited. It was stressed that these should be as inclusive as possible and a list of suggested participant groups was provided. Detailed instructions were drawn up as to how the conferences should be conducted, including overhead projector slides that were to be used to explain the purposes and the procedures to be followed. Much of the time was to be spent in small focus groups addressing the questions posed in the Review Framework. Chairs and scribes for these groups were to be appointed before the conferences. They were to take part in pre-conference meetings which would enable them to become familiar with the Framework; anticipate issues that might emerge from the process; and identify any LEA materials which it might be useful to collect prior to the conference.

Indicator 1   LEA POLICIES ENCOURAGE INCLUSIVE SCHOOLING

1.1   In what ways do policy documents, plans and guidelines (e.g. literacy strategy, equal opportunities, behaviour support, working with parents/carers) deal with inclusion?

1.2   How far are these policies understood and accepted within the LEA?

1.3   In what ways do LEA funding strategies impact upon inclusion?

1.4   How do LEA policies influence links between special and mainstream schools?

1.5   What is the role of the LEA in fostering and monitoring progress towards inclusive schooling?

1.6   What is the impact of statutory assessment procedures on progress towards inclusive education?

Indicator 2   PUPILS ATTEND A LOCAL MAINSTREAM SCHOOL

2.1   What proportion of pupils are in different forms of non-mainstream provision? (e.g. resource units, special schools, pupil referral units)

2.2 To what extent do school buildings impact upon access for persons with all disabilities?

2.3 In what ways do pupils from special schools participate in mainstream education? (e.g. part-time placements, reintegration)

2.4 How do schools' admission policies and practices influence access for all pupils?

2.5 What are the different patterns of school attendance across the LEA? (e.g. schools, cohorts, districts)

2.6 What are the patterns of exclusion (permanent and time-limited) across the LEA?

2.7 In what way does the quality of specialist provision impact on progress towards inclusive education?

Indicator 3 SCHOOLS ARE ORGANIZED TO RESPOND TO PUPIL DIVERSITY

3.1 In what ways do whole-school policy documents, plans and guidelines deal with inclusion?

3.2 How far are these policies understood and accepted within schools?

3.3 How far do the curriculum and classroom arrangements respond to diversity?

3.4 To what extent are pupils given access to assessment and examination processes?

3.5 In what ways are available human resources (e.g. pupils, parents/carers, support staff, governors) used to support inclusion?

3.6 To what extent do schools' staff development policies and practice influence the development of inclusion?

3.7 In what ways do schools foster and monitor progress towards inclusive education?

3.8 To what extent do schools collaborate in relation to inclusive education?

Indicator 4 AGENCIES WORK TOGETHER TO SUPPORT THE DEVELOPMENT OF INCLUSIVE PRACTICES

4.1 In what ways do local authority INSET and staff development programmes (e.g. for teachers, governors, health professionals) encourage inclusive practice?

4.2 In what ways do the organization and provision of LEA support services (e.g. advisers, educational psychologists) influence inclusion?

4.3 How do the priorities and practices of other agencies (e.g. health, social services) impact upon inclusion?

4.4 How does the work of community support groups (e.g. voluntary, parents/carers) impact upon inclusion?

4.5 In what ways do different agencies work together (at all levels) in developing inclusive practices?

Figure 9.1   LEA Review Framework

Coordinators were asked to prepare a report as a result of this process, focusing in particular on the following:

- examples of interesting practices in relation to the four indicators;
- priorities for further development within the LEA; and
- comments on the design and use of the review framework.

All but one of the LEAs in the study were able to carry out the procedure and return detailed reports of the outcomes of the discussions that took place.

The overall reaction to the Framework and the way in which it was used was very positive. Many LEAs reported that it had been an effective and, indeed, efficient means of facilitating a process of review upon which they can now build. Some also suggested that they would use the instrument to hold further meetings of representatives of stakeholder groups and staff groups within schools. The idea of taking account of pupil voices was also widely welcomed, and two LEAs submitted supplementary reports of additional discussions held with groups of young people.

Some small amendments to the language used in the instrument were recommended and, of course, the data themselves threw further light on changes that might be desirable (the version provided in Figure 9.1 has been modified in the light of this information). It was reported that the least satisfactory part of the instrument was the section dealing with school responses to diversity, in that it was difficult to bring together the necessary data to make effective judgments. How far this was a criticism of the content of the instrument or the particular way it was used in this study remains uncertain. Clearly the effective evaluation of school policies and practices does require a range of data based on some level of direct observation. Inspection reports and LEA school monitoring procedures should provide at least some of this evidence. In addition, the on-going study to develop the 'Index of Inclusive Schooling', described in Chapter 7, will also provide a means of looking in much greater detail at school and classroom responses to pupil diversity.

Detailed reports were analysed from 11 of the LEAs. In considering these, the team felt that it was important to be sensitive to their limitations. Whilst we were confident that the evidence represented an account of perspectives from an impressive range of stakeholders within the local authorities, it was impossible to be sure of the exact status of the ideas that were reported. For example, we did not know how many participants at a particular meeting supported each comment. Also, some reports had been edited in a way that made them far more readable but left the reader unclear as to whose 'voice' was being reported. There were also issues of definition that could not be overlooked. Most significantly, we were asking for evidence of 'effective practice in inclusion' in contexts within which these very concepts remain problematic and probably contested.

Bearing these concerns in mind, our approach to each data set helped to highlight possible themes, examples of interesting practice and questions for further consideration. It did so in a way that used the varied experiences and perspectives of members of the research team in order to critique decisions made during the process of analysis and interpretation. What emerged was then subject to further detailed scrutiny when it was read and debated by the members of the LEA teams.

The procedure used was as follows:

1   Each report was read a number of times in order to highlight possible themes (i.e. recurring themes that the respondents suggest facilitate and/or hinder moves towards inclusion), plus illustrative comments and examples.

2   During this process possible questions (i.e. 'our questions') were generated for each theme within that LEA's material.

3   In reporting our ideas to one another we also drafted initial reflections on each LEA's material, theme by theme and then more generally.

4   Each of these LEA summaries were then reviewed by the team in order to develop a cross-case analysis that included overall themes, illustrative examples and questions to be pursued. Initial interpretations of these were reviewed at two meetings of academic colleagues with expertise in special education at the University of Manchester.

The second meeting with the LEA coordinators proved to be particularly valuable in clarifying our thinking about the data and testing our emerging understandings against their own experiences. Prior to the meeting, they were sent a discussion paper in which we explained in some detail the themes that had emerged as a result of our engagement with the reports they had submitted. These were characterized as an 'initial map of the territory' which could be used to guide further investigations.

During the day the coordinators took part in a series of small group discussions, each of which was led by a member of the research team and focused on one of the emerging themes. The discussions addressed specifically the following questions: Have we got the correct themes? Are some key elements missing? Participants were also asked to consider our emerging theory that each of the themes could act as either a barrier to, or a means of facilitating moves towards, inclusive education, and, where possible, provide further illustrative examples. Detailed records of these discussions were kept for later consideration.

Developing an Inclusive Approach: Barriers and Opportunities

Following the second meeting with the coordinators, the research team further refined the themes that had emerged from the study as a whole. These are as follows:

• Policy development

• Funding strategy

• Processes and structures

- Management of change

- Partnerships

- External influences

In what follows I discuss these themes in some detail, providing a map of the different perspectives that are present in the data. In so doing I also illustrate how these themes suggest factors that can act as either facilitators or barriers to development. As a result of this analysis my colleagues and I also generated a series of questions that have implications for future policy direction and, in some cases, point to aspects that require much more detailed investigation.

As well as providing an overall map, the six themes seem to overlap and interconnect in a way that begins to suggest a 'story' of what is involved in the process of moving towards more inclusive ways of working within an area. Indeed, it may well be that moves towards successful practice are dependent upon addressing **all** of these six areas, sooner or later, not least since each of them has the capacity to present a barrier to further development. Having said that, however, we must remain cautious of the danger of underestimating the complexities that exist within each context. As I will demonstrate, whilst certain patterns and even similarities may be apparent between LEAs, each has its own 'journey', reflecting local traditions and experiences, including previous debates and disputes that have occurred in relation to the question of how best to provide educational opportunities for pupils seen as having special needs. This being the case I would argue that more intensive research is needed in order to explore the detailed aspects of the six themes and to develop understandings that could be used to guide policy makers. In the meantime, the findings provide a conceptualization of an aspect of educational policy development which has so far been given little attention.

Policy Development

Within and across the data sets it was apparent that there were enormous differences of opinion about inclusion policies and what they might involve. Here much debate focused on the difference between the terms 'integration' and 'inclusion'. While many different positions were reported, a common view was to see integration as the movement of pupils from special provision into the mainstream, and inclusion as being about the degree of participation of these pupils into mainstream activities and experiences. Many argued that simply integrating pupils was insufficient and examples were given of how such pupils may be seen as having a different status from others in the school and, as a result, continue to be marginalized. In some instances, too, they were referred to as 'integration' or 'inclusion' pupils whose presence in the school was conditional upon the presence of additional support. Indeed one LEA officer described examples of such pupils being sent home on days when the support teacher or classroom assistant was absent. Such stories led some to argue that inclusion must involve a deeper commitment to develop classroom practices and forms of school organization that respond positively to pupil diversity.

Actual policy statements help to illustrate these different perspectives. For example, officers in one LEA saw their integration policy as a commitment to close all special schools. Other LEAs have policies that focus rather narrowly on the need to integrate pupils with special educational needs, whenever possible. For example, one LEA was clear that its current policies encourage integration but not inclusion. Meanwhile, another states that the LEA:

> . . . recognizes its specific duties towards children and young people with special educational need, and is committed to make for them, no less than others, the best educational provision it can within as normal an education setting as possible.

Others adopt a form of words that suggest a much more fundamental desire to develop schools that can respond to pupil diversity in a way that is linked directly to the raising of educational standards for all. For example, one LEA suggests that the goal of its inclusive education policy is:

> . . . to make it possible for every child, whatever special educational needs they may have, to attend their neighbourhood school, and to have full access to the National Curriculum and to be able to participate in every aspect of mainstream life and achieve their full potential.

Another LEA goes beyond the special educational needs perspective in a way that echoes the overall orientation taken in this book, in order to take an even wider view of what inclusion involves. Its policy and supporting strategy seeks to:

> . . . remove the boundaries between special and mainstream schools and to promote our commitment to inclusion by enhancing the capacity of the latter to respond to diverse abilities, backgrounds, interests and needs. Inclusion in education may be seen as the process of increasing the participation of children in, and reducing their exclusion from, the community, curriculum and culture of the local school, thereby raising education standards for all.

It was reported that many of the LEAs are currently reconsidering their policy statements in relation to the issue of inclusion, not least because of the impact of the government's Green Paper and, indeed, as a result of their participation in this study.

A striking feature of certain of the data sets was the noticeable disagreements about the meaning and value of some of these written policy documents. This led some to suggest that the key difficulty is that of dissemination; whereas others seemed to believe that ignorance or misunderstanding of LEA policies may be more to do with the ways in which they are developed within that particular LEA. In this respect it was noticeable that there was a high degree of consensus about overall policies for inclusion within a small number of these LEAs, all of which invites the question, how does this occur?

Another position that was apparent in some of the data was one that implies that policy documents are of minimal importance. Rather, what is needed is a close scrutiny of practice. On this position, policy is much more to do with how resources are allocated within the LEA and, indeed, within individual schools. It is also reflected in people's attitudes and values as shown in the way they respond to the situations and problems they face on a day-to-day basis.

Across the data, there was considerable reference to the complex and sometimes contradictory ways in which people's attitudes impact on policies and practices. In those contexts where progress towards inclusion is said to have been made, this was often illustrated by examples of how attitudes have changed as part of these movements. Thus the positive views and opinions of teachers, parents and pupils are presented as indicators of success as well as one of the means by which this success has been achieved. In rather striking contrast, some of the data sets present negative attitudes amongst the same groups as being one of the main reasons why progress may be impossible.

A connection here may be made with certain comments about how policies are developed and how they are supported over a period of some years. Certainly in a number of these LEAs there are indications that those leading developments have been able, by whatever means, to develop an agreed set of principles that appear to influence attitudes across the various stakeholder groups.

Further analysis of the data, and subsequent discussion with the coordinators in participating LEAs, indicate a degree of agreement across a range of issues. This suggests a number of tentative conclusions, some of which were supported unanimously by LEA participants but which nevertheless require more detailed investigation. It was suggested, for example, that an effective LEA policy on inclusive education could in fact be described on 'a single side of A4 paper'. Such a policy would describe the basic values and principles which form the basis of all further planning, and from which a clear vision can be derived. This central idea was expressed by participants in several of the LEAs, albeit using different language. Phrases like 'strategic aims', 'mission statement', 'values and principles', and 'vision' were used frequently. However, further discussion seemed to indicate a consistent view that the most effective LEA policy statement is short. It should contain: a view of the future, where the authority wants to get to, or a vision; and the key values and principles upon which that vision is founded.

It was further suggested that an LEA policy, described in these terms, has to be stable. It should be regarded as a long-term view that does not need constant review and revision. It should be capable of 'being internalized'; 'shaping attitudes'; 'becoming a part of the way people think'; and 'being transported and applied to an ever-increasing range of planning issues faced by LEAs and individual schools'. In these ways it becomes almost memorized, known and understood by all stakeholders, and at the heart of all planning processes. It is, therefore, the opposite of a 'bolt-on' approach to policy development which allows all other aspects of policy to continue unchallenged.

The conferences organized by the participating LEAs provided an indication of the number of stakeholders and partners who, in one way or another, feel that they are involved in inclusive education. It was felt by many of the coordinators that the development of a policy statement, designed to shape future provision and practice in a locality, needs to engage all of those stakeholders. Such a process in itself needs to be inclusive and will, therefore, almost inevitably be high-profile. 'Ownership' was a word frequently used by many in the participating LEAs, and it was suggested that ownership is most effectively achieved through active participation.

The evidence from most LEA conferences indicated diversity and differences of opinion across many key policy issues within LEAs. This suggests that an inclusive policy development process should not be allowed to become a matter of reducing policy to bland or benign statements which can mean all things to all stakeholders. All stakeholders should be given an opportunity to be involved, and all voices must be heard. However, a common message from many of the conferences, especially from school-based colleagues, was that the 'LEA must take the lead'. A clarity of vision and values is essential. Complete agreement, therefore, is almost inevitably unattainable.

Questions relating to the nature of the policy development process exercised participating LEAs, both in their conferences and in their work with the research team. Should the policy development process be top-down or bottom-up? Should the policy inform practice? Or, should practice inform policy? The emerging view from participants was that the answer to each question is 'both'. Ultimately, the LEA must write and publish the policy and be responsible for its implementation at local level. To this extent, the process is top-down. However, to the extent to which all stakeholders are actively engaged in the development process, it is also bottom-up. Equally, best practice should help shape policy, but in the same way policy should influence practice.

It was felt by many of the LEA officers that the relationship between a policy on inclusive education and other policy initiatives is vitally important. The pace of change in the education service is relentless, and a range of major government initiatives has been launched since May 1997. These have included: the requirement on LEAs to have an Education Development Plan; the publication of a draft LEA Code of Practice suggesting new relationships between the LEA and its schools; the introduction of a programme of OFSTED inspection of LEAs; the Early Years Development Plan; the Behaviour Support Plan; policies to ensure 'Best Value'; and, very recently, guidelines regarding educational finance, known as 'Fair Funding', and the National Childcare Strategy. All of these, without exception, are likely to influence, or be influenced by, inclusive practices. There are, therefore, crowded agendas in individual schools and at the LEA level, with professionals working under severe pressure to tight timescales. If an LEA policy on inclusion is not to be marginalized within this context, it needs to sit at the heart of other initiatives and planning processes. In this respect, school-based colleagues insist that LEAs must 'take the lead' and, unsurprisingly, LEA colleagues asserted that they in turn need government support in the form of a clear policy steer. A government lead is needed to 'legitimize' local initiatives and to provide the necessary impetus within a context of many competing, and in certain cases incompatible, demands. Without such a lead, significant progress towards inclusive practices will probably depend upon the vision and determination of key individuals at school and LEA level. At best, therefore, progress is likely to be 'patchy'.

Participating LEA teams were also keen to discuss policy implementation. Whilst the existence of a clear policy statement was seen to be imperative, its mere existence, of course, offers no guarantee of change. What does such a policy mean for stakeholders in practical terms? What is its impact on the rights, roles and responsibilities of the stakeholders? What does it mean for existing LEA processes and structures? How can these be redesigned to support the policy? How do we know how we're doing? And how will we know when we've got there? Participating LEAs felt strongly that policy implementation will not happen systematically unless it is managed. It will not occur by osmosis. Here the role of the LEA was again seen as central. Within the context of diminishing control over schools and, almost certainly, increased levels of delegation, the responsibility for developing and then implementing an inclusive education policy can be carried forward by no other agency but the LEA.

The management of policy implementation will generate considerable additional documentation, such as: business plans, action plans, targets, service specifications, service level agreements, evaluation procedures and so on. Policy implementation is, of course, dynamic, involving constantly changing 'plan–do–review' cycles. However, LEA colleagues were clear that such additional documentation is not policy. The vision on the side of A4 remains the same.

A number of tentative conclusions regarding policy development emerge from this analysis. These suggest that an LEA's policy for inclusive education should be: short, containing a view of the future and basic values and principles; stable and relatively unchanging; capable of being internalized and applied to other areas of planning; developed through the active engagement of all stakeholders; clear, despite diversity of opinion amongst stakeholders; led by the LEA; supported by a clear government lead; and carefully and systematically managed throughout its implementation.

Bearing this formulation in mind, not least the changing relationships between central government, LEAs and their schools, we concluded that it would be helpful if further, more detailed consideration be given to the following issues:

- How can LEA policies be designed to influence the development of inclusive classroom practices?

- What are the areas of practice over which the LEA continues to have direct control?

- What other aspects of LEA planning should be influenced (or permeated) by the inclusive agenda?

- In what ways can LEAs create a greater consensus amongst stakeholder groups about inclusive education?

Funding Strategies

Within the data sets considerable attention was paid to the way funds are distributed within LEAs and in relation to overall policies. Here a striking feature of those LEAs that appeared to have made firm progress towards more inclusive arrangements was the way in which they had been able to redirect finance in ways that appear to support these moves. Some talked specifically of the need to have policies for finance that are consistent with overall principles and strategic plans, and, more particularly, to maintain these policies from year to year.

On the other hand, the evidence from some of the LEAs indicated very strongly that existing funding arrangements were seen as representing major barriers to development. In some cases these arrangements led people to suggest that, unless additional resources could be found, little change could be anticipated. In this respect it seemed that there was an unwillingness or inability to make changes to traditional funding allocations. This led some to argue that things should continue as before and that changes would need to be introduced slowly; perhaps 'added on' alongside the status quo.

All of this suggests that a much closer look is needed at those LEAs that have been able to set up financial policies that appear to foster moves towards greater inclusion in order to see if these suggest principles and strategies that could be applied more generally.

Again, further analysis of the data, and discussion with colleagues from participating LEAs, led to a degree of agreement across a range of funding issues. It should be emphasized, however, that these are tentative conclusions that need further, more detailed examination at local level, using the findings of the earlier study carried out by Coopers and Lybrand (1996) as a further starting point.

While the factors which affect progress towards inclusive practices are, of course, numerous and interdependent, the strategy for financing special needs provision in mainstream schools was felt to be a key factor in this complex interaction. For example, it was clear from participating LEAs that the level of special needs funding within each LEA's scheme for the local management of schools (LMS), the degree of differentiation between the budgets of the 'most needy' and 'least needy' schools, and the mechanisms used to determine the distribution of available funding are all enormously variable. This has a direct bearing on each individual school's capacity to respond to their pupils without recourse to support from external agencies or statutory assessment. More particularly, by virtue of either written policy or 'custom and practice', each LEA has a 'position' on the level of financial support which can be provided for an individual pupil in a mainstream setting which is affordable and sustainable.

The central point of this argument was that each LEA's funding policy will inevitably have a significant and direct bearing on progress towards inclusive practices. Put another way, the way in which special educational needs provision is funded in mainstream schools has a very considerable potential to facilitate or inhibit progress towards inclusion. It follows, therefore, that to be effective, an LEA's inclusive education policy should be underpinned by a funding strategy that has been designed specifically to support that policy. Ideally, of course, there would be wide support for, and ownership of, the policy, and hence an understanding of why and how the funding arrangements are so constructed.

There was also considerable agreement among participating LEAs that special needs funding practices should in some way seek to reflect the notion of a 'continuum'. In particular, it was observed that large discrepancies in funding levels allocated to groups of pupils who do not have large discrepancies in their level of need, leads to inevitable tensions and a 'scramble' to access higher funding levels. In other words, the continuum of funding needs to reflect the continuum of needs, and 'cliff-faces' or 'hikes' in the level of funding between one group of children and another should be avoided. The most obvious illustration of this problem is a funding system which does not provide adequate levels of financial support for children at stages one to four of the special needs Code of Practice but which allocates generous support for children with Statements. The result, inevitably, is an insatiable demand for statutory assessment as being the only route available for headteachers and parents/carers to access significant increases in funding. It was reported that this can lead to situations where policies for special educational needs funding allow resources to be moved from the most disadvantaged groups to the least disadvantaged. For example, mention was made of how funding for additional teaching hours for individual pupils, categorized as having specific reading difficulties, had been taken out of the overall special needs budget in a way that meant reduced support for other pupils experiencing difficulties.

With the amount of funding available for delegation through the LMS scheme being finite, there was unanimous agreement among participating LEAs that transparency and fairness are imperative. These are well-established principles of LMS more generally, but a couple of more specific issues emerged through discussion. It is apparently not unusual in some LEAs for those colleagues in individual schools with a particular responsibility for special needs, such as the special educational needs coordinator or the designated governor, to be unaware of the additional special needs funding delegated to their own school. It could be argued that the principle of transparency should mean that this information is known to the whole school community and not merely to the headteacher. An extension of the transparency principle, common practice in some LEAs but not others, is that special needs funding within the LMS scheme is published school by school to all schools. That is, complete transparency with each school being aware of the level of additional delegated funding to all other schools in the LEA.

A related funding issue which concerned most LEA delegates was the question of monitoring or accountability. There was a concern to ensure that delegated special needs funding is used for the purposes for which it is intended: to enhance the educational opportunities of children and young people with special educational needs; and to raise the educational standards of those pupils. Whilst the DfEE's recent Fair Funding document provides for LEAs to retain funding centrally for special needs services, the spirit of the initiative is clearly to drive up levels of delegation. This merely serves to underline a perceived need within LEAs to put in place effective monitoring procedures which hold schools accountable for their spending in the area of special needs. In this respect, one officer noted that whilst his LEA had in place systems for monitoring how delegated funding is spent, this did not include a focus on how **effectively** it was spent. It was suggested that this type of monitoring should become necessary, however, in relation to the introduction of Education Development Plans.

The principles of fairness, transparency and accountability in funding policy can be seen to be compatible and capable of being fitted together neatly in a variety of ways. Indeed, there were a number of examples of funding strategies across participating LEAs which had been designed to observe these principles. However, it was felt by a number of LEA delegates that there was a fourth principle, that of flexibility in their funding arrangements to enable creative solutions to be found to locally defined problems. Sophisticated and wholly transparent funding arrangements which have built-in systems of monitoring by the LEA can be inherently inflexible, with resources tied down and hence not available to be vired as necessary to tackle problems flexibly as they emerge. Designing a funding strategy which is tailored to support a clear policy, and which is fair, transparent, properly monitored and flexible was seen to be a major challenge. Clearly, as LEAs review their funding arrangements for special needs in the light of the 'Fair Funding' policy document, much more detailed work will need to be done in this vitally important area. Indeed, Fair Funding might be seen as an opportunity by some LEAs to address some of these issues.

The SEN Tribunals set up to investigate disputes about provision for children seen as possibly requiring special provision were reported by many LEAs to present significant difficulties in maintaining a fair and transparent funding policy. Such a policy acknowledges that resources are finite, and arrangements are required which allocate levels of support to pupils fairly. These decisions are highly contextualized and taken with regard to a host of complex local circumstances. The problem is that members of such Tribunals cannot possibly understand the local context sufficiently. As a consequence, de-contextualized decisions may be taken which are perceived locally to be profoundly unfair.

Finally, it was evident that participating LEAs were acutely aware that successive government initiatives in this area, since the Warnock Report of the late 1970s, have not resulted in any significant injections of new funding. Of course, there has been the ebb and flow of money for training and staff development. Major changes to policy and practice in schools and LEAs, however, which have flowed, for example, from the 1981 Education Act and more recently the introduction of the special needs Code of Practice, have been presented as 'resource neutral'. It was felt that if the move towards inclusive practices is to gain momentum nationally, it would need to be explicitly supported by the government and properly funded.

This general point needs to be qualified. It was not argued that, without additional earmarked funding, no progress could be made towards inclusive education. There were many examples, in individual schools and across whole LEAs, where significant progress has been made without additional funding, but it was argued that progress across the country will be brought about in response to a clear government initiative. Moreover, stakeholders were fully aware that the government is prepared to spend money on those educational issues to which it is wholly committed. It follows that, to an extent, the government's commitment to inclusion will be measured by its financial support to LEAs and schools.

It is clear that the highly complex issue of funding has to be at the heart of moves within LEAs to develop more inclusive arrangements. This being the case, we concluded that particular attention should be given to examining in more detail the ways in which the government and LEAs are dealing with this area of policy. In this context we suggested that attention should focus on the following issues:

- How can funding policies be made transparent and fair?

- In what ways can schools be held accountable for using additional special needs funding effectively?

- How can LEA funding policies be designed to foster the development of inclusive practices?

- How might government funding policies be used to encourage such developments?

- What percentage of the overall education resources should be dedicated to differentiating schools' budgets according to social disadvantage?

Processes and Structures

In engaging with the data we were surprised at the extent to which local circumstances seemed to have had such a strong impact on attitudes and expectations in relation to the issue of inclusion. This left us with little doubt that the policies of LEAs do have a considerable bearing on how provision and practices develop. All of this tended to confirm other research that indicates how various existing social structures and processes within any educational context bear upon and influence the development of local ways of responding to situations and challenges (e.g. Hargreaves, 1995). In this respect the accounts from each LEA provide a strong sense of how complex local histories have led to the current patterns of provision, services, practices and attitudes, all of which come together in order to help define current expectations.

Interestingly, these historical accounts often make reference to how particular individuals or, sometimes, groups (e.g. officers, headteachers, educational psychologists) within an LEA have had a powerful influence on the development of policies. The story was told of how the actions of one headteacher in developing an active policy towards the closure of his special school had led to the creation of an overall LEA move in this direction. Such individual influences may, of course, be sometimes positive and sometimes negative in relation to moves towards inclusion. Either way, it is clear that they should not be underestimated in any consideration of how patterns of local policy and practice emerge.

There was evidence that local historical factors of various kinds bear on the creation of definitions, not least in respect to how terms such as integration and inclusion come to be defined at the local level. More specifically, a number of respondents made reference to how recollections of earlier policy initiatives, particularly those that were seen as being unsuccessful, continue to have an influence when new proposals are discussed. In some instances these seem to have created a sense of 'fear' that in itself can act as a barrier to current proposals. A number of instances were reported of situations where parents of special school pupils had resisted attempts at reintegration into the mainstream because these would involve their child 'going back' to where they had previously failed.

Formal processes within LEAs, such as the arrangements for assessing children seen as having special needs, including the guidance offered in the government's Code of Practice, were also regarded as a significant influence on the success or failure of moves towards more inclusive arrangements. Once again, the ways in which such arrangements have been interpreted within each local context has to be seen as a key factor. Some LEA officers felt that mistakes had been made in setting up these arrangements and that they had been introduced far too quickly and, in consequence, misunderstandings had occurred which in themselves had influenced the way practices had developed. For example, many felt that the idea of 'Individual Education Plans' had gone badly wrong in some schools where they had effectively become a way of marginalizing some pupils. Particular difficulties were noted about arrangements in secondary schools. A number of LEAs also reported that arrangements based on the special needs Code of Practice had contributed to 'overspending' and the creation of a local culture which sees special needs as being an on-going struggle between schools and officers about the provision of extra resources for some pupils. Such situations are seen as severe barriers towards more inclusive arrangements. Two local authorities reported that they had experienced some success in 'moving back' from such a position.

Some comments suggested that the language associated with special needs assessment can encourage an emphasis on segregation. This is clearly another aspect of LEA policy that warrants much closer scrutiny in order to understand more about what hinders and what facilitates developments. Once again, however, it is important to be sensitive to the importance of local factors in determining what occurs. So, for example, it was reported that the admissions policies of certain grant-maintained schools were having a significant shaping effect on where some children were educated. In addition, of course, demographic factors have also to be kept in mind.

The place and roles of special schools in relation to moves towards more inclusive arrangements varied considerably across the LEAs, as did the populations in these schools. One LEA that has launched a high profile public consultation about proposals to create a more inclusive policy reported that admissions to special schools had already declined. It was felt that the publicity given to the issue within that community had in itself changed expectations and influenced decision making amongst professionals and parents. Meanwhile another authority reported that its special schools were 'absolutely full', with long waiting lists existing in some instances. In a number of LEAs the existence of relatively well-resourced special schools sometimes appears to encourage parents and others to see this as the 'safest' option for their child. Then, in some instances, it was evident that special schools have defined a very separate way of working such that links with the mainstream are almost non-existent and examples of reintegration are few and far between. Interestingly in one LEA this situation was said to have been encouraged by the fact that there are now so few special schools (catering for pupils with relatively extreme disabilities) that links are not seen as being feasible. It seems, then, that as LEAs become more successful in catering for diversity in their mainstream schools this can have the effect of further isolating those special schools that remain. In such situations the wide gulf that develops in relation to the nature of the curriculum offered in the two sectors may be seen as making meaningful links much more difficult.

On the other hand, some LEAs referred to well-established link arrangements, with pupils going back and forth between special and mainstream schools; whilst others have arrangements whereby special school staff act as outreach support teachers. One LEA in particular seems to have developed this as an overall strategy of working and officers reported that this is proving to be a positive factor in encouraging moves towards greater inclusion. However, most of the other examples tended to be on a district basis, or as a result of initiatives taken by particular schools. Two authorities also reported moves towards 'co-locating', with special schools being moved *en bloc* on to the site of a mainstream school or with new schools being built to cater for the two populations. One secondary school was described which has a specialist suite for up to 43 pupils with physical and severe learning difficulties at its 'organic heart'. These pupils are now seen as full members of the school and reported to experience opportunities for 'functional inclusion'. Adaptations to the building have been made in order to facilitate this. In this same LEA a new secondary school is being built which will accommodate up to 60 pupils with severe learning difficulties. The aim is to increase the interchange between pupils and staff so as to facilitate more extensive and meaningful inclusion experiences.

Some comments referred to the difficulties associated with special schools — mainstream links. Concern was expressed in some contexts, for example, about organizational problems when special school staff (i.e. teachers or assistants) were asked to spend some time providing support in mainstream schools. It was felt by some that allowing the most effective staff to act as a support for outreach arrangements could be to the disadvantage of those pupils remaining in the special school. Some special school staff were reluctant to work in the mainstream where, perhaps, they might feel deskilled by unfamiliar systems and practices. It was also reported that such arrangements can cause tensions between special school staff acting in a support capacity and other LEA support services.

A noticeable feature of more successful link arrangements was that these were seen as a form of school-to-school partnership within which each contributor was seen as having resources and expertise to offer but in a way that recognized that there was potential for professional development on both sides.

Considerable discussion took place between the LEA coordinators about the contribution of various types of additional provision within mainstream schools. Again there was considerable diversity here between LEAs and, in certain cases, even within LEAs. Many LEAs have units that were set up to support the integration of particular disability groups (e.g. pupils who have a sensory impairment; those defined as having specific learning difficulties). Others have developed 'resourced schools' which are given additional resources for pupils with special needs and then expected to provide some places for pupils outside their normal populations, an approach that has been referred to elsewhere as involving the creation of 'mainstream special schools' (Booth et al., 1998). Here the debate focused on the degree to which such arrangements can help to foster moves towards greater inclusion. Some felt that they simply become a new form of separate provision that creates a separate identity and ethos, albeit on the site of a regular school. It was noted that in one such context parents valued the intensive help and support provided for their children and were very reluctant to support attempts to move them into mainstream classes. Others saw such additional arrangements as being a 'pragmatic' response. For example, one officer suggested that the creation of an attached unit had enabled the authority to overcome parental fears regarding the movement of their children into the mainstream context. Even more positively, there was evidence from a number of authorities that such arrangements had fulfilled a transitional role that had eventually led to much more inclusive practices. In a number of these instances particular note was made of how the relocation of former special school teachers into the mainstream had helped to provide parents with the security of knowing that their children would continue to receive an element of individual, specialist help. On the other hand, it was reported that some of these teachers appeared to take much longer than their pupils to accommodate the day-to-day demands of life in a mainstream school.

The availability and roles of various groups of support staff is given considerable attention in some of the data sets. In this respect, a rather surprising feature of some situations was the central importance placed on the work of classroom assistants to the feasibility of more inclusive arrangements. In one LEA, for example, some argued that their availability was *the* most important factor in determining whether progress towards inclusion might occur. On the other hand, there were many comments expressing concern that assistants can become a new form of segregation within the mainstream, with the rather worrying dimension that some of the most challenging pupils are effectively being taught by the least qualified members of staff. There were even suggestions in some contexts that as assistants developed skills in working with certain pupils this had the effect of de-skilling teachers.

Examples of good practice were also reported, however, and it was encouraging to find that some LEAs had established training arrangements for classroom assistants and, in some instances, training for teachers in how to work more effectively with another adult in their classrooms. A number of reports suggested that such training might be most effectively located within schools in ways that enabled teams of staff to explore and trial ways of working that made more effective use of additional adults in the classroom.

The evidence of this study indicates that existing arrangements within an LEA, shaped by local history, can and do have a profound effect on the development of more inclusive practices. Past experiences shape reactions to new proposals and where there have been earlier difficulties there is a 'fear factor' that nees to be overcome. For this reason some authorities have found it helpful to set up various types of interim arrangements to help move things forward. The problem here is, however, that such arrangements can themselves become barriers to progress. Throughout all of this there is a sub-text regarding individuals and how they can sometimes be a key element in relation to the success or failure of particular initiatives. This would suggest that development plans must be seen as requiring a strong human dimension.

Bearing all of this in mind, we suggested that further consideration be given to the following issues:

- What interim strategies have helped overcome 'fear' of moves towards more inclusive arrangements amongst staff and parents?

- How can the special educational needs Code of Practice be used to support moves towards greater inclusion?

- What can LEAs do to help create and support effective mainstream/special school partnerships?

- How can teachers and classroom assistants work together more effectively to support the participation and learning of all pupils?

Management of Change

As already indicated, there was strong support for the suggestion that progress towards inclusion demanded the development of consistent policy over time, supported by strategies for problem solving at the local level and firm financial policies for ensuring that resources are mobilized in order to support the process of change. Indeed, a striking feature of the data sets from a few of the LEAs was the consensus that seemed to exist amongst their respondents that these overall conditions already exist to a large degree. Elsewhere the data were more often characterized by significant differences of perceptions about these matters. All of this suggests that an understanding of how to move towards more inclusive education within an LEA has to include a close look at what is needed to manage change.

Interestingly, whilst the academic literature is now rich in analytical accounts and theoretical contributions as to how school level change is brought about, there is very little available, either in this country or overseas, about local authority change and how it can be achieved.

An emphasis on tensions of various kinds related to the process of change seemed to permeate much of the data. Once again this takes many forms and can vary both within and between LEAs. For example, there was reference to difficulties between headteachers and officers regarding resource allocation; boundary disputes between special schools that have attempted to develop an outreach role and existing support services; and unease that may be created as a result of the different priorities and working patterns of the various support agencies. There was also a suggestion that when 'boundary disputes' of various kinds do occur, attempts to resolve these by the sharpening of definitions of roles and responsibilities can result in a reduction of the very flexibility that seems to be necessary for the creation of more inclusive responses.

Other tensions are said to arise as a result of the aspirations of parents that their children should attend local schools and the judgments made by professionals that suggest that this might not be consistent with the efficient use of resources. One contributor suggested that these types of situations are creating an increasingly litigious culture which may well inhibit schools from attempting arrangements which they consider to be 'risky'.

It seems that LEAs, and particularly those within them that are responsible for policy development, face a complex series of tensions in relation to the directions they might take. A senior officer in one LEA that appears to have made significant progress towards more inclusive arrangements felt that in the current context this was the key to success. The task is, he argued, one of balancing tensions and finding a positive way of going forward. A fundamental dilemma faced by many of the LEA officers concerned the management of so-called interim arrangements. Put simply, the issue is how to maintain the quality of provision that already exists and at the same time, and within the same overall resources, put energy into bringing about the changes in attitudes, practice and patterns of provision necessary in order to establish more inclusive arrangements. Some felt that it was essential to develop the capacity of mainstream schools to respond to pupil diversity before making significant changes in placement policies. Others argued that this is simply a delaying mechanism which in the current context of competing priorities will further marginalize excluded groups.

Many of the officers explained that often the way forward has been to formulate approaches that involve compromises, as, for example, in the creation of resourced mainstream schools that can act as a 'half way house' between placement in special schools and integration into a child's neighbourhood school. However, some felt that there was evidence that such compromises can themselves create new barriers to the development of more inclusive arrangements.

All of this leads us to a consideration of the roles and approaches of the LEAs in relation to the management of change. Here differences between LEAs become obvious, particularly in terms of their relationships with their schools. Some seem to have well-established ways of working that suggest that the LEA is to a large extent leading development. In contrast, others emphasize a much more facilitating role within which likely developments may be identified and then supported in a much more light-handed way. Interestingly, within the data sets there is considerable emphasis on the importance of LEAs providing a lead to schools. However, ideas about what form this lead should take varied, perhaps reflecting the different relationships and patterns of working referred to above. Certainly the introduction of a Code of Practice on LEA–School Relations provides an opportunity for LEAs to review their strategic planning role and relationship with schools and their governing bodies.

As noted earlier, some respondents suggested that schools simply want to be told what to do. In particular, they argued that whilst there was interest and sympathy with the general idea of inclusion, there was also considerable confusion about exactly what it meant. In one LEA, where a number of primary and secondary schools have developed inclusive ways of working, a senior officer suggested that progress had been achieved by pressurizing some schools to try to become more inclusive. Sometimes unexpected events, such as a fire in a special school, had provided opportunities for this to happen. He went on to explain how schools were told that they might not necessarily become 'excellent' in this way of working, but that they were simply being asked to 'give it a go'. Their experience had been that attitude change within these schools occurred later, in the light of having to work together in order to develop teaching and organizational responses to 'new' groups of pupils. This suggested that a key role for the LEA involved pushing things forward and then establishing monitoring systems to help schools to learn from experience in ways that encouraged such processes of capacity building. Indeed, throughout the data sets there was considerable emphasis on the importance of monitoring and evaluation in relation to the development of policy in this area.

On the other hand, some felt that the important thing was for the LEA to have a clear stance, to make its values clear to everybody involved and then to find ways of 'taking people with you'. Here the importance of different stakeholder groups was often noted. In addition to headteachers, school staff, parents, governors and support services, particular mention was made of senior LEA officers who may see the issue of inclusive education as being solely the responsibility of those charged with managing special needs policies. It was argued that this represents a potentially powerful barrier to development in that other LEA policies may ignore the issue of inclusion or, even worse, be designed in ways that limit possibilities for movement. Certainly there was evidence that LEA progress was associated with an approach whereby inclusion was seen as a fundamental principle that guided decisions on all aspects of LEA policy. Of course, this matter is of considerable importance in an era when LEAs are required to establish targets in relation to Educational Development Plans.

Specific mention was also made of the importance of involving members of the local council in the change process. It was noted that in certain LEAs the competing pressures on members to support different approaches to special needs had created a further barrier to change, for example, reference was made to the difficulties created when members experience 'flak in the wards' as a result of proposals to close local special schools in order to develop provision in the mainstream.

In making sense of what all of this means, then, it is important to remember that the management of change in educational contexts involves a complex set of social processes within which those at different levels within the service (e.g. LEA, school and classroom levels) construct their own interpretations of what a particular set of proposals mean. In this sense, all stakeholders are to some degree policy makers, not least individual teachers as they develop their own version of the proposals through the minute-by-minute decisions they make during their lessons. Consequently, it can be argued that the development of inclusive practices has to be seen as involving a process of staff and institutional development. Certainly accounts of many schools were reported that seem to confirm this conclusion.

An account of a primary school in an economically advantaged area illustrates how moves towards greater inclusion can be linked to and, indeed, help to foster overall school improvement efforts. In 1996 it was designated as a resource school for a small number of pupils with severe learning difficulties. Initially, some of the teachers were not very enthusiastic about the change, expressing their concern that they would not be able to cope with the new pupils. As a result of teachers being given time to work with the school's resource teacher, confidence has gradually developed amongst the whole staff. Apparently, the presence of 'unusual children' has stimulated what was described as a problem solving approach, with staff learning how to work together in order to develop new teaching responses. It was reported that the school had recently had a very favourable OFSTED inspection report which commented specifically on the quality of its teaching.

Similarly, the story was told of one inner city secondary school that has placed the principle of inclusion at the heart of its development strategy and, as a result, has in its population young people with many different disabilities. During that time policies have been developed that emphasize equality of opportunity for all students, regardless of race, gender, disability, aptitude and social background. The school has a learning support team that works with subject teachers in order to develop practices that attempt to reach all members of the class. It was reported that as the school's inclusive ways of working have developed over recent years its examination results have continued to improve significantly. A recent OFSTED inspection report drew attention to the ways in which the permeation of this 'support for learning' policy seems to have benefited the whole school community. The report noted that 'the school does much to foster its students' self-esteem and encourages them to be proud of their achievements', and concluded that it 'is a popular, highly regarded and improving school which serves its community well'.

The attitudes and contributions of LEA officers, advisers, educational psychologists and parents were frequently mentioned in relation to the management of change. In particular, examples were reported of how these groups influence the development of policies as they argue for what they see as being the most appropriate avenues to pursue. Often, therefore, tensions manifest themselves in the form of dilemmas to be addressed as decisions are required and as people at the various levels of the education service attempt to resolve their different positions and aspirations. Inevitably disagreements and disputes will arise and, as we have suggested, these can occur both within and between levels.

In the light of this analysis we concluded that further consideration might usefully focus on the following issues:

- What roles should LEAs take in order to facilitate moves towards inclusion?

- What strategies are effective in taking the various stake-holder groups forward?

- How can the dilemmas associated with change be addressed and what lessons can be learnt from existing literature on the management of change?

- How will the proposed Code of Practice on LEA–School Relations affect practice in managing major policy changes?

- How should LEAs manage policy change towards inclusion within the context of the modernization of local government?

Partnerships

Each section of the LEA Review Framework generated comments on the theme of partnerships although, not surprisingly, the majority emerged from a consideration of the final indicator on inter-agency working. Responses focused in particular on: the role of support services; inter-agency cooperation; and partnership with parents. Across each of these issues comments can broadly be divided into those which highlighted positive developments and those which indicated barriers to progress.

The fact that the main agencies with responsibility for children seen as having special educational needs, namely LEAs, District Health Authorities (DHAs) and Social Services Departments (SSDs), work under separate management systems and in non-overlapping areas can cause difficulties for effective inter-agency partnership. Furthermore, these agencies have different priorities and responsibilities in relation to policy and practice for pupils with special needs. These structural issues often exert a major influence on the development of effective partnership in planning inclusive education services. Indeed many respondents reported that different agencies have competing views about inclusive education and, not only does this have an impact on effective multi-agency cooperation, but it means that parents often receive conflicting advice from professionals about where their child should be placed.

There were contrasting responses regarding the work of health service personnel in schools. Some LEAs specifically mentioned the expertise which they bring. However, others referred to the fact that many medical personnel have not worked in schools and need training in the knowledge and skills needed to work effectively in an unfamiliar setting. On occasions, it was reported, they simply withdraw pupils into a separate room for 'therapy', and do not work collaboratively with teaching staff so as to ensure an overall coherence to the educational programme. In this way the provision of therapy becomes a form of segregation.

This problem is particularly acute for speech and language therapy services which are often recommended as part of a Statement of Special Educational Need.

It was felt that as these services tend to be in short supply, using the therapy time available limited to withdraw pupils, sometimes to a clinic several miles from the schools, is not a valuable use of scarce resources and highlights a need for multidisciplinary training to help teachers and therapists to work effectively together. One authority which has a strong commitment to inclusion had requested its support services to avoid such arrangements.

All respondents referred to the vital role that LEA support services can play in fostering inclusive practices. Examples were given of such services working collaboratively with teachers and learning support assistants in providing training, advice and support. However, other respondents expressed concern about a lack of clarity in the role of support services; that some services were 'frozen into their case loads' and were not working flexibly as part of a team.

Many respondents stressed the vital importance of inter-agency collaboration and some good examples were reported. These almost always referred to localized initiatives within an LEA, however, there were more examples of effective authority-wide inter-agency working for pupils under the age of 5. Reference was made in one authority to the Early Years Development Plan that had been produced through a partnership of representatives of the main organizations involved in early years services, including the statutory, private and voluntary sectors. The objectives are to provide high quality and well coordinated services for all school children, including those with special needs. Systems have been put in place to review and update the plan on a regular basis.

One LEA suggested that effective inter-agency collaboration can be facilitated when the management of local education and social services come under the same umbrella, as has happened in some smaller unitary authorities. This would be further facilitated if District Health Authorities also worked within the same boundaries. Indeed one LEA suggested that all local authority children's services should be managed by a single organization and so provide a more holistic and collaborative service, which different agencies with their conflicting priorities and philosophies are unable to provide at present.

Despite structural problems which impact upon successful inter-agency co-operation, respondents reported that, through increasing opportunities for joint training between staff from different agencies, many of the issues concerning developments in inclusive education could be addressed. All agreed that collaboration is most effective when there is commitment from all parties and when channels of communication, both formal and informal, are used well.

Many respondents stressed the vital importance of effective partnership with parents/carers as LEAs develop more inclusive practices. In particular, it was seen as being crucial for there to be good communication between parents and professionals as problems or misunderstandings can complicate matters, result in parents feeling distressed and not properly consulted, and ultimately may lead to them taking their grievances to the SEN Tribunals. Many mentioned the important role played by parent partnership officers in supporting parents and in ensuring that communication between all parties remains effective, but it was acknowledged also that the wishes of parents/carers of one child may not be compatible with the wishes of the majority. Parents understandably want what is best for their child while the LEA has to consider the needs of all children. These problems are not new but, at a time when provision for pupils with special needs is becoming more inclusive, it may become increasingly difficult for LEAs to offer provision which meets the needs and wishes of all parents.

Many respondents referred to the potentially important role of parent and community support groups in helping to promote inclusive education and in developing partnership between parents and LEA officers. It was reported that in one LEA the Parent Partnership Project had played a huge part in developing parents' understanding and confidence in mainstream provision. In another authority a Supporting Parents Inclusive Network offers independent support and advocacy to families from a range of cultural backgrounds as well as to schools. Such groups seem to be particularly effective in promoting inclusion if they remain generic and represent pupils with a variety of needs. If, however, they represent single interest groups (i.e. only concerned with one category of children) they can operate without reference to the needs of other pupils and their families. Indeed in these circumstances they may often act as advocates for specialist segregated provision.

Some LEAs referred to the increased involvement of parents and carers in school life as being a positive and helpful development in the establishment of effective inclusive education.

A number of key questions emerged from our analysis of responses under the theme of partnerships. These were:

- How can different LEAs, health and social services departments work together to formulate a coherent policy on inclusion which is understood and agreed by all parties, including parents?

- How can support staff, in particular from health and education, work with teachers and learning support assistants in mainstream schools to provide the highest quality service in the limited time available?

- What are the combination of factors which facilitate the development of a shared philosophy and maximum commitment and collaboration between different agencies?

- How can parent and community support groups be established in all LEAs to support the development of inclusive education?

External Influences

Policies and practices in relation to the idea of inclusion do not develop in a vacuum. As we have noted, LEAs in England and Wales are having to take account of a whole range of recent government initiatives in all areas of education. Any moves towards inclusive education, therefore, have to be set against other pressures with which LEAs and schools are currently faced. Respondents referred to a number of specific external factors which influence developments in inclusive education. These can be grouped into the following overlapping sub-themes: the link between all government initiatives and inclusion; the impact of National Curriculum assessments and LEA target setting; the effect of the literacy and numeracy strategies; and provision for pupils categorized as having emotional and behavioural difficulties.

Several respondents expressed concern that government initiatives in education are not always compatible with moves towards the principle of inclusion. In particular, it was felt that a culture which seems to measure quality in terms of narrowly focused examination and test results may not acknowledge the excellent work going on in schools to support pupils experiencing difficulties. Furthermore, the plethora of recent government guidance on educational issues led one respondent to refer to inclusion as 'a bit of an add on', whilst another reflected that inclusion may be 'slipping off' the agenda.

In answer to these concerns, many respondents suggested that inclusive education should be seen as a permeating principle that should be at the heart of all planning, at the school level, at the LEA level and, most important of all, at government level. Some argued that schools could not be expected to adopt this principle if it was not seen to be valued by the LEA. And, of course, the same might be said of LEAs, if government is not seen to make inclusion a priority within its educational reform agenda.

For some, a helpful connection was made here between notions of inclusion and the government's overall concern to raise standards in schools. One LEA, for example, had developed an 'Inclusive Education Audit' which suggests that inclusion is about aiming for 'high levels of achievement for all children and young people'. Specific examples were reported from a number of LEAs of where progress towards greater inclusion within individual primary and secondary schools appeared to have led to overall improvements in educational attainment and social behaviour for all pupils. This is consistent with a view which is emerging from recent research evidence which indicates that the development of inclusive education can, under certain conditions, be directly related to improving the quality of education for all pupils (e.g. Sebba and Sachdev, 1997).

A large number of respondents complained that the publication of national examination and test results, and school performance league tables act as a disincentive for some mainstream schools to accommodate pupils categorized as having special needs. As one LEA put it the 'blame and shame mentality can influence schools' thinking' implying that even more efforts are being directed towards improving results. It was felt by some that, as currently construed, the target setting agenda may be incompatible with the successful inclusion of pupils with special needs in mainstream schools. However, some LEAs referred to the existing expertise among special education teachers in target setting and argued that good practice in this area could, if managed correctly, inform good practice for all pupils. In addition, there was a strong message from the majority of respondents that alternative ways of recognizing school achievements should be developed so that all pupils could be included. It was felt that this would help to offset the current trend, reinforced through the publication of school league tables, to assess schools solely in terms of traditional academic indicators.

On the whole, the government's recent National Literacy and Numeracy Strategies were seen as potentially very positive for inclusion, partly in a preventative sense in that they should provide a mechanism for the early identification of pupils likely to experience learning difficulties. This should enable appropriate action to be taken early which may prevent pupils being referred for statutory assessment later in their school careers. It was argued that, for this to be effective, further training should be offered to special educational needs coordinators and other staff.

A final external influence on policy and practice in inclusion, referred to by colleagues in all the LEAs, are the difficulties posed by 'pupils with emotional and behavioural difficulties'. Recent trends in LEAs have indicated a rise in the number of such pupils being referred for statutory assessment and the consequent increase in the numbers being recommended to special schools or units. In addition there is the well-documented rise in the numbers of pupils being excluded from mainstream schools, the majority of whom may have problems which are indistinguishable from pupils described as having emotional and behavioural difficulties. This is the one group of pupils who appear to be the most difficult to accommodate in mainstream schools. At the same time, however, there is a worrying proportion of special schools that work with such pupils being placed in special measures as a result of OFSTED inspections.

Some LEAs stressed the need for early intervention and better training of mainstream staff in responding to pupils seen as having emotional and behavioural difficulties. However, few LEAs referred to examples of good practice in this difficult area, although one mentioned a special team of education welfare officers whose role was to reintegrate excluded pupils back into mainstream schools. Another positive account in this respect is provided by Barrow (1998), who describes the success of the London Borough of Merton in developing an inclusive approach to difficult behaviour that concentrates on providing for so-called disaffected pupils by supporting mainstream schools.

The following key questions emerged from the data on the effect of wider influences that we felt need further consideration:

- How should schools, LEAs and government connect policies for inclusion into the wider reform agenda?

- How can the progress made by all pupils, including those with special needs, be included in the overall assessment of a school's performance?

- How can mainstream schools be encouraged to reduce pupil exclusion rates and offer more inclusive education for pupils with emotional and behavioural difficulties?

- How can special schools be included in target setting and the LEA's Educational Development Plan in ways that may help to foster moves towards inclusion?

Implications

The agenda for this particular study was wide and complex, necessitating a much longer and deeper process of investigation than was possible within the available time. Nevertheless, it was possible to make a firm start in refining the agenda, mapping the issues for further study and, at the same time, establishing research procedures that can be followed. The study also provides the basis for a conceptual analysis which throws considerable light on how inclusive education policies should be defined and what factors are likely to have a bearing on their introduction. Furthermore, it proved to be valuable to the participating LEAs in assisting them to review existing arrangements as a basis for their own development planning.

In this section I discuss the implications of the analysis provided, looking in particular at what this suggests in relation to the roles of LEAs and their schools, how the task of developing inclusive policies might be conceptualized, and what strategies might be worth considering. All of this leads me to consider how all that we are proposing here might relate to the government's wider reform agenda.

As we have seen, the issue of inclusion has considerable support within the LEAs in this study. Few, if any, voices were heard to argue against the general principle that schools should seek to cater for all pupils, as far as possible. The problems became much more apparent when the discussion focused in more detail on what is meant by inclusive education and how policies might be introduced in order to encourage developments in that direction. It will be recalled that our own starting point was the formulation used in the Green Paper (DfEE, 1997), where inclusion is seen as a process of developing ways of facilitating the participation and learning of pupils seen as having special educational needs in the mainstream. Like the authors of the Green Paper, however, we remained very concerned that the term 'special educational needs' can be misleading and may lead to unhelpful assumptions. We were aware, however, that within the field many versions of this overall position existed and, of course, these are in various ways evident in the data that was collected. For example, some see inclusion as being about the provision of the best of special needs practices inside mainstream regular schools and along-side other practices. Indeed, some would argue that such a move would be to the advantage of many other pupils who would benefit from these more specialized responses. On the other hand, some would see all of that as yet another form of separate provision, albeit located within the mainstream context, but in a way that is largely 'bolted on' to the standard arrangements for all pupils. On this position, moves towards inclusion have to involve a more fundamental push towards school reform such that overall organizational arrangements, curricula, assessment and pedagogy are developed in response to the learning characteristics of all members of the school. The fear, expressed by some of the respondents in this study, about this more reformist orientation is that it requires a much longer term process which would leave many children vulnerable as a result of any reductions in current specialized provision and support.

And so we return to the tensions and dilemmas faced by those in LEAs who are charged with formulating and coordinating moves towards greater inclusion. In the light of this study, what can we suggest in relation to their tasks? The evidence suggests that some of the LEAs in the sample have made and are making significant progress. Common sense would suggest that it would be helpful to look in more detail at their experiences. Having said that, we would want to guard against any suggestion that solutions can be simply lifted from one place and transplanted in another. The evidence shows very clearly that each LEA does have a unique biography that explains what has happened in the past and, at the same time, continues to help shape current events. The problem is that these biographies are immensely complex, involving many interconnected elements that may not even be remembered by those who were involved in them.

Bearing all of this in mind, it is possible to suggest patterns and possibilities that may help colleagues within an LEA to look at their own situation and, in so doing, strengthen their existing strategies for encouraging moves towards a more inclusive school system.

The central dilemma faced by LEAs is very similar to the one that I have already referred to in discussing school development in Chapter 7. It is the tension between *development and maintenance*. As I have explained, schools tend to generate organizational structures that predispose them towards one or the other. Schools (or parts of schools) at the development extreme may be so over-confident of their innovative capacities that they take on too much too quickly, thus damaging the quality of what already exists. On the other hand, schools at the maintenance extreme may either see little purpose in change or have a poor history of managing innovation. Moving practice forward, therefore, necessitates a careful balance of maintenance and development. It seems, then, that LEAs have to address a similar maintenance–development dilemma and all its associated difficulties.

Attempting to move policy and practice forward within LEAs also involves forms of turbulence that arise as attempts are made to change the status quo. As we know, turbulence may take a number of different forms, involving organizational, psychological, technical or micro-political dimensions. At its heart, however, it is frequently about the dissonance that occurs as people struggle to make sense of new ideas. It is important to remember, however, that without periods of turbulence, successful, long-lasting change is unlikely to occur (Hopkins et al., 1994). In this sense turbulence can be seen as a useful indication that the LEA and its schools are 'on the move'.

LEAs are clearly facing maintenance–development dilemmas. Specifically, how do they ensure quality provision for today's pupils within existing arrangements while, at the same time and within the same resources, making even better provision for tomorrow's pupils? People in some of the LEAs believe that because of this dilemma little progress can be anticipated unless significant new resources are made available. In a sense their way of resolving the maintenance–development dilemma is to continue as before whilst developing new responses alongside existing arrangements. This manifests itself in some respects in the various 'interim arrangements' that have developed in certain LEAs, but what might be seen as compromises can, in effect, lead to the creation of new structural barriers that may prove difficult to overcome in the future.

It is also evident that LEAs in England are experiencing various forms of 'turbulence' as they seek ways of 'balancing the tensions and finding a positive way to go forward'. The question is, how can those involved be supported in coping with such periods of difficulty? What organizational arrangements are helpful in encouraging moves towards more inclusive practices?

Reflecting both the patterns that are evident in the LEAs in this study and the processes explored within the study for reviewing current arrangements, it is possible to suggest some strategies that may be helpful in addressing the maintenance–development dilemma in order to create action plans. Here use could be made of the LEA Review Framework to involve stakeholder groups in a consideration of current provision as perceived from different perspectives within the local community. As we have seen, the Framework has proved to be effective in helping often 'hidden voices', such as pupils and parents, to be heard in a way that can enrich the discussion and, at the same time, present necessary challenges to the status quo. The experience of using the Framework in the way suggested, proved to be efficient in relation to the use of time and effective in ensuring that varied perspectives are considered. The weakest element in this process related to Indicator 3 (i.e. 'Schools are organized to respond to pupil diversity'). Essentially those involved felt that they did not have sufficient information available to make judgments in relation to the questions in this section of the Framework. This difficulty could be overcome if those who know the schools in the LEA well (e.g. headteachers, school staff, pupils, LEA inspectors and advisers) are charged with preparing relevant material prior to the meeting. This could include extracts from OFSTED reports, internal school review documents and copies of the findings of regular LEA monitoring processes.

It is now a well-established practice for English LEAs and schools to set targets that can be used to guide and monitor the effects of improvement efforts in areas of priority. In such a context it seems likely that anything that is not seen as being worthy of targeting is likely to receive less attention. I am suggesting consequently, that as a result of the process using the LEA Review Framework, LEA targets should be identified that can be used in a similar way to foster moves towards greater inclusion. Given the findings of this study it seems clear that such moves are much more likely to be successful where the LEA has made its own position clear through the publication of mission statements that emphasize a commitment to inclusive principles. In addition, the evidence also suggests that the active involvement of representatives of all the relevant stakeholder groups in determining targets is likely to be supportive of actions that are then taken.

Finally, the evidence of this study indicates that the six themes that have been explored have an enormous relevance to the likely success of LEA moves to develop more inclusive arrangements. As we have seen, the themes suggest factors that have the capacity to help foster or act as a barrier to such developments. Furthermore, even where progress is being made none of them can be ignored since sooner or later they are likely to have some bearing on what occurs. So we see these as a series of organizational conditions that exist in every LEA and that need to be reviewed and, where necessary and possible, modified in order to create more supportive arrangements. These will, we suggest, be of particular importance during the inevitable periods of turbulence.

Having said all of that, it is necessary to draw attention once again to the complexities of the contexts I am describing and the profound difficulties faced by those within LEAs who have the task of managing policy development. My suggestions imply that they have almost complete control over the development agenda, such that they will be able to set targets and establish timelines for change in a way that will enable them to manage turbulence by balancing maintenance and development activities. In fact, many LEA officers suggest that their current working context is such that government priorities dominate the agenda and timescales for development activities. As a result they see their task as mainly involving the management of turbulence that is created by **not** being able to balance the maintenance–development dilemma.

As my colleagues and I have looked at the findings of this study and considered the possible implications for future policies of LEAs, it has become very obvious that the issue of inclusion has to be considered in relation to the government's overall agenda for raising standards in education, in all schools and for all pupils, as introduced in the White Paper 'Excellence in Schools' (DfEE, 1997a). Within the overall national arrangements for achieving this goal, four major policy documents provide the overall context within which LEAs are required to operate. These are:

- Educational Development Plans — these will include the LEA's proposals, for approval by the Secretary of State, setting out performance targets and a school improvement programme designed to address and achieve these targets, plus supporting information to underpin the proposals.

- Code of Practice on LEA — School Relations — in which the principles, expectations, powers and responsibilities that must guide the work of LEAs in relation to schools are made explicit. As the Educational Development Plan prescribes what LEAs are required to do, the Code focuses on how it should be done.

- Fair Funding — which sets out to clear the 'funding fog' surrounding education budgets by requiring funds to be allocated transparently and in line with a clearer definition of the respective roles of schools and LEAs.

- A Framework for the Inspection of Local Education Authorities — this defines the basis of the inspection programme which will identify the strengths and weaknesses of each LEA inspected, including the effectiveness of its support for school improvement.

Together these policy documents provide the means for determining what LEAs will address, how they will operate, how all of this will be funded and how the whole strategy will be monitored and evaluated. This being the case, it seems reasonable to argue that if the commitment to inclusion is to be turned into action then it must **permeate** all of the frameworks and processes that are involved, otherwise it is likely that it will become marginalized alongside what is clearly a dynamic strategy which is being implemented with an enormous sense of urgency. Given the historical tendency for special education to remain as a separate field that works largely in parallel with the mainstream system, this could mean that the term 'inclusive education' would simply become a new way of referring to traditional special education practices. On the other hand, the current context does provide an outstanding opportunity to put inclusion on the agenda in such a way that it would inform all aspects of policy development.

The Wider Context

Returning to the international context that was addressed at the start of this chapter, the account of developments in English LEAs illustrates very clearly the need to place the issue of inclusion at the centre of policy discussions. In this sense it has to be seen as an essential element of the international movement known as 'Education for All'.

In recent years the issue of special needs has become much more focused on issues of integration and, now, inclusion. However, the concern has remained with pupils who have disabilities and others categorized as 'having special educational needs'. Thus the preoccupation remains with this particular group amongst the many others who are also vulnerable to exclusionary pressures within education systems. So, whilst there has been some movement of pupils from special settings into the mainstream, this approach has not had the hoped for success in ending the problems of separation *within* the mainstream. Where pupils have come into the mainstream from special provision they have often remained relatively isolated. As we have seen, they may be referred to as 'integration' or 'inclusion' pupils in contrast to 'mainstream' or 'our' pupils. Often, too, their presence is contingent upon the continued provision of extra resources. Thus they are in the school on a conditional basis; they and the extra resources are allowed to remain in a school that may, in practice, make little effort to develop ways of working that will reach out to them as learners.

What I have proposed, then, is an alternative, **transformative** approach to inclusion, which requires attention to all policies and processes within an education system through a principle of permeation. This is of course very difficult to achieve, not least in that it challenges so much of existing practice and demands significant changes in the use of available resources. However, some interesting examples of national reform programmes that are seeking to encourage moves in these directions exist and these are worthy of more detailed attention. Interestingly, these developments are occurring in both economically advantaged and disadvantaged parts of the world.

In Laos, for example, the Ministry of Education is developing a policy of providing educational opportunities for children with disabilities as an essential part of the national strategy to provide education for all children (Ministry of Education, Laos, 1997 and 1998a). In this sense inclusion is seen as an opportunity to improve the overall quality of education through the improvement of teaching and management skills, and the development of a new attitude that stresses that teachers have responsibility to ensure that learning is taking place. By the middle of 1998 36 schools had joined a project that involved them in exploring these ideas and developing new approaches. The evaluations that have been carried out indicate that 273 pupils who might otherwise have been out of school are now enrolled. Meanwhile there is evidence that the changes that have been made in these schools in order to support the participation of these children have improved overall learning conditions. In particular, there has been a marked reduction in repetition and drop out rates in the project schools.

Moving to a very different context, during the last few years New Zealand has been developing a new national strategy known as 'Special Education 2000' (Ministry of Education, 1998b). Whilst from my perspective the title itself is rather unfortunate, with its continued use of language that may still signal separate arrangements for some children, its aims are encouraging. Specifically, the stated purpose is 'to achieve a world class inclusive education system that provides learning opportunities of equal quality to all students' and 'to ensure that students with special educational needs can attend the school of their family's choice'. The strategy has two major components. First of all, it provides information, education and specialist support to assist families, schools and teachers achieve the best possible learning environment for all students with special educational needs. Secondly, it involves increased funding to provide assured and predictable resourcing for individual students and schools. The implementation of the strategy is supported by an extensive research programme.

In Uganda a policy of universal primary education (UPE) was introduced in 1997. It states that four children from each family are entitled to free schooling, that this should include an equal number of girls and boys, and that if a family has a child with a disability he or she should be given first priority (UNESCO, 1998). It was anticipated that UPE would develop over some years but an overwhelming number of families took advantage of the new opportunity and enrolment of children in primary schools increased by more than three million from one year to the next. With not enough schools, classrooms, materials or teachers to deal with this enormous influx, many children are taught under mango trees and although the teacher–learner ratio is meant to be 1:55, in reality it is 1:110 in the first two primary grades. Within a very short space of time, however, the participation of children with disabilities in the schools has increased dramatically. The challenge now is to provide teachers with the training and support that will help them to provide all children with as good a quality of education as present resources will permit.

Another very interesting educational reform programme is underway in the 'new' South Africa, where inclusion is seen as being a central guiding principle. For example, the Schools Act of 1996 provides clear guidelines for admissions of pupils that attempts to eliminate discriminatory practices. Meanwhile, a national commission on the future of special needs education has led to the publication of a report, 'Quality Education for All', which recommends a shift from the idea of special educational needs towards the notion of 'overcoming barriers to learning and development' (Department of Education, 1997). In these ways the historical opportunities created by national reform are enabling a recognition that moves towards inclusion have to involve a scrutiny of contextual pressures that inhibit the participation of many different groups of pupils. There are, however, many difficulties that need to be overcome in order to implement this way of working. There are, for example, severe economic constraints, including the massive inequities in the distribution of resources inherited from the previous regime. For example, I was told recently that whilst most white children with disabilities are educated in expensively resourced special schools, something like 98 per cent of black children with disabilities receive no formal schooling of any kind. Attitudinal barriers also exist, not least amongst members of the special education community, some of whom wish to see the maintenance of the existing framework of provision.

These examples illustrate the overall approach to policy development I am suggesting, that of permeating the principle of inclusion within an overall strategy for transforming schools within a country or district. Indeed, to varying degrees they draw our attention to yet another possibility: perhaps inclusion is the *means* of bringing about such a transformation.

Chapter 10

Some Final Reflections

As must be obvious by now, there is a strong autobiographical strand through-out this book. Much of it is about shifts in my own thinking and practice that have occurred as a result of experience in the field, set against the many changes that have been going on in education systems in different parts of the world. What is reported here, therefore, should be seen as yet another interim report. All I can say is this is as far as I have got so far. In that sense the book provides a record of my 'journey' and a summary of at least some of what I feel that I have learnt. It is also an illustration of what I see as the central message, that of developing better understandings of moves towards inclusion through processes of what I have called collaborative inquiry.

Writing the book has forced me to reflect further on the elusive idea of inclusion in education. My current approach is to define inclusion as a process of increasing the participation of pupils in, and reducing their exclusion from, the cultures, curricula and communities of their local schools, not forgetting, of course, that education involves many processes that occur outside of schools. As Keith Ballard argues, all of this has to be seen as part of the wider struggle to overcome exclusive discourse and practices, and against the ideology that asserts that we are each completely separate and independent. This leads him to conclude:

> We cannot put people away from ourselves any more than, as environmentalists have shown, we cannot throw something away. There is no *away*. We live in complex interdependencies with the planet we inhabit. Whatever we do, whatever is done, includes us all, no matter what strategies we may use in an attempt to distance and isolate ourselves. Actions that exclude and diminish others exclude and diminish ourselves. (Ballard, 1997; p. 254)

The agenda of inclusive education has to be concerned with overcoming bar-riers to participation that may be experienced by any pupils. As we have seen, however, the tendency is still to think of inclusion policy or 'inclusive education' as being concerned only with pupils with disabilities and others categorized as having 'special educational needs'. Furthermore, inclusion is often seen as simply involving the movement of pupils from special to mainstream contexts, with the implication that they are 'included' once they are there. In contrast, I see inclu-sion as a never ending process, rather than a simple change of state, and as dependent on continuous pedagogical and organizational development within the mainstream.

A narrow view of inclusion has particularly limited validity in economically poorer nations, though, as I have illustrated, experiences in such countries may cause reflection on the appropriate focus of policy in economically richer countries. It is clear that in any one country, a lack of facilities, the need for curriculum reform, insufficient or inappropriate teacher education, poor school attendance, problems of family poverty, cultural dislocation, the conditions giving rise to street children, problems of disease, and differences between the language of instruction and the home language may be as important as issues of disability in affecting participation in schools.

All of this moves the issue of inclusion to the centre of discussions about the improvement of schooling. Rather than being a somewhat marginal theme concerned with how a relatively small group of pupils might be attached to mainstream schools, it lays the foundations for an approach that could lead to the transformation of the system itself. Of course none of this is easy, not least in that it requires the active support of everybody involved in the business of schooling, some of whom may be reluctant to address the challenges that I have presented. In this respect my book has a particular message for those, like me, who have made their careers in the special needs field. We have to be clear about our purposes and self-critical about the approaches we use. Too often in the past our contributions have themselves acted as barriers to the development of more inclusive forms of schooling.

Bearing these concerns very much in mind, this book has attempted also to illustrate how an engagement with less familiar contexts can stimulate a process of critical reflection, thus enabling previous experiences to be reconsidered and new possibilities for improvement to be recognized. In my own case, this has drawn attention to a series of propositions that I currently use to guide my school improvement efforts. For the reasons I have outlined, these do not represent a recipe that can be applied in any context. Rather they might be seen as a series of possible 'ingredients' that may also be of use to others who are interested in the development of schools that can become more effective in reaching out to all learners. In summary they are as follows:

- usc cxisting practiccs and knowledge as starting points for development;

- see difference as opportunities for learning rather than problems to be fixed;

- scrutinize barriers to pupil participation;

- make effective use of available resources to support learning;

- develop a language of practice amongst teachers; and

- create conditions in schools that encourage a degree of risk-taking.

As we have seen, these ingredients are overlapping and interconnected by the idea that attempts to reach out to all learners within a school have to include the adults as well as the pupils. It seems that schools that do make progress towards more inclusive arrangements do so through a process of growth that leads to the development of conditions within which every member of the school community is encouraged to be a learner.

Neil Postman, the co-author of the 1960s classic, *Teaching as a Subversive Activity*, was reported as suggesting that recent years have seen far too much emphasis on technology and additional information as the means of solving the world's problems (*Postman in New Statesman*, 23 August 1996). Talking about starvation, for example, he noted that we already have enough knowledge to feed everybody on the planet. He concluded:

> As you go through and look at our most serious problems, you'll see they have very little to do with information. They are not amenable to technological solutions. But a lot of people think that technology is the only way we should go. So there is a real sense that we may be distracted from addressing the real causes of these problems.

In many ways the arguments that I have developed in this book reflect a similar view. They reject the idea that inclusion is an empirical question that requires us to first of all prove that providing a shared education for all children within a community is effective. They also cast considerable doubt on the assumption that further technological progress is necessary in order to achieve more inclusive forms of schooling. Instead, they focus attention on a scrutiny of the barriers that prevent this from happening within particular contexts and how these can be overcome. This leads me to conclude that we already have enough knowledge to teach all of our children successfully. As I suggested in Chapter 1, the big question is, do we have the will to make it happen?

A Final Thought

As I worked on the evaluation of the initiative to reform kindergarten education in Anhui Province, China, referred to in Chapter 3, I saw many examples of what I saw as good practice. Indeed, it was evident that the initiative had been very successful, not least in drawing the attention of teachers in the project schools to new possibilities for reaching out to children in their local communities who had previously been excluded. Over the gateway to one of the kindergartens was a motto which seemed to be guiding their efforts. It is one that I try to keep in mind as I go about my own work. It read, 'All for the children, for all the children'.

References

ADAMS, F. (ed.) (1986) *Special Education*, Harlow: Councils and Education Press.

ADELMAN, C. (1989) 'The practical ethic takes priority over methodology', in CARR, W. (ed.) *Quality of Teaching*, London: Falmer Press.

AINSCOW, M. (ed.) (1989) *Special Education in Change*, London: Fulton.

AINSCOW, M. (ed.) (1991) *Effective Schools for All*, London: Fulton.

AINSCOW, M. (1994) *Special Needs in the Classroom: A Teacher Education Guide*, London: Jessica Kingsley/UNESCO.

AINSCOW, M. (1995a) 'Education for all: Making it happen', *Support for Learning*, **10**, 4, pp. 147–157.

AINSCOW, M. (1995b) 'Special needs through school improvement: School improvement through special needs', in CLARK, C., DYSON, A. and MILLWARD, A. (eds), *Towards Inclusive Schools?*, London: Fulton.

AINSCOW, M. (1996) 'The development of inclusive practices in an English primary school: Constraints and influences'. Paper presented at the American Education Research Association Annual Meeting, New York.

AINSCOW, M. (1997) 'Towards inclusive schooling', *British Journal of Special Education*, **24**, 1, pp. 3–6.

AINSCOW, M. (1998) 'Developing links between special needs and school improvement', *Support for Learning*, **13**, 2, pp. 70–75.

AINSCOW, M., BARRS, D. and MARTIN, J. (1998) 'Taking school improvement into the classroom'. Paper presented at the International Conference on School Effectiveness and Improvement, Manchester, UK, January, 1998.

AINSCOW, M., BOOTH, T. and DYSON, A. (1999) 'Inclusion and exclusion: Listening to some hidden voices', in BALLARD, K. (ed.) *Inclusion and Exclusion in Education and Society: Voices on Disability and Justice*, London: Falmer Press.

AINSCOW, M., ECHEITA, G. and DUK, C. (1994) 'Necesidades especiales en el aula', *Aula*, **31**, pp. 70–77.

AINSCOW, M., FARRELL, P. and TWEDDLE, D.A. (1998) *Effective Practice in Inclusion and in Special and Mainstream Schools Working Together*, London: Department for Education and Employment.

AINSCOW, M. and FLOREK, A. (eds) (1989) *Special Educational Needs: Towards a Whole School Approach*, London: Fulton.

AINSCOW, M., HARGREAVES, D.H. and HOPKINS, D. (1995) 'Mapping the process of change in schools: The development of six new research techniques', *Evaluation and Research in Education*, **9**, 2, pp. 75–89.

AINSCOW, M. and HART, S. (1992) 'Moving practice forward', *Support for Learning*, **7**, 3, pp. 115–120.

AINSCOW, M. and HOPKINS, D. (1992) 'Aboard the "moving school"', *Educational Leadership*, **50**, 3, pp. 79–81.

AINSCOW, M. and HOPKINS, D. (1994) 'Understanding the moving school', in SOUTHWORTH, G. (ed.) *Readings in Primary School Development*, London: Falmer Press.

AINSCOW, M., HOPKINS, D., SOUTHWORTH, G. and WEST, M. (1994) *Creating the Conditions for School Improvement*, London: Fulton.

AINSCOW, M. and MUNCEY, J. (1989) *Meeting Individual Needs in the Primary School*, London: Fulton.

AINSCOW, M. and SOUTHWORTH, G. (1996) 'School improvement: A study of the roles of leaders and external consultants', *School Effectiveness and School Improvement*, **7**, 3, pp. 229–251.

AINSCOW, M. and TWEDDLE, D.A. (1979) *Preventing Classroom Failure*, London: Fulton.

AINSCOW, M. and TWEDDLE, D.A. (1984) *Early Learning Skills Analysis*, London: Fulton.

AINSCOW, M. and TWEDDLE, D.A. (1988) *Encouraging Classroom Success*, London: Fulton.

ARTHUR, H. (1989) 'Inset and whole school policies', in AINSCOW, M. and FLOREK, A. (eds) (1989) *Special Educational Needs: Towards a Whole School Approach*, London: Fulton.

ARTILES, A.J. and TRENT, S.C. (1994) 'Overrepresentation of minority students in special education', *Journal of Special Education*, **27**, pp. 410–437.

BALLARD, K. (1995) 'Inclusion, paradigms, power and participation', in CLARK, C., DYSON, A. and MILLWARD, A. (eds) *Towards Inclusive Schools?*, London: Fulton.

BALLARD, K. (1997) 'Researching disability and inclusive education: Participation, construction and interpretation', *International Journal of Inclusive Education*, **1**, 3, pp. 243–256.

BALSHAW, M. (in press) *Help in the Classroom, 2nd edition*, London: Fulton.

BARROW, G. (1998) *Disaffection and Inclusion: Merton's Mainstream Approach to Difficult Behaviour*, Bristol: Centre for Studies on Inclusive Education.

BARTH, R. (1990) *Improving Schools from Within*, San Francisco: Jossey-Bass.

BARTOLOME, L.I. (1994) 'Beyond the methods fetish: Towards a humanizing pedagogy', *Harvard Education Review*, **64**, 2, pp. 173–194.

BARTON, L. (1988) (ed.) *The Politics of Special Educational Needs*, London: Falmer.

BARTON, L. (1993) 'Disability and education: Some observations on England and Wales', in PETERS, S.J. (ed.) *Education and Disability in Cross-cultural Perspectives*, London: Garland.

BASSEY, M. (1990) 'Crocodiles eat children', *CARN Bulletin No. 4*, Cambridge: Cambridge Institute of Education.

BOOTH, T. (1995) 'Mapping inclusion and exclusion: Concepts for all?', in CLARK, C., DYSON, A. and MILLWARD, A. (eds) *Towards Inclusive Schools?*, London: Fulton.

BOOTH, T. and AINSCOW, M. (1998) (eds) *From Them To Us: An International Study of Inclusion in Education*, London: Routledge.

BOOTH, T., AINSCOW, M. and DYSON, A. (1998) 'Understanding inclusion in a competitive system', in BOOTH, T. and AINSCOW, M. (eds) *From Them To Us: An International Study of Inclusion in Education*, London: Routledge.

BRANTLINGER, E. (1997) 'Using ideology: Cases of nonrecognition of the politics of research and practice in special education', *Review of Educational Research*, **67**, 4, pp. 425–459.

BRENNAN, W. (1979) *Curricular Needs of Slow Learners*, Milton Keynes: Open University.

BROUILLETTE, R. (1993) 'Theories to explain the development of special education', in MITTLER, P., BROUILLETTE, R. and HARRIS, D. (eds) *World Yearbook of Education: Special Needs Education*, London: Kogan Page.

BURGESS, R.G. (1982) 'Keeping a research diary', *Cambridge Journal of Education*, **11**, 1, pp. 75–83.

CARR, W. and KEMMIS, S. (1986) *Becoming Critical: Knowing Through Action Research*, London: Falmer.

CENTRE, Y., WARD, J. and FERGUSON, C. (1991) *Towards an Index to Evaluate the Integration of Children with Disabilities into Regular Classes*, Macquarie Special Education Centre, Sydney, Australia.

CHAMBERS, R. (1992) *Rural Appraisal: Rapid, Relaxed and Participatory*, Brighton: Institute of Development Studies.

CLARK, C., DYSON, A., MILLWARD, A. and SKIDMORE, D. (1997) *New Directions in Special Needs: Innovations in Mainstream Schools*, London: Cassell.

CLOUGH, P. and BARTON, L. (eds) (1995) *Making Difficulties: Research and the Construction of Special Educational Needs*, London: Paul Chapman.

COHEN, M. (1997) 'A workshop in the workplace: A study in school-based teacher development', *Support for Learning*, **12**, 4, pp. 152–157.

COOPERS AND LYBRAND (1996) *The SEN Initiative: Managing Budgets for Pupils with Special Educational Needs*, London: Coopers and Lybrand.

DAUNT, P. (1993) 'The new democracies of Central and Eastern Europe', in MITTLER, P., BROUILLETTE, R. and HARRIS, D. (eds) *World Yearbook of Education: Special Needs Education*, London: Kogan Page.

DAVIES, L. (1996) 'The management and mismanagement of school effectiveness', in TURNER, J.D. (ed.) *The State and the School: An International Perspective*, London: Falmer.

DELAMONT, S. (1992) *Fieldwork in Educational Settings*, London: Falmer Press.

DEPARTMENT OF EDUCATION (1997) *Quality Education for All: Overcoming Barriers to Learning and Development*, Pretoria, South Africa: Department of Education.

DEPARTMENT FOR EDUCATION AND EMPLOYMENT (1995) *Exclusions from School*, London: HMSO.

DEPARTMENT FOR EDUCATION AND EMPLOYMENT (1997a) *Excellence in Schools*, London: HMSO.

DEPARTMENT FOR EDUCATION AND EMPLOYMENT (1997b) *Excellence for All: Meeting Special Educational Needs*, London: HMSO.

DEPARTMENT FOR EDUCATION AND SCIENCE (1978) *Report of the Committee of Enquiry into Special Educational Needs (The Warnock Report)*, London: HMSO.

DESSENT, T. (1987) *Making the Ordinary School Special*, London: Falmer Press.

DYSON, A. (1990) 'Special educational needs and the concept of change', *Oxford Review of Education*, **16**, 1, pp. 55–66.

EBBUTT, D. (1983) *Educational Action Research: Some General Concerns and Specific Quibbles*, Cambridge: Cambridge Institute of Education mimeo.

EICHINGER, J., MEYER, L.H. and D'AQUANNI, M. (1996) 'Evolving best practices for learners with severe disabilities', *Special Education Leadership Review*, pp. 1–13.

EISNER, E.W. (1990) 'The meaning of alternative paradigms for practice', in GUBA, E.G. (ed.) *The Paradigm Dialog*, London: Sage.

ELLIOT, J. (1981) *Action Research: A Framework for Self-evaluation in Schools*, Cambridge: Cambridge Institute of Education.

ELMORE, R.F., PETERSON, P.L. and McCARTHY, S.J. (1996) *Restructuring in the Classroom: Teaching, Learning and School Organization*, San Francisco: Jossey-Bass.

FUCHS, D. and FUCHS, L.S. (1994) 'Inclusive schools movement and the radicalisation of special education reform', *Exceptional children*, **60**, 4, pp. 294–309.

FULCHER, G. (1989) *Disabling Policies? A Comparative Approach to Education Policy and Disability*, London: Falmer Press.

FULLAN, M. (1991) *The New Meaning of Educational Change*, London: Cassell.

FULLER, B. and CLARK, P. (1994) 'Raising school effects while ignoring culture? Local conditions and the influence of classroom tools, rules and pedagogy', *Review of Educational Research*, **64**, 1, pp. 119–157.

GALTON, M.J., SIMON, B. and CROLL, P. (1980) *Inside the Primary School*, London: Routledge.

GIPPS, C., GROSS, H. and GOLDSTEIN, H. (1987) *Warnock's 18%: Children with Special Needs in the Primary School*, London: Falmer Press.

GLASSER, W. (1990) *The Quality School*, New York: Harper & Row.

GOACHER, B., EVANS, J., WELTON, J. and WEDELL, K. (1988) *Policy and Provision for Special Educational Needs*, London: Cassell.

GOSLING, L. and EDWARDS, M. (1995) *Toolkits: A Practical Guide to Assessment, Monitoring, Review and Evaluation*, London: Save the Children.

HAMMERSLEY, M. (1992) *What's Wrong with Ethnography?*, London: Routledge.

HARGREAVES, A. (1995) 'Renewal in the age of paradox', *Educational Leadership*, **52**, 7, pp. 14–19.

HARGREAVES, D.H. (1995) 'School culture, school effectiveness and school improvement', *School Effectiveness and School Improvement*, **6**, 1, pp. 23–46.

HARRE, R. (1981) 'The positivist-empiricist approach and its alternative', in REASON, P. and ROWAN, J. (eds) *Human Inquiry*, Chichester: Wiley.

HART, S. (1992) 'Differentiation. Part of the problem or part of the solution?', *The Curriculum Journal*, **3**, 2, pp. 131–142.

HART, S. (1996) *Beyond Special Needs: Enhancing Children's Learning Through Innovative Thinking*, London: Paul Chapman.

HARTNETT, A. and NAISH, M. (1990) 'The sleep of reason breeds monsters: The birth of a statutory curriculum in England and Wales', *Journal of Curriculum Studies*, **22**, 1, pp. 1–16.

HAWES, H. (1988) *Child-to-Child: Another Path to Learning*, Hamburg: UNESCO Institute for Education.

HEGARTY, S. (1990) *The Education of Children and Young People with Disabilities: Principles and Practice*, Paris: UNESCO.

HEGARTY, S. (1993) 'Reviewing the literature on integration', *European Journal of Special Needs Education*, **8**, 3, pp. 197–200.

HESHUSIUS, L. (1989) 'The Newtonian mechanistic paradigm, special education and contours of alternatives', *Journal of Learning Disabilities*, **22**, 7, pp. 403–421.

HOLLY, M.L. (1989) 'Reflective writing and the spirit of inquiry', *Cambridge Journal of Education*, **19**, 1, pp. 71–80.

HOPKINS, D., AINSCOW, M. and WEST, M. (1994) *School Improvement in an Era of Change*, London: Cassell.

HOPKINS, D., WEST, M. and AINSCOW, M. (1997) *Creating the Conditions for Classroom Improvement*, London: Fulton.

HOPKINS, D., WEST, M. and AINSCOW, M. (1996) *Improving the Quality of Education for All: Progress and Challenge*, London: Fulton.

HOUSE, E., LAPAN, S. and MATHISON, S. (1989) 'Teacher inference', *Cambridge Journal of Education*, **18**, 1, pp. 53–58.

HUBERMAN, M. (1993) 'The model of the independent artisan in teachers' professional relationships', in LITTLE, J.W. and McLAUGHLIN, M.W. (eds) *Teachers' Work: Individuals, Colleagues and Contexts*, New York: Teachers College Press.

IANO, R.P. (1986) 'The study and development of teaching: With implications for the advancement of special education', *Remedial and Special Education*, **7**, 5, pp. 50–61.

JANGIRA, N.K. and AHUJA, A. (1992) *Effective Teacher Training: Cooperative Learning Based Approach*, New Delhi: National.

JOHNSON, D.W. and JOHNSON, R.T. (1989) *Leading the Cooperative School*, Edina: Interaction Book Co.

JOHNSON, D.W. and JOHNSON, R.T. (1994) *Learning Together and Alone*, Boston: Allyn and Bacon.

JOYCE, B. (1991) 'Cooperative learning and staff development: Teaching the method with the method', *Cooperative Learning*, **12**, 2, pp. 10–13.

JOYCE, B. and SHOWERS, B. (1988) *Student Achievement Through Staff Development*, London: Longman.

KEDDIE, N. (1971) 'Classroom knowledge', in YOUNG, M.F.D. (ed.) *Knowledge and Control*, London: Macmillan.

KISANJI, J. (1993) 'Special education in Africa', in MITTLER, P., MITTLER, P., BROUILLETTE, R. and HARRIS, D. (eds) *World Yearbook of Education: Special Education*. London: Kogan Paul.

LANZARA, G.F. (1991) 'Shifting stones: Learning from a reflective experiment in a design process', in SCHON, D.A. (ed.) *The Reflective Turn*, New York: Teachers College Press.

LATHER, P. (1986) 'Research as praxis', *Harvard Educational Review*, **56**, 3, pp. 110–129.

LEVIN, H.M. (1993) 'Empowerment evaluation and accelerated schools'. Paper presented at the American Evaluation Association Annual Meeting, Dallas.

LEVIN, H.M. and LOCKHEED, M.E. (eds) (1993) *Effective Schools in Developing Countries*, London: Falmer.

LEWIN, K. (1946) 'Action research and minority problems', *Journal of Social Issues*, **2**, pp. 34–36.

LINCOLN, Y.S. and GUBA, E.G. (1985) *Naturalistic Inquiry*, Beverley Hills: Sage.

LIPMAN, P. (1997) 'Restructuring in context: A case study of teacher participation and the dynamics of ideology, race and power', *American Educational Research Journal*, **34**, 1, pp. 3–37.

LOUIS, K.S. and MILES, M. (1990) *Improving the Urban High School: What Works and Why*, London: Teachers College.

LUNZER, E. and GARDNER, K. (1984) *Learning from the Written Word*, Edinburgh: Oliver & Boyd.

KEMMIS, S. and MCTAGGERT, R. (1998) *The Action Research Planner*, Victoria: Deakin University.

MACBEITH, J., BOYD, B., RAND, J. and BELL, S. (1996) *Schools Speak for Themselves*, National Union of Teachers.

MEHAN, H., VILLANUEVA, I., HUBBARD, L. and LINTZ, A. (1996) *Constructing School Success: The Consequences of Untracking Low-achieving Students*, Cambridge: Cambridge University Press.

MILES, M. (1989) 'The role of special education in information based rehabilitation', *International Journal of Special Education*, **4**, 2, pp. 111–118.

MILES, M. and MILES, C. (1993) 'Education and disability in cross-cultural perspective: Pakistan', in PETERS, S.J. (ed.) *Education and Disability in Cross-cultural Perspective*, London: Garland.

MINISTRY OF EDUCATION (1997) *Management of the Integrated Education Programme Guidelines*, Vientiane, Lao PDR: Ministry of Education/Save the Children (UK).

MINISTRY OF EDUCATION (1998a) *Report: Inclusive School and Community Support Programmes in Lao PDR*, Vientiane, Lao PDR: Ministry of Education/ Save the Children (UK).

MINISTRY OF EDUCATION (1998b) *Special Education 2000*, New Zealand Ministry of Education.

MITTLER, P. (1993) 'Childhood disability: a global issue', in MITTLER, P., BROUILLETTE, R. and HARRIS, D. (eds) *World Yearbook of Education: Special Needs Education*, London: Kogan Page.

MORDAL, K.N. and STROMSTAD, M. (1998) 'Adapted education for some?', in BOOTH, T. and AINSCOW, M. (1998) (eds) *From Them To Us: An International Study of Inclusion in Education*, London: Routledge.

MOSES, D., HEGARTY, S. and JOWETT, S. (1988) *Supporting Ordinary Schools*, Windsor: NFER-Nelson.

Moss, H. and Reason, R. (1998) 'Interactive group work with young children needing additional help in reading', *Support for Learning*, **13**, 1, pp. 32–38.

Nias, J. (1987) 'Learning from difference: A collegial approach to change', in Smyth, J. (ed.) *Educating Teachers: Changing the Nature of Pedagogical Knowledge*, London: Falmer Press.

Nias, J., Southworth, G. and Yeomans, R. (1989) *Staff Relations in the Primary School*, London: Cassell.

Norwich, B. (1990) *Re-appraising Special Needs Education*, London: Cassell.

Norwich, B. (1997) *A Trend Towards Inclusion: Statistics on Special Schools Placement and Pupils with Statements in Ordinary Schools, England 1992–96*, Bristol: Centre for Studies on Inclusive Education.

O'Hanlon, C. (ed.) (1995) *Inclusive Education in Europe*, London: Fulton.

Oliver, M. (1988) 'The political context of educational decision making: The use of special needs', in Barton, L. (ed.) *The Politics of Special Educational Needs*, Lewes: Falmer Press.

Peters, S.J. (ed.) (1993) *Education and Disability in Cross-cultural Perspective*, London: Garland.

Peters, S.J. (1995) 'Disabling baggage: Changing the education research terrain', in Clough, P. and Barton, L. (eds) *Making Difficulties: Research and the Construction of SEN*, London: Paul Chapman.

Pijl, S.J. and Meijer, C.J.W. (1991) 'Does integration count for much? An analysis of the practices of integration in eight countries', *European Journal of Special Needs Education*, **3**, 2, pp. 63–73.

Poplin, M. and Weeres, J. (1992) *Voices from the Inside: A Report on Schooling from Inside the Classroom*, Claremont, CA: Institute for Education in Transformation.

Porter, A.C. and Brophy, J.E. (1988) 'Synthesis of research on good teaching: Insights from the Institute of Research on teaching', *Educational Leadership*, **48**, 80, pp. 74–85.

Reason, P. (1988) *Human Inquiry in Action: Developments in New Paradigm Research*, London: Sage.

Reason, P. and Rowan, J. (1981) *Human Inquiry: A Sourcebook for New Pardigm Research*, Chichester: Wiley.

Reynolds, D. (1991) 'Changing ineffective schools', in Ainscow, M. (eds) *Effective Schools for All*, London: Fulton.

Reynolds, M.C. and Ainscow, M. (1994) 'Education of children and youth with special needs: An international perspective', in Husen, T. and Postlethwaite, T.N. (eds) *The International Encyclopedia of Education, 2nd Edition*, Oxford: Pergamon.

Robinson, V.M.J. (1998) 'Methodology and the research-practice gap', *Educational Researcher 27*, pp. 17–26.

Rosenholtz, S. (1989) *Teachers' Workplace: The Social Organization of Schools*, New York: Longman.

SAXL, E.B., LIEBERMAN, A. and MILES, M. (1987) 'Help is at hand: New knowledge for teachers as staff developers', *Journal of Staff Development*, **8**, 1, pp. 7–11.

SCHEIN, E. (1985) *Organisational Culture and Leadership*, San Francisco: Jossey-Bass.

SCHINDELE, R. (1985) 'Research methodology in special education: A framework approach to special problems and solutions', in HEGARTY, S. and EVANS, P. (eds) *Research and Evaluation Methods in Special Education*, Windsor: NFER–Nelson.

SCHON, D.A. (1987) *Educating the Reflective Practitioner*, San Francisco: Jossey-Bass.

SCHWAB, J.J. (1969) 'The practical: A language for the curriculum', *School Review*, **78**, pp. 1–24.

SEBBA, J. and AINSCOW, M. (1996) 'International developments in inclusive education: Mapping the issues', *Cambridge Journal of Education*, **26**, 1, pp. 5–18.

SEBBA, J. and SACHDEV, D. (1997) *What Works in Inclusive Education?*, Ilford: Barnardo's.

SENGE, P.M. (1989) *The Fifth Discipline: The Art and Practice of the Learning Organization*, London: Century.

SERGIOVANNI, T.J. (1992) *Moral Leadership*, Boston: Allyn and Bacon.

SKRTIC, T.M. (1991) 'Students with special educational needs: Artifacts of the traditional curriculum', in AINSCOW, M. (ed.) *Effective Schools for All*, London: Fulton.

SKRTIC, T.M. (1986) 'The crisis in special education knowledge: A perspective on perspectives', *Focus on Exceptional Children*, **18**, 9, pp. 1–15.

SLAVIN, R.E., MADDEN, N.A. and LEAVEY, M. (1984) 'Effects of cooperative learning and individualized instruction in mainstreamed students', *Exceptional Children*, **50**, 5, pp. 434–443.

SLEE, R. (1996) 'Inclusive schooling in Australia? Not yet', *Cambridge Journal Of Education*, **26**, 1, pp. 9–32.

SMITH, D.J. and TOMLINSON, S. (1989) *The School Effect: A Study of Multi-racial Comprehensives*, London: Policy Studies Institute.

STOLL, L. (1991) 'School effectiveness in action: Supporting growth in schools and classrooms', in AINSCOW, M. (ed.) *Effective Schools for All*, London: Fulton.

STUBBS, S. (1995) 'The Lesotho National Integrated Education Programme: A case study of implementation', MEd Thesis, University of Cambridge.

SWANN, W. (1991) *Segregation Statistics*, London: Centre for Studies on Integration in Education.

TALBERT, J.E. and MCLAUGHLIN, M.W. (1994) 'Teacher professionalism in local school contexts', *American Journal of Education*, **102**, pp. 120–159.

THOUSAND, J.S. and VILLA, R.A. (1991) 'Accommodating for greater student variance', in AINSCOW, M. (ed.) *Effective Schools for All*, London: Fulton.

TOMLINSON, S. (1982) *A Sociology of Special Education*, London: Routledge.

TRENT, S.C., ARTILES, A.J. and ENGLERT, C.S. (1998) 'From deficit thinking to social constructivism: A review of theory, research and practice in special education', *Review of Research in Education*, **23**, pp. 277–307.

UDVARI-SOLNER, A. (1996) 'Theoretical influences on the establishment of inclusive practices', *Cambridge Journal of Education*, **26**, 10, pp. 101–120.

UNESCO (1994) *The Salamanca Statement and Framework for Action on Special Needs Education*, Paris: UNESCO.

UNESCO (1995) *Review of the Present Position in Special Education*, Paris: UNESCO.

UNESCO (1998) *From Special Needs Education to Education for All: Discussion Paper for the International Consultative Forum on Education for All*, Paris: UNESCO.

VAMVAKDOU, N. (1998) 'Developing inclusive teaching strategies in the early years: A case study', MEd dissertation: University of Manchester.

VISLIE, L. (1995) 'Integration policies, school reforms and the organization of schooling for handicapped pupils in Western societies', in CLARK, C., DYSON, A. and MILLWARD, A. (eds) *Towards Inclusive Schools?*, London: Fulton.

WANG, M.C. (1991) 'Adaptive education: An alternative approach to providing for student diversity', in AINSCOW, M. (ed.) *Effective Schools for All*, London: Fulton.

WANG, M.C. and REYNOLDS, M.C. (1996) 'Progressive inclusion: Meeting new challenges in special education', *Theory into Practice*, **35**, 10, pp. 20–25.

WASLEY, P., HAMPEL, R. and CLARK, R. (1996) 'Collaborative inquiry: A method for the reform minded'. Paper presented at the Annual Meeting of the American Educational Research Association, New York.

WEDELL, K. (1981) 'Concepts of special educational needs', *Education Today*, **31**, 1, pp. 3–9.

WEICK, K.E. (1985) 'Sources of order in underorganized systems: Themes in recent organizational theory', in LINCOLN, Y.S. (ed.) *Organizational Theory and Inquiry*, Beverley Hills: Sage.

WEST, M. and AINSCOW, M. (1991) *Managing School Development*, London: Fulton.

WEST, M., AINSCOW, M. and HOPKINS, D. (1997) 'Making sense of school development from the inside'. Paper presented at the International Conference on School Effectiveness and Improvement, Memphis, January, 1997.

WINTER, R. (1989) *Learning from Experience: Principles and Practice in Action Research*, London: Falmer.

WOLFENDALE, S. (1987) *Primary Schools and Special Needs: Policy, Planning and Provision*, London: Cassell.

Index